Nordic Defense:
Comparative Decision Making

Nordic Defense:
Comparative Decision Making

Edited by

William J. Taylor, Jr.
Center for Strategic and
International Studies
Georgetown University

Paul M. Cole
Center for Strategic and
International Studies
Georgetown University

Lexington Books
D.C. Heath and Company/Lexington, Massachusetts/Toronto

Library of Congress Cataloging in Publication Data
Main entry under title:

Nordic defense.

  Bibliography: p.
  Includes index.
  1. Scandinavia—Military policy—Decision making—
Addresses, essays, lectures. 2. Finland—Military policy
—Decision making—Addresses, essays, lectures.
I. Cole, Paul M. II. Taylor, William J. (William Jesse),
1933–
UA646.7.N67   1985   355'.0335'48   85-4533
ISBN 0-669-09746-2 (alk. paper)

Copyright © 1985 by D.C. Heath and Company

All rights reserved. No part of this publication may be reproduced
or transmitted in any form or by any means, electronic or mechanical,
including photocopy, recording, or any information storage or retrieval
system, without permission in writing from the publisher.

Published simultaneously in Canada
Printed in the United States of America on acid-free paper
International Standard Book Number: 0-669-09746-2
Library of Congress Catalog Card Number: 84-48683

Contents

Foreword vii
Amos A. Jordan

Preface ix
William J. Taylor, Jr. and *Paul M. Cole*

Introduction xi
William J. Taylor, Jr. and *Paul M. Cole*

1 **Denmark** 1
   Christian Thune and *Nikolaj Petersen*

   Introduction 1
   Principal Actors and the Structure of Decision Making 4
   Danish Policy Making for Defense: Two Cases 14
   Conclusion 31

2 **Finland** 37
   Trond Gilberg

   The Setting 37
   Soviet Strategy, Tactics, and the Position of Finland in the 1980s 39
   Domestic Constraints on Finnish Decision Making for Defense 43
   Decision Making for National Defense: Structures and Process 46
   Economic and Technological Constraints 52
   The Goals and Objectives of Finnish Defense Policy 53
   Execution of Finnish Defense Policy: Forces and Training 54
   Defense Strategy 57
   Conclusion 59

3 **Iceland** 63
   John Fairlamb

   Current Defense Policy 65
   Icelandic Perceptions of Threat 66

The Defense Community   70
The News Media   78
Public Opinion and Civil–Military Relations   79
Decision-Making Constraints   80
Conclusion   85

4 Norway   91
James Stark

The Actors   91
The Process   104
The Constraints   108
Security Guidelines   113
The Policy Process: Two Cases   114
Conclusion   120

5 Sweden   127
William J. Taylor, Jr.

The Backdrop of Swedish Defense Decision Making   127
The Fighter Aircraft Controversy   131
The Defense Community   132
The News Media   146
Public Opinion and Civil–Military Relations   147
Decision-Making Constraints   152
Channels of Decision Making   160
Putting the Pieces Together: The Fighter Aircraft Controversy   166
Conclusion   179

6 Comparative   187
Paul M. Cole

The Setting   188
Structures   191
Defense Issues   193
Lessons from the Study of Nordic Defense Decision Making   203

Index   205

About the Contributors   215

About the Editors   217

Foreword

Amos A. Jordan

President

Georgetown University
Center for Strategic and International Studies

The comfortable circumstances that have allowed the Nordic countries to anticipate great stability in their international security environment are today eroding. For decades these countries have existed as Europe's "quiet corner," where detente and diplomacy were the cornerstones of a sufficient national security policy. Armed forces have been maintained on the basis of the perception that the military threat from the Soviet Union has been relatively low.

Given a preference, the Nordic nations would choose to maintain this status quo. But circumstances have changed. Well-known Soviet submarine violations of Swedish territory are but one aspect of a much broader trend, as reflected in the growth of the Soviet military presence at Murmansk, express Soviet interest in the Svalbard, and numerous territorial violations of several Nordic nations by Soviet armed forces.

Nordic perceptions of the changing environment have changed somewhat more slowly, but the trend is now fully in evidence. The perennial debate about the upgrading of armed forces and the level of forces sufficient to meet the perceived threat has taken on a new urgency. Of special importance is the emerging discussion, throughout the Nordic region, in which existing notions about the role of force in regional security policies is being reassessed.

Though Western security will be fundamentally influenced by the evolution of this debate, there is little understanding outside of the Nordic nations of the character of the debate or of its key players. This book is intended to fill this need by providing information about and analysis of the defense decision-making processes of the five Nordic nations. Other Western nations, and especially the United States, have much to learn from the way these decisions are taken, since many of the efficiencies and approaches used in these countries are relevant to our own experience.

Readers will find this volume to be useful on a number of counts. It provides useful information on an under-studied set of issues. It does so in a balanced, objective fashion. It educates about issues that are certain to assume much higher prominence in the years ahead. As such, I believe it makes a useful contribution to the understanding of this central component of Western security.

Preface

William J. Taylor, Jr.
Paul M. Cole

The genesis of this book was comparative research performed in Sweden by Dr. William Taylor, Jr., for a previous book (*Military Unions: U.S. Trends and Other Issues* (Sage, 1977)). Dr. Taylor's discussions with Brigadier General Nils Frederic Haegerström of the Swedish Army, Dr. Mats Bergquist who at the time was the political counselor at the Embassy of Sweden in Washington, D.C., and with colleagues in the Department of Social Sciences at the U.S. Military Academy surfaced three important points. First, many similarities and dissimilarities between the national security structures and decision-making processes of the Nordic countries and the United States were identified. Second, northern Europe was becoming increasingly important geopolitically. Third, there was little literature that analyzed the national security decision-making processes in the Nordic countries.

Since 1977 several opportunities occurred to push this effort along. In 1978 preliminary findings were discussed at the Biennial Conference of the Section on Military Studies, International Studies Association, and again in 1979 at the Annual Conference of the International Studies Association. Another opportunity to examine this research was provided in 1979 at a conference in Norway co-sponsored by the Norwegian Defense Institute and the Georgetown University Center for Strategic and International Studies.

One result of these efforts emerged in 1979 when it was decided that Finland and Iceland should be included in the study. Dr. Trond Gilberg of Pennsylvania State University agreed to undertake research on Finland, and Major John Fairlamb of the U.S. Military Academy agreed to study Iceland. In 1980 *Problems of Communism* published a major article which incorporated some preliminary findings of this expanded effort ("The Soviet Union and Northern Europe," *Problems of Communism,* March–April 1981).

In 1983 the co-editors of this volume decided to move ahead with the project toward publication. By that time it was necessary to find a substitute for the chapter on Denmark, and we were fortunate to find Dr. Christian

Thune and Dr. Nikolaj Petersen, both well-respected Danish professors, to contribute a new chapter on Danish defense decision making.

This multi-year effort would not have been possible without the assistance of several special people. Among them Alan Tapsell stands out. Alan, official translator for the Office of the Defense Attaché, U.S. Embassy Stockholm, provided regular translations from the Swedish press and helped us understand the proper context of defense decision making in Sweden. Numerous translations from Swedish and Norwegian were also provided by Louise Haegerström-Taylor, for which we are grateful.

Without the assistance of Julia Culver this book would still be a manuscript sitting on the shelf. We thank Julia for her research support. Morrie Ruffin also contributed valuable research and editing support. Lynda Husband and Ed Formosa prepared the bulk of the manuscript for which we thank them. We would like to acknowledge and thank the Carthage Foundation for its support of northern European studies at CSIS.

The substance of the book, of course, is the work of the authors and editors who are responsible for any errors.

Introduction

William J. Taylor, Jr.
Paul M. Cole

This book purports to be one of the first published studies on the subject of comparative defense decision-making processes. To our knowledge it is the first to focus on the Nordic nations. Two general observations are central to this study. First, policy is not process, and the distinction is important. Second, the study of national security decision-making processes, the input side of decision making, has inherent value as a companion approach to the study of national security (or defense) policy, which is the output side of decision making.

National security *policy* is not process. A policy is a general course of action designed to achieve national security, to provide a framework for establishing national security objectives and for designing programs to achieve objectives. Although some policies may be personal decisions of a head of state or a minister, determination of policy and policy execution generally involve people and organizations of a national security bureaucracy in decision making. Thus, policy *per se* generally is an output of a decision-making bureaucracy. This is not to deny that policy is often conditioned by previous or ongoing programs. An old adage in policy studies is: "Show me your programs and I'll tell you your policy." But most would admit that previous and ongoing programs were developed on the basis of previously decided policy.

Jordan and Taylor, in *American National Security*,[1] tell us that national security policy may be defined as that part of government policy having as its objective the protection of a nation's people and territory from physical assault and the protection by a variety of means of vital economic and political interests, the loss of which would threaten the vitality and fundamental values of the state. Even for neutral nations some aspects of national security policy decision making involve cooperation and coordination with other states. Very few aspects of national security policy involve combined, allied decision making. However, it is clear that the vast preponderance of security decisions are indeed "national" or internal to the state, despite the fact that most national security policies are designed to influence political behavior and conditions outside the nation. One might suggest that national security policy studies *inter alia* are a special subset of the overall field of public administration studies. Arguably, public administration studies might deal with only some aspects of the process by which policy is both decided and implemented. More important, it is clear that the study of national security is inherently interdisciplinary. At peril, one disregards studies of human society, human nature, history, and economics. And the struggle for power which some political scientists tell us is the object of all politics certainly resides in the organizational and bureaucratic relationships which some have found to be the "essence of decision."

Most studies of comparative national security policy share two characteristics. First, they focus on policy outcomes, not on the processes by which policies are decided. Second, they have very little comparative content. The study of policy outcomes is important in telling us what a state's policies have been and are. Sometimes these studies offer projections of future policy directions with both heuristic and policy science value. More often than not, projections are based on possible or probable international interactions, external to the state.

It is extremely rare that one finds comparative decision-making content in national security studies. Undeniably, the study of a single state's national security decision-making process from one or more perspectives can have great explanatory value. The very few extant companion studies of several states' decision-making processes included in a single volume, although valuable, do not constitute a "comparative approach." The latter must identify differences and similarities and clarify their significance. This is precisely where most comparative studies of policy or process fall short; they do not take the final, most important and more difficult step. This volume does so.

The study of decision-making processes in a comparative context has great explanatory and, perhaps, predictive value for the policy analyst or decision maker. At minimum, studies of the input side of policy or strategy should serve as valuable cross checks on what strategic analysts think they observe as strategy, that is, the manifestation of policy output. Variables or factors external to the state (international variables) obviously have major impact upon national security decisions made by political leaders. For example, the actual or potential national security capabilities of friends and foes are central. However, the significance of otherwise "objective factors" is conditioned by perceptions because information is filtered through the images or psychological predispositions of political leaders and various segments of the polity before becoming relevant to decision making.

Important, too, for decisions are the ways in which a government organizes for national security. As Allison and Szanton tell us in *Remaking Foreign Policy*,[2] it is the structures of government agencies with their various missions and authorities, the processes by which decisions are made and executed, and the people whose characteristics and values interact in discussions and studies that determine how government works.

Our study considers the above factors and focuses on four areas of inquiry:

1. *The Defense Community.* Identifies the participants, elements and sectors (public and private) that are involved in or have influence on defense policy making at various stages.
2. *The Channels.* Maps out the formal and informal interactive processes within the defense community through which defense policy is formulated and executed.
3. *The Constraints.* Identifies the salient strategic, technical, resource, and political restraints that affect defense decision making.
4. *The Functions.* Identifies the policy results that are produced by the defense community, for example, strategy, doctrine, force structure, procurement, and personnel.

In each chapter a case study demonstrates how the defense decision-making process in a particular Nordic country actually works.

These four areas of inquiry are the same as those found in James Roherty's *Defense Policy Formulation*[3], which investigates national security decision making in Australia, South Africa, India, Japan, and France. Our research into the defense decision-making processes of the five Nordic nations—Denmark, Finland, Iceland, Norway, and Sweden—and our comparison of the five was conducted along the same lines. Students and government practitioners alike will find that Roherty's work and this volume are useful companions.

Perhaps the most important concept to master if one is to understand defense decision making in the Nordic countries is the "Nordic Balance." As Arne Brundtland, Norwegian security analyst, said in 1981, this concept "refers to a balance in the limitations of the applications of political or military power,"[4] which can be defined in either dynamic or static terms. The dynamic approach suggests that there has been and is a linkage between the security policies of the Nordic countries. Brundtland makes this case well, but attaches a greater degree of significance to it than others are prepared to accept, certainly more than the governments involved have been willing to admit. There are many reasons for this reluctance, including an unwillingness on the part of Sweden and Finland to compromise the obligations of neutrality. Thus we will stay with the static analysis, as it is the better way to describe the Nordic Balance in peacetime.

The five Nordic nations have developed a network of formal and informal relationships that has successfully tempered superpower interests in the region. This network, which has developed in the post–World War II years, helps regulate the regional security obligations that each Nordic nation has accepted. In practice this means that before a security issue is decided, it is examined for the impact that it will have on the other Nordic states. The Nordic Balance is not codified by law, nor is it a formal structure that regulates all aspects of security policy. But as an analytical tool the Nordic Balance helps explain the special, often unique, elements found in the security policy of each Nordic nation. A brief summary will illustrate some of these special characteristics.

Denmark

Denmark's geo-strategic position poses special problems for Danish defense policy planners. Historically, the frustration of how to deal with Denmark's perceived strategic value to the Great Powers made it difficult for the Danes to develop a coherent defense policy. Questions of whether to choose alignment with Germany to the south, with England to the west, with Russia to the east, or to maintain guaranteed neutrality as an alternative to alignment, have created what one scholar described as a defense policy since 1864 akin to "a walk through the wilderness."

Today Denmark's geo-strategic position is no less important than it was in the latter nineteenth century or first half of the twentieth century. By virtue of their geographic location the Danes dominate the belts and sounds from the Baltic Sea to the North Sea and the Atlantic Ocean. Their territory also represents the northern flank of NATO's central region and forms a natural connection between Germany and Norway. The country is flat with very few obstacles. Its 5 million inhabitants are distributed over one peninsula (Jutland) bordered by a seemingly unmanageable number of large and small islands that are characteristically indefensible because of their long, readily accessible coastlines. The dilemma of being perceived as a strategic piece of territory by both superpowers while at the same time possessing limited resources and population essential for mounting a credible defense has left Denmark with few options. Some observers would suggest that in the nuclear age this strategic dilemma has fostered feelings of hopelessness and futility, leading some to advocate complete disarmament. The other alternative, the status quo of membership in the NATO alliance ensuring that reinforcements will arrive as soon as possible, is advocated by those who remember the nightmare of World War II.

Prior to World War II the Soviet Union dominated only some 40 kilometers of the Baltic coast. The situation changed greatly after the war when the Soviets dominated an area covering approximately 2000 kilometers of the Baltic coast. During this period of domination the Soviets have greatly expanded the harbor and shipbuilding capacity of the area. It is estimated that more than 50 percent of the total shipbuilding and maintenance capacity required for keeping the Soviet Navy at sea is now available in the Baltic area.[5] The Danish Straits provide the only international passageway to this enormous industrial and military center. Therefore the geo-military importance of Denmark may be characterized as:[6]

1. *Transit area,* with the Danish Straits being the link between the Baltic Sea and the oceans.
2. *Barrier,* where the area may be used to block the exits from the Baltic Sea for Warsaw Pact naval units and merchant shipping and also for preventing NATO naval forces from entering the Baltic Sea. In addition, control of the area may preclude hostile air activity over and through the area.
3. *Surveillance area,* from which passage to and from the Baltic Sea can be observed and registered. Such monitoring of Soviet and Warsaw Pact naval forces are especially important to the NATO countries.
4. *Assembly and base area,* enabling offensive and defensive operations, including either a NATO counterattack against a possible Warsaw Pact attack across the North German plain or a Warsaw Pact attack from the north into the rear of NATO forward defense in the northern part of the Federal Republic of Germany.

Finland

Finland is a neutral nation which exists in the shadow of Soviet power. Finnish security policy is constrained both by the Paris Peace Treaty of 1947, which established specific limits on the size of Finnish armed forces, and by the Treaty of Friendship, Co-operation and Mutual Assistance (TFCMA) signed with the USSR in 1948. The TFCMA has been extended twice, first in 1955 and again in 1970. The latter extension is to remain valid until 1990. The essential elements of the TFCMA are:

1. Any armed attack on Finland (or the Soviet Union through Finland) by Germany or any of its allies will require Finnish resistance and, if necessary, armed assistance by the Soviet Union.
2. The pact requires consultation between the high commands of both countries in the case of a threat of such an attack.
3. Finland is prohibited from entering any alliance directed against the Soviet Union (this obligation is also assumed in reciprocity by the Soviets).
4. The contracting parties pledge to respect the sovereignty and integrity of each other.

These formal agreements are only part of the milieu in which Finnish leaders consult with the Soviets fairly regularly on important foreign policy issues, though such consultation does not necessarily imply cooperation. For example, in the fall 1979, the Finns rejected a Soviet proposal for combined maneuvers.

The Finns state repeatedly both in publications and in interviews that they are concerned that all external powers understand the dedication of their nation to real neutrality, made credible by a strong "total defense." The general goals and objectives of Finnish defense are:[7]

1. the preservation of the territorial integrity of Finland in peacetime and in war;
2. denial of Finnish territory to any would-be aggressor whose purposes may focus either on the subjugation of Finland proper or on the utilization of Finnish land, sea, or air space for aggression against third parties; and
3. preservation of the political, socioeconomic and legal systems of Finland.

In order to execute these fundamental tasks, the defense forces and the political authorities immediately responsible for them have established a number of more specific functions, chief of which are:

1. maintenance of the forces authorized under existing treaties and proper training of personnel;
2. production procurement, and maintenance of equipment needed by the defense forces; and
3. enhancement of the population's support for the defense effort and development of physical education and sports, thereby improving the ability of all Finns to participate in this national effort.

Iceland

The broad outlines of Iceland's foreign policy were established in the period 1949–51. Tradition, history, and culture favor neutrality as a basic approach to Icelandic defense policy. Iceland's exposed position in the cold war environment which quickly followed the end of World War II imposed on Iceland the requirement to tilt from a policy of neutrality toward the developing framework of collective security.[8] In a politically agonizing and highly contested decision, Iceland joined NATO in 1949. Simultaneously, Iceland declared her intention never to raise a military force and never to accept the presence of foreign troops during peacetime. Amidst the deepening cold war and the deteriorating international climate, Iceland signed a Bilateral Defense

Agreement with the United States in 1950, which remains the basic contractual relationship. Under the terms of the 1951 agreement, Iceland temporarily accepted the presence of an American-manned, NATO Defense Force (IDF) of Keflavík, 47 kilometers from the capital of Reykjavík.

These key decisions, NATO membership and the Bilateral Defense Agreement, serve to define present Icelandic defense policy, and all discussion in the Icelandic polity is focused on issues directly related to these two policy decisions. It is conventional wisdom that a greater involvement in NATO is politically unacceptable. The trend from 1951 to the present has been toward lessening the foreign presence in Iceland. Conflicts arising from the clash of defense interests with the more visible perception of resource threats have periodically strained the NATO connection, sometimes to the point of suggesting Iceland's withdrawal from NATO, the Bilateral Agreement, or both.

For a number of reasons the populace has never totally accepted these broad outlines of Icelandic defense policy. As a result, defense policy has become a very important and divisive political issue. While present defense policy is defined by the same contractual agreements established in 1949–51, the drift away from neutrality in 1951 is still contested. Icelanders demonstrate a general awareness of the fact that the Soviet navy has expanded in recent years and that Iceland's geography makes it strategically important to NATO and to the Soviets as well. This awareness is not accompanied by any real sense of urgency concerning Icelandic national security. However, bearing in mind that political opinion on any issue in Iceland runs the ideological spectrum from left to right, it is possible to detect a consensus concerning the Soviet Union.

Some analysts have made much of the fact that the Soviet diplomatic mission is by far the largest in Reykjavík. The most common response to this by the average Icelander is to refer to well-known stereotypes of Russian bureaucratic inefficiency and the Soviet need to insure political reliability by overlapping functions and redundancy of personnel. There are other contributing factors. Russians perform all functions in the Soviet mission, whereas in Western embassies the bulk of nonrepresentative functions are performed by Icelandic employees. Nevertheless, the former reason is the one most frequently cited by Icelanders.

Norway

Norway's security is based upon several interrelated policies. The most important of these is membership in the North Atlantic Alliance. This, like neutrality for Sweden, is the cornerstone of Norwegian security. And, although this implies a rejection of bilateral security arrangements in favor of multilateral guarantees, it is also apparent that Norway places major reliance upon the two major naval powers, the United States and Great Britain.[9]

Closely related to this are Norway's unilateral measures for reassurance and nonprovocation of the Soviet Union, with which it shares a 196 kilometer border. The restrictions influence the nature of Norway's participation in the NATO alliance. The most important of these are "base and ban" policies: a ban against the positioning of nuclear weapons or foreign troops in Norway. Despite the fact that domestic social and political considerations are also responsible for these restrictions, Norway has consistently sought to lessen the risk of crisis or conflict, first through its early postwar "bridge building" and UN policies, and later by attempting to defuse incidents which might lead to confrontation with the USSR. With technology expanding the potential problem areas between Norway and the Soviets, it is uncertain whether this policy of nonprovocation will be able to be applied as readily to new issues. Events of recent years on Svalbard, negotiations over boundaries and fishing zones, incidents in North Norway and, most recently, the Norwegian decision to prestock equipment for a U.S. marine brigade, might be indicative of continuing and possibly expanding problems.

A third major policy guideline is the Norwegian rejection of a purely Nordic solution to its problems. This was manifest in Norway's attitude during the 1948 Nordic defense pact negotiations, when Norway was the least enthusiastic of the three participants. Subsequent reviews of this policy have continued to support that position. This does not, however, imply any decrease in Norwegian support for Scandinavian cooperation. Moreover, Norway considers specifically the impact of its own decisions upon the policies of its Nordic neighbors.

In order to maintain a credible deterrent, Norway has kept a consistent level of defense spending and maintained a strategy which emphasizes defense of North Norway against a limited attack using forces in place. This not only protects against a possible limited attack with little or no warning, but also provides a delaying force to enable Norway to bring its mobilized reserves to bear. The system is heavily reliant on early warning of Soviet preparations for attack.

A January 1981 decision to prestock U.S. military equipment in Norway has led to serious debate. The rationales for that decision will be discussed below, but it should be noted that shortening the time required to introduce U.S. troops into Norway means that in a time of crisis the Norwegian government might be able to put off the decision to request introduction of non-Norwegian NATO forces. There clearly were political as well as military reasons for both the prestocking agreement and the location of the prestocked equipment.

Sweden

Sweden also is a neutral country. Whether the result of historical necessity or rational choice, this nation of only 8.3 million people has not been involved as a belligerent in war since the Napoleonic era. Through a combination of decisions over the years, Sweden has adopted a foreign policy of "non-alignment (or freedom from alliances) between power blocs in peace, aiming at neutrality in war."[11] The foreign policy objective is *de facto* neutrality unsupported by international guarantees or by conventional international law such as the cases of Swiss or Austrian neutrality. Sweden's policy of neutrality presupposes a *tous azimut* strategy under which total defense preparations should provide the capability to meet an attack from any quarter. Sweden's defense is deemed to play an important role in maintaining the Nordic balance by preventing instabilities which might result in direct confrontation in the Nordic area between the superpowers.

Swedish defense doctrine calls for "Total Defense", including:

1. military defense,
2. civil defense,
3. economic defense,
4. psychological defense, and
5. "other defense," for example, telecommunications and medical care.

Military strategy planned for meeting the marginal attack has in reality been a combination of territorial defense based on rapid mobilization of a large conscript force and home guard, and a technologically advanced air force.

The Nordic Balance

Despite the formal differences in the status of their foreign and defense policies, there are important similarities in the cultures and traditions of the Nordic nations which have led to a relatively high degree of cooperation. The Nordic Council, established in 1952, is a common forum in which each of these nations discusses matters related to industry, trade, agriculture, labor markets, and culture. Foreign and defense policy matters generally are kept outside the council.[12] For dicussions of common policies related to the latter, the Nordic Ministers of Foreign Affairs meet twice annually. These meetings generally cover such matters as joint sponsorship of aid programs to developing nations, but there is also periodic focus on common defense concerns such as those subsumed by various proposals for a Nordic nuclear free zone.

The Nordic balance exists at two levels, the political and the military. The first level includes the subjective, political ambience borne out of the bilateral diplomatic, trade, and cultural relations each of the Nordic countries maintains with the USSR and those relationships and understandings that the Nordic nations maintain among themselves. The second level includes the more objective aspects of military force structure, doctrine, and strategy of each of the Nordic nations, couched in the contexts of both their legal commitments to NATO or to neutrality and of the military strategic relationship between NATO and the Warsaw Pact. The Nordic balance is best conceptualized as a carefully orchestrated zone within which the inherent tensions born out of mutual superpower hostilities and capabilities are to be attenuated. Acts in the region which might be considered hostile on the part of either superpower or their respective allies are drawn quickly into international public focus. International prestige is an element of national power and, in this respect, the public positions taken by the Nordic nations can impact in important ways upon the policies adopted in peacetime by the superpowers. Too, the certainty that the considerable military capability possessed by most of the Nordic nations would be exercised efficiently in their own defense must serve as an important consideration in the calculations of Soviet military planners and the Soviet leadership.

Notes

1. Jordan, Amos A., William J. Taylor, Jr., and associates. *American National Security,* second edition, (Baltimore: Johns Hopkins University Press, 1984), vii–viii.
2. Allison, Graham, and Peter Szanton, *Remaking Foreign Policy,* (New York: Basic Books, 1976).
3. Roherty, James, ed., *Defense Policy Formation,* (Durham, N.C.: Carolina Academic Press, 1980).
4. See Arne Olav Brundtland, *The Nordic Balance,* (Oslo: Norwegian Institute of International Affairs, 1981), 1.
5. "Denmark Between the Superpowers." Danish Foreign Policy Society, 1975.
6. "Warsaw Pact Aggression Possibilities Against Denmark," Danish Defense Intelligence Service, August 1980, 4–6.
7. Vego, Milan, and John C. Burton, III. "Fulcrum of Power: Scandinavia," *Defense and Foreign Affairs,* January 1981.
8. Grøndal, Benedikt, *Iceland From Neutrality to NATO Membership,* (Oslo: Universitetsforlaget, 1971), 14.
9. Frydenlund, Knut, "The Security of Norway and the Atlantic Alliance," *NATO Review,* June 1976, 3.
10. Perhaps this is what Norwegian Foreign Minister Knut Frydenlund meant when he said prestocked U.S. equipment would permit Norway to "keep a lower pro-

file in the event of a crisis with the Soviet Union . . ." See "Russians Assail Norway on Arms Stockpile," *New York Times,* December 28, 1980.

11. Andrén, Nils, *et al, The Future of the Nordic Balance,* (Stockholm: Ministry of Defense, Secretariat for National Security Policy and Long-Range Defense Planning, 1977), 85. For further background, see Johan Jørgen Holst, ed., *Five Roads to Nordic Security,* (Oslo: Universitetsforlaget, 1973), 208–212.

12. "Nordic Cooperation," (Stockholm: P.A. Norstedt et Söner, 1971), 1–2.

1
Denmark

Christian Thune
Nikolaj Peterson

Introduction

Denmark's membership in NATO may today seem obvious enough given the strategic situation of the country and the perceived nature of the Soviet threat. The Danish decision to join NATO in 1949 was backed by a substantial majority of the *Folketing* (parliament) including the major party, the Social Democrats.[1]

At the time, however, the decision was viewed by many as a sharp break with the posture of neutrality that had formed the basis of Danish security policy during the first half of the century. Danish neutrality policy had been coupled with a pragmatic accommodation to the fact that neighboring Germany was the largest military power in central Europe. However, neutrality did not protect Denmark when Germany occupied it on April 9, 1940 in order to secure bases and lines of communication for the simultaneous attack on Norway. Danish military resistance was feeble due partly to a snap political decision to put up only token resistance and partly to the fact that during the 1930s Danish defense forces had been cut back to the absolute minimum.

After the Second World War sentiments among a majority of the Danes could be summed up in the often repeated sentence "Never again an April ninth." The onset of the Cold War further made it clear to most Danes that it would pose great difficulties for a small country with limited resources like Denmark to muster the kind of credible defense capabilities which would make its neutrality respected in case of another major conflict in Europe.

It is significant, however, that before Denmark's decision to join the North Atlantic Treaty Organization there were for more than half a year serious deliberations among Denmark, Norway, and Sweden on a scheme for a Scandinavian collective security arrangement. The Danish Social Democratic government of the day vigorously supported this effort.[2] These negotiations eventually foundered on the gap between Swedish insistence on the strict neutrality of a Scandinavian Defense Union and Norwegian—and to a lesser degree Danish—insistence on military ties with the Western powers. The historical circumstances surrounding Denmark's decision to join NATO are important to the extent that the political discussion on defense issues may even today be described as a debate between the view that Danish defense must be strong and firmly committed to the alliance and the view that Denmark should keep as low a profile as possible vis-à-vis superpower rivalry and weaponry, that Danish defense and alliance commitments should be kept at a low level in political as well as economic terms, and that the possibilities of further basing Danish security on arrangements in a Nordic or United Nations context should be explored.[3]

Accordingly, successive Danish governments have stressed the importance of Danish efforts in the UN in the fields of disarmament and assistance to Third World countries. While a significant amount of diplomatic and financial resources have gone into securing an adequate profile for Denmark in the UN it must be realized that Nordic cooperation has nothing but the very slightest results to show on a politically operational level.

Actually Denmark's decision to join the European Community in 1973 has led to much more radical changes in Danish foreign policy. The so-called European Political Cooperation increasingly constitutes the framework for Danish foreign policy.[4] To a large extent the raison d'etre of the Political Cooperation can be described as the harmonization and formulation of a common Western European platform vis-à-vis the superpowers but especially the United States. Thus Danish membership tends to reinforce the European dimension in Danish foreign politics and to diminish the U.S.-based Atlantic dimension which was at the core of the 1949 decision to join NATO. The European Political Cooperation is slowly approaching and may soon cross the formal demarcation line between political issues and security/defense issues which have not till now been covered by the Cooperation. Denmark opposes this trend, but may well quite soon be compelled to choose between a security policy based on European cooperation within a loosened NATO framework or to turn once more toward the Atlantic concept of the United States.[5]

Denmark's Strategic Situation and the Soviet Threat

The essential vulnerability of Denmark is due to two aspects of its strategic situation. First, in an often cited expression, Denmark is placed as the cork in the bottle of the Baltic. The power which effectively controls the Danish straits is able to prevent any fleet from leaving or entering the Baltic. Second, Denmark is situated on the flank of the European central front and thus control of Danish territory, especially the peninsula of Jutland, is essential from the viewpoint of defending as well as attacking forces in this theater.[6]

During the first decades of Danish NATO membership the attention of military defense planning focused primarily on the first mentioned aspect.

Further, the NATO perception of the Soviet threat was that the main hazard for Denmark was a surprise attack concentrated on securing control of the Danish straits. From this threat perception the obvious strategy seemed to be to give the defense forces the capability to fend off an attack without the need of a general mobilization. At the same time high priority was given to providing sufficient reinforcements.

During the 1970s the perception of the Soviet threat concentrated more on a scenario where Denmark would get involved after a major all-out Soviet attack on central Europe. Given the scale of such an attack the implication was, first, that warning time would be considerably longer. A second implication was that Denmark's position on the flank of the central front became the potentially more relevant aspect of defense planning. In 1962 Denmark and West Germany had set up a joint defense structure for Hamburg, Schleswig-Holstein, and Denmark. This joint command for the Baltic Approaches (BALTAP) has during the last decades become the foundation of the Danish defense effort to an increasing extent.[7] The resulting integration of Danish and West German planning and resources may well today constitute a considerably more effective military guarantee for Denmark than the Allied forces which, according to the Rapid Reinforcement Plans of NATO, are earmarked for Denmark.

The Politicization of Defense and Security Issues

Danish defense is thus today highly integrated with and dependent upon the West German armed forces. Strangely enough this development has not really been contested in a Danish political context. Three other issues, however, have been targets for the significant politicization of Danish debate on security and defense issues which has occurred in recent years.

First the nuclear issue more or less erupted on the Danish political scene—as in the rest of Western Europe—in the months preceeding the Intermediate-range Nuclear Force (INF) double-track decision of December 1979.[8] The remarkable growth of the antinuclear protest movement was partly inspired by the West German peace movement; partly by a general mistrust of U.S. strategic and global policies, which was from 1981 reinforced in many Danish eyes by what was perceived as the offensive strategies of the Reagan administration; and partly self-evidently from the fears of a nuclear holocaust for which the INF debate acted as a catalyst.

The nuclear issue took on a special direction when the peace movement, the left-wing parties, and eventually the Social Democrats took up seriously the prospect of a Nordic Nuclear Free Zone.[9] This idea, which originally was a Norwegian Social Democratic initiative, succeeded in becoming the common denominator for political action for the rather heterogeneous forces of antinuclearism. Thus the nuclear issue brought into the political focus not only NATO's INF modernization program but also other aspects of the alliance commitment.

The second highly politicized issue was the matter of allied reinforcements.[10] It is a long established symbol of Denmark's low profile in the alliance that Denmark accepts neither allied bases nor the prepositioning of nuclear warheads on its soil. But the intense debate in 1980–81 concerning the implications of the Rapid Reinforcement Program and the program for U.S. fighter reinforcements (Collocated Operation Bases) was surprising and probably explained by the way in which the nuclear issue had reinforced apprehensions about military integration into the alliance. The debate focused on the issue of prepositioning of heavy U.S. military equipment which by the critics was seen as diminishing Danish independence and freedom to maneuver in a crisis.

The third major issue became the Danish adherence to the 1978 NATO decision of an annual 3 percent growth in real terms in the defense budgets of the member countries. This issue will be covered in more detail below in connection with the presentation of the defense agreements of 1982.

The politics of security and defense were transformed in two or three years from a state of relative tranquility and consensus to one of extreme politicization and visibility.[11] The following presentation of the structure of decision making should be viewed in this light.

Principal Actors and the Structure of Decision Making

The Government and the Ministry of Defense

For the Danish Government, its ministries and agencies are of course the principal actors in the formulation and implementation of Danish defense policy, even if the constraints of parliamentary democracy occasionally make themselves very much felt.

The Danish defense administration or bureaucracy is divided between the Ministry of Defense and the Defense Command. The division of work and the spheres of authority tend to be somewhat blurred to the outside observer. In principle the ministry, which consists of the minister and the Defense Department, handles the *political* framework for Danish defense policies, for example, the part of defense administration that relates to the political apparatus generally and to other branches of government—and NATO—bureaucracy.

The Defense Command on the other hand is entrusted—again in principle—with the more routine and *technical* administration of defense. However, given its extensive staff resources, quantitatively as well as qualitatively, the Defense Command has in recent years come to play an important role in the planning and execution of political initiatives. In the formal structure the Defense Command's channel of command to the minister goes through the department. But actually the minister often consults or decides directly with the chiefs of the Defense Command, or they make good use of the fairly easy and direct access which they enjoy with the minister as well as with other centrally placed politicians.

Apart from the defense minister other ministers play a varying but often central role in defense decision making. Due to the fact that security and defense policy is often highly politicized the prime minister and the foreign minister will follow the preparations of defense decisions closely. Though these ministers can draw on nothing like the administrative apparatus which is as the disposal of the defense minister, the prime minister includes in his small staff a security policy adviser and the foreign ministry has a small but centrally placed NATO section.

Obviously the defense minister, the department, and the Defense Command have a comparatively free hand in the formulation and implementation of more general or technical defense matters. But along with the accelerating politicization of defense issues the trend is toward more involvement from the prime and foreign ministers. This state of affairs is of course reinforced in the present four-party coalition government by the fact that the leaders of the major coalition parties, the Conservatives and the Liberals, occupy the posts of prime and foreign minister, respectively. The finance minister will of course also have an opinion as to the overall room for defense expenditures in the strained budgets of today's Denmark. Accordingly, these four ministers will often constitute a special "inner cabinet" in defense decision making.

An interesting offshoot of the involvement of several branches of government in defense issues is the Coordinating Committee for Security Questions which includes senior staff from the prime minister's office, the Foreign Ministry, the Defense Ministry, the Defense Command, and Military Intelligence. This committee coordinates and channels relevant information between the departments. In the event of a major emergency or crisis this committee should be the central coordinating and steering unit.

The government may occasionally want to base its decisions on the analyses and proposals of government-appointed committees of experts and advisers.[12] In 1968 the nonsocialist coalition government appointed the Seidenfaden Committee to analyze the options for Danish security politics. The occasion was the upcoming twentieth anniversary of Denmark's entry into NATO, which had given rise to some public debate over continued membership. The committee consisted mainly of senior government officials, officers, and researchers. Not too surprisingly the committee concluded in its extensive report that there was no real option for Denmark other than continuing membership in NATO.[13]

After the onset of an extensive politicization of defense and security issues in the late 1970s the Social Democratic government in 1981 set up a permanent Commission on Security and Disarmament Affairs. This commission has members from the research community, the political parties, and various government departments including defense representatives. Interestingly enough the mandate of this commission is not so much to give the government good advice as to stimulate and participate in a qualified public debate.

The Folketing and the Political Parties

Denmark is a constitutional monarchy and a parliamentary democracy. Since 1913 no single party has been able to command a majority in the Folketing and accordingly governments have either had to be based on a coalition of parties which together constitute a majority or to be a minority government of one or more parties which rely on other parties outside the government to furnish the necessary parliamentary support. The latter constellation is the rule rather than the exception. The Danish political system can safely be described as multi-party. At present nine parties of greatly varying size are represented in the Folketing.[14] See table 1-1.

Between the 1880s and the First World War defense questions were the most hotly debated issues among the political parties of the time and there has since been a consistently high level of politicization of defense budgets in particular.

The largest party since 1924, the Social Democratic party, commands a central position in this as well as other issues. The decision to join NATO was more than anything promoted by the shift in the Social Democratic party away from the neutralist stance of the 1930s toward an acceptance of alliance membership, and the resulting necessity of a reasonably strong Danish defense. However, during the last decade the party has generally been disposed toward letting defense suffer, along with other fields of public expenditure, from the effects of economic recession. The party line has moreover been greatly influenced by the extent to which the nuclear issue has become controversial in a Danish context. Accordingly the Social Democracts have become generally adamant in their opposition to important aspects of NATO's present nuclear strategy, such as INF modernization. In this view, such opposition does not affect Denmark's basic commitment to NATO membership and to an adequate Danish defense effort. The Conservatives and the Liberals along with their two small coalition partners, the Center Democrats and the Christian People's party, are consistently in favor of NATO membership and generally receptive toward the calls for stronger defense allotments from the Defense Command and from NATO. However, in the present political situation even the NATO and defense commitments of

Table 1-1
The Danish Parliament as of October 1984: Based on Results of National Elections Held January 1984

Party	Votes	Seats	Change from 1981	Percentage of Seats
Conservative Party	787,764	42	+16	23.5
Liberal Party	405,623	22	+2	12.3
Center Democratic Party	154,533	8	-7	4.5
Christian People's Party	91,521	5	+1	2.8
Social Democratic Party	1,063,201	56	-3	31.3
Socialist People's Party	387,170	21	0	11.7
Radical Liberal Party	184,274	10	+1	5.6
Progress Party	120,701	6	-9	3.3
Left Socialist Party	89,042	5	0	2.8
Others	76,498	4	-1	2.2
Total	3,360,327	179		100

Note: Denmark's current government is led by a minority coalition consisting of four center right parties: the Conservatives, the Liberals, the Center Democrats and the Christian People's party. The coalition controls only 77 of the 179 seats in the Folketing (parliament). The remaining seats are held by the Social Democrats, the Socialist People's party and other smaller political groups. Since the Danish Constitution only requires 2 percent of the national vote for parliamentary representation, a large number of parties (currently nine) often hold seats in the Folketing.

these four parties have been given second priority to the perceived need to remain in governmental power and carry through the coalition program for economic recovery. Thus the coalition government has during the last two years suffered a series of almost humiliating defeats in the Folketing over nuclear policy issues.[15] The Social Democratic opposition, acting in a coalition with the left-wing parties and the small but influential Radical Liberal party, have caused these setbacks.

The fact that the government coalition is forced to base its existence on this kind of "selective" parliamentarism is mainly due to the influence of the small Radical Liberal party. This party provides the government with the necessary majority in economic and social policies. However, in nuclear policy issues it sides with the Social Democrats and the left-wing parties, and in defense issues it has been outside the governing consensus since the mid-1970s. This stand is consistent with the Radical Liberals' traditional bias toward defense expenditures and their lukewarm attitude toward NATO.

The two left-wing parties, the Socialist People's party and the Left Wing Socialists are against NATO membership and want a sharply reduced defense based on a Danish decision to disarm unilaterally. The Communist party has not in recent elections been able to pass the threshold of 2 percent of the votes which is necessary to secure seats in parliament according to Danish election laws. However, the party when in parliament has consistently voted against any defense expenditures, and of course attacked Danish NATO membership. To the right of the government coalition is the Progress party. This party was founded in 1973 as an antitax and anti-government-spending party and after initial electoral successes in the 1970s which made it at times the second largest party, it has now dwindling electoral support. Its security and defense policies have been somewhat erratic. The founder, Mogens Glistrup, did not exclude defense from the government expenditures he was campaigning against and has often been cited for his suggestion that Danish defense should be traded for a telephone answering service with the recorded message "We surrender." However, the majority of the party has without reservations supported a strong defense posture as well as NATO membership.

The government has to answer to the Folketing for its defense policies in three different ways. First, members of the Folketing may pose questions or interpellations to the defense minister. There has been a marked growth in the number of questions during the last few years. In 1979 the foreign minister and the defense minister had to answer eleven questions which to a large extent were made by members of the left-wing parties. In 1983 the number had gone up to forty-four. This rise reflects the growing politicization during the period and not surprisingly a majority of the questions were concerned with the INF issue and the issue of allied reinforcements to Denmark. It should be noted that apart from the political difficulties these questions may occasionally pose for the government, they create a considerable burden for the Ministry of Defense in administrative terms. Whereas the procedures connected with a question ensure a short debate mainly between the minister and the questioner, the procedures concerning interpellations are more elaborate and imply speeches from the spokesmen of all the parties. The debate will usually end in a vote between one or more proposed resolutions. If the Folketing decides on a resolution which goes against the government, the latter will usually be forced to step down according to the principle of parliamentarism. While the present nonsocialist government coalition has been in power it has been voted down in a succession of interpellation debates on the INF issue. However, as already mentioned the government has decided not to let this have any parliamentary consequences and has instead accepted the rather humiliating prospects of presenting a policy to its allies which is not government policy but that of the Social-Democratic-led opposition.

Second, the Folketing debates and decides on the necessary laws in connection with the operation of the defense system. These debates, however, seldom constitute a problem in themselves, inasmuch as they usually reflect the consensus which the government may or may not have secured in previous negotiations with its supporting parties. These negotiations constitute the third arena for the Government-Folketing relations. Negotiations may take place in a formalized setting in the Folketing's seventeen-member Defense Committee or more informally in the ad hoc committees composed of representatives of those parties who secure the majorities for the various defense settlements. The workings of these parliamentary mechanisms will be described in greater detail below in connection with a presentation of the making of the defense settlements of 1982 and 1984.

Pressure Groups and Lobbying

In Denmark, as in any other open democracy, decision makers are the object of the efforts of a variety of pressure groups that try to influence political decisions. Some of these groups have an almost formalized status in defense decision making. This applies to the various unions of defense personnel, who like all employees lobby for better working conditions and higher wages. In recent years, the organization of professional soldiers and NCOs has acquired increasing influence over defense policy making by virtue of close contacts with the Social Democratic party.

Denmark's armament industries are negligible and accordingly there is no lobbying on behalf of any "military-industrial complex." However, since the major politicization of defense occurred in 1979 there has been a marked growth in the number of private organizations that try to influence decision makers and public opinion. Only a few of these are presenting prodefense viewpoints. The major organizations, The Atlantic Association and Defend Denmark ("Værn om Danmark"), both have rather limited membership. One major grassroots movement in favor of a strong defense is of course the Home Guard with its 78,000 members. However, the Home Guard, being part of the defense, does not speak out as an organization, even if its individual members make themselves frequently heard in the public debate.

Measured in terms of membership and support the old and new peace organizations in contrast have a significant impact on the direction and content of the current public debate on defense issues.[16] The grassroots character of these organizations is reflected in the plethora of pamphlets, meetings, and mass demonstrations which have manifested themselves in recent years under the slogans of "No to war, NATO, INF, defense expenditures," and the like. In political terms the major impact of the peace movement seems to have been on the attitudes of the Social Democrats. Members and supporters of the peace movement are increasingly represented in the Social Democratic party organization and the party leader, Anker Jørgensen, is himself a fervent spokesman for skepticism toward NATO nuclear strategy. Several of the major trade unions have similarly made the peace cause part of their platform.

One further source of (fluctuating) influence on decision makers are the experts on defense and security issues from the universities and research institutes. However, their number is very small and their efforts to make their viewpoints heard among decision makers suffer from the well-known difficulties in translating expert analyses into identifiable political impact on decision makers.

The Media

The treatment of defense and security issues in the Danish media is neither quantitatively nor qualitatively at a high level. The treatment is mostly focused on single issues, those that are hotly contested in the political debate, and there is rarely an ambition to treat the more general or for that matter technical aspects of the overall issue. Even if it may thus be said that the media are more reflective than provocative in the public arena of debate they may still constitute a considerable influence on the perceptions of the populace in general, for example by presenting and eventually gradually magnifying the importance of single issues, such as the INF issue.

Public Opinion

The Danes are regularly polled on their attitudes towards security and defense.[17] The results have in recent years presented a somewhat puzzling picture. On the one hand the polls reveal a consistent majority in favor of Danish membership in NATO. See table 1–2. In a 1983 poll the results were 69 percent in favor, 15 percent against and 16 percent undecided. On the other hand a majority of those polled have come out against increased defense budgets (36 percent in favor, 51 percent against) and NATO deployment of Pershing IIs in Western Europe (24 percent in favor, 58 percent against).

These polls indicate that the contradictions in Social Democractic policy reflect similar contradictions among the voters, and may thus be sound electoral strategy. And at the same time the polls may explain why the present government coalition is reluctant to make a stand and force an election on defense and security issues. If such an election were held it would obviously be a contest between the government parties' attempt to make NATO membership the central issue and the Social Democrats' and left-wing opposition's attempt to focus attention on the nuclear issue.

External Influences

The major external influence on Danish defense decision making naturally enough stems from NATO. Of course Danish governments loyally go through the various phases of NATO consultation when major defense decisions are made. However, at the time when NATO is consulted on a specific

Table 1-2
The Danish Gallup Polls: 1949-1984
"Are you for or against Danish membership in NATO?"

	For %	Against %	Do not know %	Total %
March 1949	47	26	27	100
September 1950	53	26	21	100
April 1951	49	27	24	100
March 1952	50	28	22	100
October 1952	44	28	28	100
February 1953	49	23	28	100
August 1953	48	25	27	100
April 1954	39	25	36	100
August 1954	47	24	29	100
December 1955	27	24	29	100
August 1957	54	19	27	100
November 1957	67	15	18	100
March 1958	55	18	27	100
February 1959	42	15	43	100
June 1959	44	6	50	100
February 1960	33	11	56	100
July 1960	41	11	48	100
January 1961	49	11	40	100
August 1961	58	9	33	100
March 1962	47	10	43	100
November 1962	50	12	38	100
June 1963	50	11	39	100
June 1964	49	13	38	100
April 1965	45	19	36	100
November 1965	41	13	46	100
June 1966	41	17	42	100
January 1967	42	14	44	100
October 1967	47	14	39	100
June 1968	39	20	41	100
Aug./Sep. 1968	54	16	30	100
April 1969	53	11	34	100
September 1969	45	13	42	100
October 1970	52	15	33	100
March 1972	50	22	28	100
November 1972	45	18	37	100
November 1973	49	25	26	100
March 1974	52	19	29	100
May 1975	51	22	28	100
June 1976	49	17	34	100
August 1977	52	26	22	100
September 1978	57	21	22	100
August 1979	55	19	26	100
September 1980	58	18	24	100
November 1981	59	18	23	100
May 1983	69	15	16	100
November 1984	56	19	25	100

Source: Berlingske Tidende and The Gallup Institute.

proposal the government has usually already been through intricate maneuvering to secure a parliamentary majority behind it. Accordingly the government will be extremely reluctant to compromise the laboriously reached domestic consensus by accepting major amendments from NATO.

Denmark's relations with NATO have recently been especially strained by the many footnotes to NATO communiques on the INF issue which stress Danish reservations to NATO policy in this area. This trend which earned Denmark the sobriquet "footnote country" is of course the consequence of the Social-Democratic-led Folketing majority's successes in forcing the nonsocialist government coalition's hand on this issue as described above.

Whereas NATO has normally been reduced to expressing its official concerns about Danish defense efforts when these have been found lagging in relation to the requirements decided upon in the NATO councils and committees, individual major members of the alliance have occasionally felt free to voice their misgivings. For instance, former U.S. Secretary of Defense Harold Brown wrote in 1980 two long letters to his Danish colleague in which he stressed in precise terms U.S. dissatisfaction with the Danish failure to live up to the NATO goal of a 3 percent annual increase in defense expenditures.[18]

Denmark's Western European allies are to a varying degree uncertain about the implications of what they see as the "neutralist tendencies" especially in Danish nuclear policies. The French initiative to gather those Western European NATO members which are "responsible" about the nuclear issue into the revitalized WEU has the character of an informal signal to Danish decision makers that Denmark runs the risk of being marginalized in a NATO context if present policies are continued—even if these policies are dictated by the Social-Democratic-led majority.

The Soviet Union of course also constitutes a major "external influence," partly because it is the major perceived threat to Danish security and partly due to the extent of its access to the Danish domestic setting. The Danish Communist party has a record of consistently high loyalty to the Moscow line, and even if the party has a negligible influence in Danish party politics as such it has a major influence on parts of the peace movement. The degree of this influence is a hotly discussed subject in the Danish debate. The uncertainty around this issue is well reflected in a poll taken in 1983 where there was a majority of affirmative answers to the question whether the communists had infiltrated and controlled the organizations of the peace movement. In the same poll a majority said they did not believe that the activities of the peace movement were always to the advantage of the Soviets.

Actually the peace movement seems much more to be part of a truly transnational movement and thus reflects more than anything the growth and platforms of the West German peace movement. Another transnational movement with considerable, if rather unnoticed, impact on the Danish domestic setting is the so called Scandilux cooperation between Western European Social Democratic parties.[19] Scandilux has under the aegis of the West German Social Democratic Party gained considerable momentum during the last two or three years. Probably West Germans as well as Danes have enjoyed this quasi-international forum at a time when they were out of government. At any rate there seems to be a remarkable coincidence between the issues debated and stands taken at Scandilux meetings and the initiatives subsequently taken by Danish Social Democrats especially in the INF context.

The Demise of the Establishment

The presentation of the Danish defense decision-making structure in the preceding pages should make it clear that the degree of complexity is equal to that of any other open society. However, it must be emphasized that even within this structure there is a tendency toward the emergence of substructures.

During the 1950s, 1960s, and early 1970s one could almost identify a small "establishment" of defense decision makers. This establishment consisted of defense-oriented politicians from the major parties (the Social Democrats, the Conservatives, and the Liberals), senior officers and civil servants, and a few researchers and members of the business community. A very considerable part of the discussions relating to defense issues took place within this group and to a certain extent it could be said that if and when this establishment reached a consensus on a given issue the result would very soon be operational defense policy.

The onset of politicization of defense and security changed the composition as well as the role of the establishment. The split and shift in Social Democratic defense postures disengaged this party from the establishment. One result of this development was a growing polarization between the anti-defense majority of the Social Democrats and the now Conservative- and Liberal-dominated establishment. Another perhaps less noticed result was that the viewpoints of the military chiefs and the defense experts, which had hitherto been part of an intraestablishment dialogue, now come to sound like part of the right-of-center parties' critique of the Social Democrats. At any rate the defense decision making of the early 1980s in many ways implied a break with the procedures and structures of earlier decades. This point should be illustrated by the following study of the defense agreements of 1982 and 1984.

Danish Policy Making for Defense: Two Cases

The "Defense Settlement" as an Institution in Danish Politics

The politics of Danish defense policy has a long and distinct history of its own, which singles out this issue as one which has structured not only the policy agenda of Denmark's politics but its entire political system. The fact that the dominant left-right dimension in Danish politics does not coincide completely with the defense policy dimension has had a destabilizing effect both on coalition formation in general and on defense policy making in particular. In the area of defense policy making, this has led to a peculiarly Danish institution, the conclusion of so-called defense settlements (*forsvarsforlig*), covering several financial years, between a broad coalition of defense-oriented parties in government and opposition. This institution arose out of the 1949 decision to join NATO, which was underwritten by a coalition of Social Democrats, Liberals, and Conservatives, who also carried through the subsequent defense laws by which Danish armed forces were adapted to the new framework of collective and integrated defense in NATO. As a distinct institution the defense settlement did not come into existence until 1960 when an agreement was negotiated between the four old parties in Danish politics, including the Radicals but excluding parties to the left of the Social Democrats. The inclusion of the formerly anti-NATO and defense-skeptical Radical party was necessitated by its participation in a government coalition with the Social Democrats, but also signaled a (temporary) shift in its policies and hence a general increase in consensus. Through this broad coalition, defense was taken out of domestic policy, at least for a while, and the 1960s thus came to be the "golden era" of defense policy consensus.

At the end of the decade, cracks occurred in the coalition when the Social Democrats—temporarily in opposition (1968–71) while the three other parties to the 1960 agreement formed a joint government—threatened to abandon the coalition. After a few years of renewed politization, another broad consensus was established in 1973, however, when the four old parties negotiated a new defense settlement which was subsequently underwritten by the new nonsocialist parties that emerged after the December 1973 election.[20] This time the coalition held only a few years; in 1975 the Radicals started to part ways with the other parties over the acquisition of the F-16, and in 1977 the party, having lost heavily in a parliamentary election, chose to stay outside when after extended wrangling the coalition parties agreed to renew the 1973 settlement with minor revisions for another four years (1977–81).

As an institution *the defense settlement* is characterized by its focus on the input side of defense, such as budgets and length of conscription period, and output categories such as strength figures and organization. It focuses less on the functions and tasks of the defense force. In 1960, in 1973, and in 1977 consensus was centered around a detailed settlement which specified each year's defense expenditures for the duration of the settlement. The protracted deliberations over the budget issue, which took up more than a year in 1976–77, testify to the highly symbolic content of Danish defense politics, in which the height of the defense budget and especially its upward and downward movements are considered a symptom of the general priority of defense compared to the civilian aspects of government. (The indexing of annual defense expenditures, which started in 1960, has served to blunt the actual impact of this symbolic strife over defense expenditures.) Another traditional symbol, which has been losing importance during the last decade, is conscription and especially the length of the first conscription period. In the 1950s and 1960s, this was probably the most highly politicized defense policy issue; however, since 1973 when a major step towards the professionalization of the Danish armed forces was made, and 1977 when conscripts started being paid what are probably by far the highest salaries in the world, conscription has ceased to be the focus of the defense debate. In 1984, a differentiated increase in the conscription period was negotiated without any negative feedback.

Another characteristic of defense settlements has been the detailed prescription of output categories in terms of military strength potential. The army is defined in great detail as far as number of troops and descriptions of personnel categories are concerned and also with respect to active units (brigades) and their armament. The navy and air force are even more clearly defined; every single unit type is prescribed. A further characteristic of the detailed definition of input and output is that the two are not linked by any elaborate costings nor are output categories defined on the basis of cost-benefit analyses; on the contrary, a perennial problem with Danish defense settlements has been the discrepancy between the agreed budget and the prescribed force postures, resulting normally in suboptimal activity levels and the postponement of agreed materiel investments. After a few years this normally results in mounting tension between the organizational framework and its contents, and hence in pressures for a new settlement on an adjusted balance between input and output categories. Such adjustments usually take the form of a downward revision of force goals rather than upward adjustments of budgets.

Finally, defense settlements are usually made for a certain specified period, normally four years, which may very well be the maximum length before inbuilt tensions prove too onerous to bear. For this reason, defense settlements have sometimes been accompanied by the establishment of unofficial committees representing the participating parties, with whom the implementation and adjustment of the agreed framework is discussed, and who normally have a veto over departures from the settlement. Defense agreements are usually based on the premise that changes can only be made unanimously.

In the following case studies two recent defense settlements, concluded in 1981 and 1984 respectively, are analysed in some detail.

Case I: The Making of the 1981 Defense Settlement[21]

In 1977 the Folketing extended the 1973 defense settlement for another four years after nearly two years of political negotiations, which had centered almost entirely on such issues as the question of defense cuts, which were demanded by the Radical Liberals and to some extent supported by the Social Democrats, versus defense improvements demanded by the nonsocialist parties; the possibility for renegotiation (for example, in case of economic crisis); and the duration of the new settlement.

This rather futile experience, which was terminated when the Radical Liberals left the negotiating table, as well as the less than orderly way in which the 1973 defense settlement itself had been negotiated, was probably the main reason why in the summer of 1977 the defense minister, Orla Møller, instituted what was probably meant to be a "cookbook" process toward a new defense settlement, taking effect as of April 1981. The process was designed to consist of three consecutive phases:

1. a planning phase under the auspices of the Defense Ministry and Defense Command and under the overall direction of the ministry
2. a law-preparatory phase in the ministry
3. a parliamentary phase for the building of political consensus.

Aside from the wish to avoid the untidiness of previous defense policymaking processes, the institution of a planning process reflected the increasing role and status of planning in the Danish defense establishment during the 1970s—to a large extent inspired by the U.S. example, but in its practical design following more closely the Swedish model. In 1970 the three service commands were amalgamated in a unified Defense Command, under which a special long-term planning group (LTP) was established directly under the chief of the defense staff. Some years later (in 1976) a small planning unit (two or three officials) was created in the Defense Department, which had till then been rather skeptical of the need and possibilities of long-term planning.

The Planning and Law-Preparatory Phase (Autumn 1977–Winter 1980). In the summer of 1977 contacts were established between the Ministry of Defense and the Defense Command to initiate a planning process in preparation for the parliamentary bargaining process prior to the next defense arrangement. This would take effect in April 1981, after the 1977 settlement lapsed. In August 1977 it was agreed to concentrate the overall direction of long-term planning in the Defense Department and to establish a joint organization between the department and the Defense Command to direct and coordinate the actual planning process which would continue to be located within the Defense Command. This "Ministry of Defense project management for long-term planning in the defense establishment" was to be chaired by the permanent secretary of the department, the other members being high-ranking military leaders, namely the chief of defense staff, the chief of the operative forces (COMBALTAP), and the chief of the home guard. A joint Defense Department/Defense Command secretariat was set up to coordinate the work of the "project management" and to oversee actual planning exercises in the Defense Command. The planning process proper was initiated by a Ministry of Defense order of September 30, 1977 to the Defense Command, which detailed it to work out a small number of alternative proposals for a new defense structure after the expiration of the current defense settlement on March 31, 1981. The proposals were to be suitable as a basis for political negotiations, and planning should therefore be arranged so flexibly that political demands concerning priorities and criteria could be fitted into the process on a running basis. The entire planning process was conceived to take place in four phases:

Phase 1 would consist of an analysis of the expected status of the armed forces in 1981 compared to existing organizational goals, norms, tasks, and activities. Special attention should be paid to deficiencies compared to the recently prolonged 1973 defense structure.

Phase 2 would consist of an analysis of the cost and military effectiveness of maintaining and completing the 1973 structure, taking into consideration necessary adjustments, for example, NATO decisions for an increased defense effort.

Phase 3, considered the central aspect of the whole planning process, should consist of the elaboration of cost- and effectiveness-evaluated alternatives to the existing structure, that is, the one analysed in phases 1 and 2.

Phase 4, finally, should aim at the elaboraton of a new defense bill.

Phases 1 and 2. Because of their technical character phases 1 and 2 were designed as ordinary Defense Command exercises with the work being performed in the so-called basic organization. The two reports were finished during 1978 and showed significant deficiencies in the existing defense structure as well as rather staggering budgetary demands if this structure were to be continued and completed during the 1980s. The phase 1 report documented a significant shortfall in personnel (some 2,000 out of a peacetime force of about 40,000) as well as significant materiel deficiencies, especially with respect to armored personnel carriers, MTBs, navy helicopters, and tanks, totaling about two years' normal materiel investments.

The phase 2 report covered not only the completion and extrapolation of the 1973 structure into the late 1980s, but also the qualitative improvements foreseen in NATO's Long-Term Defense Plan (LTDP) of 1978 and in the annual force goals and biennial Ministerial Guidance exercises. The results of the analysis were rather sobering. The report not only predicted a sizeable shortfall of personnel in the late 1980s (some 6,000), but also huge potential materiel deficiencies. If the 1973 structure were to be continued during the 1980s annual materiel investments between 2.5 and 6.5 billion kroner (in 1984, $1 = 11 Dkr) would be required, which should be compared to an investment budget for FY 1979 of 866 million kroner. On the other hand operating budgets would, after an initial 15 percent rise, rise slowly during the decade. In total the defense budget was predicted to rise in real terms from some 6 billion in 1979 to some 12 billion in 1983–85 and then to drop again to a level of some 9–10 billion. Maintaining and completing the existing structure would thus mean a 70 percent increase in the defense budget or an annual increase of some 10 percent in real terms over a decade.

Although this model was later somewhat defensively termed as "Rolls Royce defense model," it was not actually based on unreasonable quantitative or qualitative norms; most of all it illustrated (in admittedly very stark terms) the long-term discrepancies between goals and performance with respect to the existing defense structure. This was also the conclusion of Defense Minister Poul Søgaard (Social Democrat, 1977–82) when he declared that with an unchanged budget it would only be possible to operate but not to renew existing materiel, which in his analysis only strengthened the need to think in alternative terms in the following phase 3 exercise.

Phase 3. While phases 1 and 2 were mainly technical, phase 3 envisaged the formulation of alternative defense structures which could be used as input into the political process proper. Therefore it was planned to be a joint planning process involving in close coordination all relevant parties, that is, the Defense Command, the Defense Department, and the minister of defense, with the minister and his department in the overall guiding and coordinating role. Ministerial guidance was exercised through various channels: through the issuing of planning directives and planning premises, through coordinating "project management," through direct communication with the defense chiefs, and through public speeches.

The main demand, which was repeatedly underlined by the minister, was the need for alternative thinking, a demand which was especially stressed after the phase 1 and 2 reports had been finished. Second, the demand for flexibility was stressed; in principle the existing defense organization, including its particular balance between the three services, should be disregarded. A third demand was for a better balance between the future tasks of the armed forces and allocated resources, in order to avoid the usual "undermining" of defense structures after a few years. The main demands as to the contents of proposed alternatives were threefold. The Danish defense forces should be viewed as part of a larger allied defense effort, in particular within the defense of the BALTAP area, the primary goal being to "work out alternatives . . . which—within the given planning restrictions—will best enable the Allied Commander Baltic Approaches (COMBALTAP) to solve his defense tasks in the planning period."[22] Specifically, planners were directed to think in terms of a balanced defense force under BALTAP rather than at a national level and thus to focus on the need for an adaptation of Danish defense efforts to the (already known) German contribution to the defense of the BALTAP area.

Furthermore, the importance of allied reinforcements was stressed as planners were directed to strengthen "the possibility and ability to secure reception and support of allied reinforcements, potentially already in the early stage of a crisis, as well as the capability for effective cooperation with allied forces."[23] Planners were also directed to upgrade the military wartime efficiency of the armed forces, if necessary through an "untraditional view of (their) existing organization, including its training and support structure" in peacetime.[24]

Finally, planning was predicated on certain budgetary assumptions which quickly became a bone of contention between the minister and the military authorities. At the NATO summit in Washington, in May 1978, the Danish government accepted in principle the goal of an annual 3 percent increase in the defense budget, but also reserved its position both as far as the existing and coming defense settlements were concerned. As a consequence the final planning directive issued in late 1978 ordered planners to work under three alternative economic frameworks: (1) zero growth, (2) 1.5 percent growth, and (3) 3 percent growth, all in real terms. Of these, the zero alternative was to be considered the basic model with the other two alternatives as additions to it on a cost-evaluated building-block principle.

To these ministerial planning principles were added priorities, issued by the defense chief, the most important of which were:[25]

1. A basically unchanged contribution to the land defense of Jutland/Schleswig-Holstein, which in effect meant that expected cuts in the army would have to be effected solely in the eastern, island part of Denmark.
2. The defense of the eastern islands and the straits should rest on a balanced three-service forward defense concept based on aircraft, ships, and mines. Other tasks, such as surveillance or exercise of sovereignty—

traditionally very important navy tasks—were to be downgraded along with the land defense of the island Zealand.[26]
3. Air defense was to be based on a mixture of aerial interdiction and missile defense, not least with a view to protecting the introduction of allied reinforcements. As possibilities for rapid reinforcement by allied air units were deemed rather good, it was found possible to somewhat reduce the number of aircraft in the Danish Air Force.

Responsibility for the actual planning exercise was originally placed in the Long-Term Planning Group (LTP) of the Defense Command and was carried out in ad hoc groups for the various services and for the defense establishment as a whole and with representatives of relevant Defense Command and service staffs. In the concluding phase, however, the exercise was transferred to the ordinary Defense Command organization, to the chagrin of both the LTP and the service staffs, in a move which to a certain extent short-circuited the entire process.

The result was three alternative defense structures, the "B-structures," which primarily reflected the preferences of the Defense Command. (Simultaneously three parallel "A structures" representing the preferences of the service chiefs were produced, which marginally diverged from the B structures.) Of these the Defense Command strongly recommended the B3 structure which was based on a 3 percent real growth as producing a "force posture, which quantitatively as well as qualitatively will enable (the armed forces) to solve (their) main tasks with reasonable certainty . . ." Conversely the B1 and B2 structures (based on zero and 1.5 percent real growth respectively) were characterized as unsatisfactory, the zero model having "so many weaknesses that its war-preventive effects as well as its tactical possibilities of solving the main task must be doubted."[27]

Despite the precautions taken to insure political and departmental control, the results of the planning process mainly reflected the attitudes of the Defense Command, and a prevalent view in the ministry was that it did not sufficiently take into account the directives and guidances issued by the department and the minister of defense. For instance, the result was criticized for not being "alternative" enough (the B3 structure was basically a marginally scaled-down version of the existing defense structure) and for not being sufficiently based on the prescribed cumulative building-block procedure. Specifically, the defense structures were criticized for not heeding the minister's expressed wish to upgrade surveillance, warning, and the exercise of sovereignty, and his directive to plan in a BALTAP rather than a national framework.

Phase 4 (Autumn 1979). After the delivery of the phase 3 report rather frantic efforts were made in the department to produce a revised basis for a new defense structure which would be more in accordance with the political directives which had been issued. This attempt was hampered, however, by the limited resources of the Defense Department and by the lack of time, it having been stipulated that a new defense bill would be put before the Folketing toward the end of 1979. The resulting proposal—termed the C1 model—which was based on the assumption of zero budget growth, therefore became more or less an adaptation of the B1 model with only minor revisions, and to all practical purposes a somewhat scaled-down version of the existing 1973 defense posture. This model was consolidated into a defense bill which was laid before the government in January 1980.

At this time, however, the political climate had undergone so many changes since the initiation of the planning process that the government decided to lay aside the bill and to initiate political discussions with potential parties to a new settlement, including the Radical Liberals, on a more open and less binding basis.

The Parliamentary Phase (Winter 1980–Summer 1981) To understand this volte-face one has to take into consideration relevant changes in the political environment of defense policy during 1977–79. At the time when the process was initiated and during most of its course, this environment was favorable insofar as defense was not a prominent political issue, and as there seemed to be a rather widespread, if usually tacit, acceptance of the need to augment defense expenditures somewhat despite official reservations as to the "3 percent principle." During most of 1978–79 the Social Democrats governed in a unique coalition with the Liberal party, which was definitely committed to a certain increase; the Social Democratic defense minister himself seemed to expect a final solution lying somewhere between a 3 percent and a zero solution.

In the autumn of 1979 this government coalition broke down in disagreement over an economic crisis program to meet the effects of the new oil crisis, and after parliamentary elections in October 1979 a new Social Democratic minority government was formed. This cabinet soon ran into severe troubles over security policy. The economic crisis unleashed by the second oil price hike hit Denmark very hard, forcing the government into a drastic economic retrenchment program. This created a highly unfavorable atmosphere for the discussion of a new defense agreement on a possible expanded budgetary basis; indeed the situation gave rise to demands for cuts in the defense budget, both on the left wing and in the government party. At the same time the INF issue, which had hitherto been largely dormant in Danish politics, gave rise to a heated public and parliamentary debate characterized by increasing pressures by the left-wing parties upon the security policy position of the Social Democrats, which had already been weakened when after the elections the Radical Liberals acquired a pivotal position as the primary parliamentary support for the government. In the winter of 1980 the new peace movement also started to make its influence felt. To cap the problem, visible cracks began to appear in the Social Democratic party over defense and security policy when a vocal left wing, numbering up to a quarter of its parliamentary group and having to some extent the ear of Prime Minister Anker Jørgensen, began to assert itself in party deliberations. In this process both Foreign Minister Kjeld Olesen, who belonged in the dominant mainstream group of the party, and Defense Minister Poul Søgaard, of the numerically and politically rather weak defense-oriented part of the party, had to accept humiliating defeats over INF and defense policy, respectively.

As indicated above, this political setting has not changed significantly since late 1979 despite the fact that the Social Democratic government was replaced by a nonsocialist cabinet in 1982, and has led to important changes in Danish security policy, mainly in the nuclear domain. It also served to make defense policy making much more complicated than had been expected when the planning process ended in late 1979.

In the Social Democratic party the left wing's unwillingness to accept any budgetary expansions for defense was acquiesced in by the majority of the parliamentary group, at least as an opening position. This led to the presentation of a broad sketch based on a zero solution, on the basis of which the government invited the potential parties to a new defense settlement, including the Radical Liberals (who had opted out in 1977), to initiate informal discussions. At the same time the defense bill and planning reports were placed in political cold storage.

It is not necessary here to follow in detail the intricate interparty negotiations which started in January 1980 and went on intermittently until August 1981 when the government and the four nonsocialist parties which had concluded the 1977 settlement agreed on the outlines of a new defense agreement covering the 1981–84 period.

The four nonsocialist "settlement parties" (*forligspartier*) kept close ranks during the discussions in reflection of the fact that their defense policy programs are highly compatible. They agreed to reject the proposed zero solution as totally inadequate and considered it to some extent a betrayal of previous understandings. Their main position tended to be that the existing defense structure was by and large satisfactory, and that the main task would be to find the necessary funding for its continuation and completion. They therefore advocated a growth in defense expenditures of at least 3 percent per year and indicated their willingness to go even higher. In the spring of 1981 the four parties presented their own compromise proposal aiming at a return to the 1973 force goals over a four-year period and predicated on an annual increase of defense expenditures of some 2.2 percent. In their arguments they pointed to the NATO 3 percent decision, the need for a credible defense posture, and the tense international climate after the Soviet invasion of Afghanistan. Gradually they also came to demand as a condition for concluding a defense agreement the acceptance of prepositioning of heavy materiel in Denmark as part of NATO's upcoming Rapid Reinforcement Plan (RRP).

The Radical Liberal party, which the government was anxious to include in the talks because of its central position in domestic policy, was basically in favor of defense cuts and took part in the interparty talks mainly to keep the Social Democrats committed to the zero solution. The party rejected any concession over this and made it a further condition that there must be no compromise over base policy which would allow the prepositioning of heavy materiel for NATO reinforcements.[28] The party also advocated the establishment of a "total defense commission" to work out a "total defense" posture, including civil defense and other nonmilitary activities.

Caught between these opposing positions, and internally split, the Social Democratic leadership had to tread lightly. Its problems were further exacerbated by heavy criticism and outright pressure from outside actors. The zero solution was heavily criticized by NATO authorities as well as by several NATO governments, including the West Germans, and in the summer of 1980 an international press campaign was launched under the banner line of "Denmarkization," which depicted Denmark as a "free rider" in NATO. A special feature of the external reaction was the two highly critical letters which U.S. Minister of Defense Harold Brown sent his Danish colleague Poul Søgaard in the spring of 1980 in which he expressed his concerns over the course of Danish defense decision making.

In defending itself against the storm of international criticism the government pointed to three factors. First, it pointed to the extensive indexing against inflation of Danish defense expenditures, which is possibly the best in the whole of NATO; second, it pointed to the internationally high level of Danish development aid which—seen in a broader perspective—also contributed to Western security, and finally the government's general wish to further detente and to refrain from fueling the arms race was mentioned.[29] Domestically, the main argument for the zero solution was that in a period of government retrenchment it would be unfair and politically self-defeating to let defense expenditures rise.

However, both international criticism and the adamant refusal of the nonsocialist parties to countenance the zero solution began gradually to affect the position of the Social Democratic government. The defense-oriented group in the party became more vocal during 1980, some influential politicians in its mainstream group started to worry about the deadlock in the negotiations which had characterized 1980, and part of the trade-union movement started to express concern over the employment aspects of the zero solution. These factors began to interact with the general preference of the party leadership for sticking to the tradition of broad defense settlements with the nonsocialist parties and were further strengthened in the spring of

1981 when the knotty problem of prepositioning more or less dissolved itself: in SACEUR's draft RRP plan there was no mention of the need for prepositioning in Denmark. As a result the government started in the spring of 1981 to move away from the zero solution by gradually increasing its offers of additional defense "packets," mainly with respect to the land defense of Zealand, the MTB fleet, and area air defense. In August 1981, when offers amounted to an annual real growth of some .75 percent, the nonsocialist parties jumped to accept an agreement out of fear of another deadlock, while the Radical Liberals decided to stay out of the settlement and to vote against it when it came up in Parliament. In the Social Democratic parliamentary group counsels were divided. Twelve members voted against the settlement, which several ministers were also known to be against, while forty-one voted for. In the concluding phase of the negotiations the decisive factors seem to have been not only the strong pressures of Foreign Minister Kjeld Olesen and Defense Minister Poul Søgaard, but also the personal intervention of Prime Minister Anker Jørgensen, not normally a supporter of increased defense budgets, in order to take the defense issue off the political agenda.

The defense settlement was finally enacted in May 1982 when it was endorsed by the Folketing by 113 votes against 28. The new Defense Act was supported not only by the parties to the compromise (including a unanimous Social Democratic group) but also by the right-wing Progress party, and was opposed by the Radical Liberals, the People's Socialists, and the Left Socialists. To discuss and guarantee the implementation of the agreement, an unofficial interparty committee, the "Committee of Eleven," was set up with three representatives for the Social Democrats and two for each of the other settlement parties. This procedure had also been followed in 1973, but had been officially discontinued after 1977 so as not to appear to exclude the Radicals from influence upon defense policy. The right-wing Progress party which had voted for the Defense Act tried to get access to the committee, but to no avail.

Relative to the existing 1973/77 structure the 1981 settlement envisaged only few changes, mostly in terms of minor reductions of force goals (see table 1–3 for armed forces' strength 1984 and 1987). The standing force of the army was reduced from about 8,500 to 7,000 men, while its mobilization force was reduced from some 70,000 to 65,000. The navy was almost unchanged with 38 fighting units, while the air force was slightly reduced: from 104 to 92 aircraft, but with a more favorable ratio of new and older aircraft (from 52/52 to 80/12). As a whole the settlement for 1981–84 did not imply significant changes in the tasks of the Danish armed forces, but it served to underline certain trends. Its purpose was clearly to increase their wartime effectiveness, with a special upgrading of surveillance and warning as well as the reception of allied reinforcements; on the other hand the defense against invasion, military defense proper, was given somewhat less priority. In this way the 1981/82 defense settlement pointed towards a

Table 1–3
Danish Armed Forces 1984 and 1987 (projected)

		End 1984	End 1987
Army			
War structure			
Field Army:	Brigades	5	5
	Combat groups	6	6
	BTNs (combat and support)	22	23
Local defense:	BTNs	13	9
	CMPs	16	4
Personnel:	Standing force, incl. supplementary force[a]	7,000	9,750
	Mobilization force	65,000	62,250
Total wartime forces		72,000	72,000
Peace structure			
Field Army:	Brigades	5	5
	Combat groups	6	6
	BTNs	8	10
Local defense:	(to be mobilized)	—	—
Personnel:	Officers	3,105	2,990
	Professional (privates and NCOs)	8,350	6,000
	Conscripts	6,665	8,050
	Civilians	3,350	3,350
Total peacetime force		21,470	20,390
Navy			
	Frigates/corvettes	5	5[b]
	Torpedo and missile boats	16	16
	Submarines	4	5[c]
	Minelayers	7	6
	Minesweepers	6	3
	Surveillance units	22	23
	Fishery inspection units	18	18[d]
	Coastal forts	2	2[e]
	Naval bases	3	3
Personnel:	Officers	1,380	1,340
	Professional (private and NCOs)	3,280	3,305
	Conscripts	1,215	1,050
	Civilians	2,560	2,460
Total peacetime force		8,435	8,155
Mobilization force		3,820	4,685
Total wartime force		12,255	12,840

Table 1-3 (continued)

		End 1984	End 1987
Air Force			
	Combat aircraft squadrons: F-16	48/3	52/4[f]
	F-104, DRAKEN	48/3	32/2
	Transports	3	3
	Fishery inspection aircraft	3	3
	Rescue helicopters	8	8
	IHAWK missile units	6	8
	Point defense units (AA cannon)	6	6
Personnel	Officers	1,380	1,395
	Professional (private and NCOs)	4,575	4,720
	Conscripts	1,230	735
	Civilian	2,365	2,275
Total peace time force		9,550	9,125
Mobilization force		10,000	10,000
Total wartime force		19,550	19,125
Home Guard[g]			
	Army Home Guard	51,570	
	Naval Home Guard	3,694	
	Air Base Defense Corps	1,521	
	Ground Observer Corps	8,787	
	Women's Army Corps	9,260	
	Women's Naval Corps	1,449	
	Women's Air Force	1,708	
	Home Guard Directorate etc.	63	
Total Home Guard		78,052	

Source: Five-party agreement on the organization of the armed forces during the 1985–87 period, dated June 29, 1984.

[a]The supplementary force consists of demobilized personnel who can be mobilized at very short notice (less than 24 hours).
[b]The two frigates will be demobilized with key crews from 1986.
[c]Including 2 on leasing arrangement.
[d]Including 8 helicopters, 4 of which are modified for combat missions.
[e]Armaments mothballed.
[f]In 1988, 57 F-16s.
[g]The Home Guard is an all-volunteer force, established in 1948. During recent years recruitement has risen signficantly.

slightly increased Danish dependence upon NATO, both with respect to allied reinforcements and to cooperation with the Federal Republic of Germany within the BALTAP Command.

Case II: The Making of the 1983 Defense Settlement[30]

To round up and put into perspective the 1981/82 defense settlement a few comments should be added about the evolution of Danish defense policy until late 1984. To a large degree, the 1981 defense agreement served to remove defense policy from the political agenda. On the other hand, from 1982 and especially after September 1982 when the government was taken over by a coalition of the four nonsocialist parties which had negotiated the 1981 compromise, security policy became a hotly contested issue between government and opposition. Disagreements mainly centered on INF policy; the Social Democratic party gradually moved towards a repudiation of NATO's dual-track decision of 1979 and—in a majority parliamentary coalition with the Radicals and the left-wing parties—forced the government to accept its views. Disagreements further focused on the proposal for a nuclear-free zone in Scandinavia, on the limits of Denmark's official no-to-nuclear-weapons policy which the Social Democrats moved to expand, and on the role of nuclear weapons in NATO strategy generally.[31]

Defense was not totally exempted from this struggle over security policy, as in late 1982 the Social Democrats forced the government to accept a reduction in the 1983 and 1984 defense budgets which more than cancelled the budget improvements agreed to a year earlier. But by and large, the implementation of the 1981 settlement was rather smoothly effected in the sheltered counsels of the Committee of Eleven, the only really contested issue being the future role of submarines in the naval forces. The government wanted to start procurement of new submarines as agreed in 1981/82, while the Social Democrats advocated a leasing arrangement with the West German navy; the party's defense spokesman Knud Damgaard wanted to go even further and transfer submarine missions to the air force.

In the spring of 1984 the government hesitantly opened negotiations for a defense agreement to replace the one which would expire at the end of the year. This time preparations were on a much more modest scale than a few years earlier, presumably both because of the general consensus that what was needed was an adjustment of the existing structure rather than a major overhaul, and because of the less than satisfactory experiences with the 1977–79 planning exercise. On the basis of a report by the chief of defense concerning the evolution of the armed forces during 1985–89, Defense Minister Hans Engell (Conservative) in March 1984 presented a draft proposal for revisions in the existing structure covering a five-year period.[32] Very few significant changes were indeed proposed, the most important being a proposal to somewhat strengthen the role of conscription by calling up a higher proportion of each age group and by lengthening the conscription period in combat units from nine to twelve months. The second main feature of the proposal was the presentation of a five-year investment program totalling some 12.5 billion kroner (i.e. some 2.5 billion per year), designed to do away with major deficiencies in the materiel of the three services. As a consequence a modest increase in defense expenditures of about 1 percent per year was foreseen.

Compared to the tortuous negotiations of 1976–77 and 1980–81 the defense settlement of 1984 was concluded almost overnight. This was possible for several reasons. First, no attempt was made to include the Radical Liberal or other parties in the negotiations, which were kept entirely within the group of parties participating in the 1981 agreement. Second, both the present government parties and the Social Democrats had special reasons of their own for working for a speedy and undramatic solution to the problem. Among the government parties, and especially in the Conservative party of Prime Minister Poul Schlüter and Defense Minister Hans Engell, the prevailing attitude was to isolate defense as far as possible from the severe disagreements over certain security policy issues which had characterized government/opposition relations since the Schlüter government was formed in the autumn of 1982. Traditionally the nonsocialist parties have been interested in keeping defense policy above party politics and often prefer a less than satisfactory compromise with the Social Democrats rather than risk the permanent politicization of defense. In the prevailing atmosphere in early 1984 such considerations had particular weight, not least with the highly pragmatic government leader. On the other hand, there were definite limits to what the Conservatives and especially the Liberal and Center-Democrat coalition partners were willing to accept on the altar of compromise.

Nevertheless, the Social Democratic opposition party was placed in a fairly favorable negotiating position, which was also deftly utilized, especially by defense spokesman Knud Damgaard. But the Social Democrats had to work within certain constraints, too. Somewhat ironically the party's revision of its nuclear weapons policy made it concerned to stress its orthodoxy in other security policy issues so as to bolster its flagging image as a "responsible" party in defense policy and as a wholehearted supporter of Denmark's NATO commitments. Over the previous few years party leader Anker Jørgensen, who had been the main exponent of nuclear policy revisionism, had repeatedly stated that the party was in favor of an effective defense structure; there were therefore limits to how far the party leadership could follow the demands for defense cuts that were being voiced in the party and its rank and file in reaction to the economic and social retrenchment policies of the Schlüter government. Such demands were likely to become highly vocal at the forthcoming party congress in September 1984 and would very likely tie down the party leadership on defense cuts if an agreement were not reached with the government before the congress convened.

Both the government and the Social Democrats were therefore interested in the early conclusion of an agreement, if one could be reached, and quickly agreed to aim for a settlement by the end of June, when the Folketing would be called in for an extraordinary meeting at a comfortable distance from the Social Democratic party congress. In a formal sense negotiations were held within the Committee of Eleven, but for practical reasons they were actually conducted between Defense Minister Hans Engell, acting on a broad mandate from the four government parties, and the three Social Democratic members of the committee: Knud Damgaard, the official defense spokesman; Poul Søgaard, former defense minister; and Kjeld Olesen, former foreign and defense minister. Defense Minister Engell kept close and continuous contacts with the eight nonsocialist members of the committee and presumably also with his chief and political protege Poul Schlüter, while the Social Democratic negotiators kept in close contact with party leader Anker Jørgensen. There were also several informal meetings, between Defense Minister Engell and Knud Damgaard and also between Prime Minister Poul Schlüter and Anker Jørgensen, to untie particular knots in the negotiations.

The Social Democratic opening gambit was presented in early June when the concluding round of talks was initiated. The main demands were for a three- instead of a five-year agreement; an unchanged defense budget with certain limitations to the existing indexing against inflation; a leasing arrangement for new submarines instead of a building program; a gradual phasing-out of larger naval units; a substitution of additional F-16s for proposed fleet helicopters; and finally the establishment of an "analysis group" to advise the defense minister independently of the Defense Command.

In the final agreement of June 29, 1984, these demands were reflected to a large degree. Its principal features were the following (see also table 1–3 which details its force and personnel goals compared to the present situation).[33]

1. The agreement is to run for three years (1985–87). The government parties acceded to this demand partially because they came to the conclusion that any settlement in 1984 would be a meager one and there might be a fairer climate for defense improvements some three years hence.
2. No changes in the purposes and tasks of the armed forces were foreseen: "Cooperation in BALTAP and with those NATO members who provide reinforcements for the defense of Denmark is accorded particular weight."[34]
3. The agreement was based in principle on unchanged defense expenditures for the next three years (that is, without restoration of the 1983 and 1984 cuts), but with certain very small additional appropriations for special purposes, namely the Home Guard and ammunition build-up. Indexing of the operating budget will be limited to 2 percent annually as for other state activities, while other parts of the budget will continue to

be about 100 percent compensated for inflation if "technological inflation" is excluded.
4. A specific agreement was reached on a three-year materiel investment plan totalling some 6 billion kroner (i.e. some 2 billion per year) out of a defense budget of 11.5 billion kroner. The main items of the plan are a strengthening of the army's air defense capability (which is almost nonexistent at the moment), the initiation of a new naval building program for the so-called Standard Flex-units, the addition of twelve F-16's to the air force, and a build-up of depleted ammunition stocks.
5. In the army, conscription is to be given a larger role by increasing the length of the conscription period from nine to twelve months in combat units. This will allow for an expansion of the standing force and also improve the quality of the mobilization force. At the demand of the Social Democrats, certain—rather unclear—safeguards were introduced to protect the interests of the professional soldiers, whose organization is closely connected with the trade-union movement, and therefore has some political clout.
6. The navy's two frigates are to be deactivated during the agreement period. This reflects an old Social Democratic skepticism as to the effectiveness of these units, and generally toward the concept of a forward naval defense in the Baltic. Also, a leasing arrangement was approved with respect to submarines, while the whole concept of submarine defense and alternatives to it is being investigated.
7. Finally, the government halfheartedly agreed to set up a small analysis group which will be independent of the Defense Command. Among its prescribed tasks will be a study of the need for submarines, the possibilities of land-based sea missiles and other aspects of new weapons technology.

After the compromise, Social Democratic leader Anker Jørgensen argued that the armed forces would have to live on a tight but still reasonable budget. It would be impossible to cut down on other government expenditures and at the same time give increased appropriations for the military. In the party there seemed to be overall satisfaction with the agreement which removed one potentially contentious issue from the party congress agenda; only a small handful of left-wing members of the parliamentary group voiced their disagreement. In the government both Prime Minister Poul Schlüter and Defense Minister Hans Engell chose to focus upon the positive aspects of the agreement while admitting that it was less satisfactory than hoped for. Other spokesmen for the government parties were less sanguine about the settlement, but the prevailing attitude still remained one of relief that after all a holding operation, which saved the traditional broad cooperation between Social Democrats and nonsocialist parties over defense policy, had been possible.

Conclusion

In many ways the processes prior to the defense settlements of 1981 and 1984 were quite different. While the 1981 agreement was preceded by tortuous political negotiations lasting more than eighteen months and before that by an extended planning process, the 1984 settlement was in reality effected in a few weeks and also lacked the elaborate planning process, even though this element was of course not absent. These differences are primarily due to the fact that the 1981 settlement was politically intended to lead to significant revisions of the existing structure, while the 1984 exercise was merely meant to result in minor adjustments of the 1981 structure. But despite this, there are also similarities between the two processes in that both produced basically similar results, namely only a marginal change of the status quo.

This status-quo orientation seems to be a basic characteristic of defense policy making in Denmark. It is evident from the central role played in the process by the notion of unchanged (but inflation indexed) defense budgets, but it is also reflected in the inflexibility of defense organization, force goals, and so on. Changes tend to be small and incremental to a degree that cannot be explained solely by the constraints that existing armaments, infrastructure, and other elements of the "defense heritage" naturally place on decision makers. Nor does the status quo reflect any basic agreement that the existing structure is the optimal one; in fact, many participants find it either inadequate, too ambitious, or just less than suitable for specific Danish conditions and defense needs.

The status-quo orientation of Danish defense policy should rather be seen as resulting from a political deadlock between the left-wing forces (which on this particular issue include the Radical Liberals) wanting to reduce defense efforts and the nonsocialist parties arguing for moderate, but not drastic improvements, with the Social Democratic party in the middle with leanings in both directions, but usually attracted by the compromise position of the zero solution.

This deadlock is basically a consequence of the perennial risk of politicization in Danish defense policy. Because politicization interferes with the "normal" domestic policy process, the institution of a defense settlement has been conceived so as to remove the issue from the day-to-day political agenda. The indexing of the defense budget serves the same purpose, as it normally takes the question out of the yearly wranglings over finance bills. By and large, defense settlements have indeed served their purpose; despite the acute politicization of other aspects of security policy during the last few years, defense policy proper has been relatively exempt from political confrontation.

But political constraints are not the only reason for the status-quo orientation of Danish defense policy. It also results from the way the military organization functions. A participant in the 1977–79 planning process recently observed that the defense leadership is not composed and organized for the task of changing defense priorities. "Like all similar bureaucracies it is organized to manage on the given basis, by including as many considerations as possible and in the greatest unity possible. The future which can be agreed upon will largely point to a continuation of the balanced defense structure, by assigning no or unchanged priorities."[34] He further argues rather convincingly that planning can have little effect in such a system, unless firm political guidance is given. The major finding of the planning process of the 1970s was exactly the realization that long-term defense planning is impossible in a political vacuum.[35]

This political vacuum is a direct consequence of the attempt to depoliticize defense policy, and is one of its most serious drawbacks. When defense policy is relegated to hectic and symbolically charged negotiation rounds every three or four years, a continuous defense debate is discouraged; such debate might penetrate the rather superficial concerns now tending to determine defense policy, and might further a deeper and more sophisticated analysis of defense needs and alternative solutions to them. When he was defense minister, Poul Søgaard made at least an attempt at funneling reasoned political priorities into the planning process, but he failed to a large extent, because he was operating in a political void; when the new defense agreement came to be decided at the political level, it was based on rather different criteria from those which had underpinned the planning process.

It might be tempting to link the lack of a sophisticated defense debate to the fact that in comparative terms—whether the measuring-rod is other small NATO members or a neighboring neutral like Sweden—the Danish defense effort is only a modest one in terms of budgets, personnel, or materiel. Denmark's position at a strategic crossroads implies a sizeable dependence on outside assistance from NATO reinforcements and the German Bundeswehr in case of an attack. This is certainly part of the explanation, but to arrive at a fuller understanding one has to include variables of political culture as well as parliamentary strategy. To a large extent Danish defense and security policy has been shaped by the Social Democratic party and colored by its tradition of skepticism towards balance-of-power politics and its preference for a nonprovocative defense posture. Even though the party has accepted the need for alliance membership and a credible defense since the Second World War, it has still been committed to certain reservations in its NATO policy as well as to a moderate defense effort. Such reservations have only been strengthened by parliamentary and electoral regard for the Radical Liberal and the left-wing parties.

To a certain extent, the nonsocialist parties have been reduced to a policy, in which the defense settlement is the principal instrument, of restraining and constraining the Social Democratic party, and of resigning themselves to underwrite less than satisfactory defense postures. It should be pointed out, however, that no political party, not even the defense-oriented Liberals and Conservatives, advocates significant increases in the Danish defense effort, for example to the level recommended by NATO. Nor is there, as has been demonstrated above, a basis in public opinion for a markedly changed defense policy.

Whether in government or in opposition, the Social Democrats will therefore continue to call the tune as far as Danish defense policy is concerned. How the party's preferences will evolve in the future is difficult to tell, as this will depend not only on the ever-fluctuating balance between its various factions, but also on the inspiration it receives from its West European sister parties, and especially the West German SPD. One of the concepts which is presently beginning to creep into the defense-policy thinking of European Social Democrats is the notion of "defensive defense," a defensive posture which clearly lacks offensive capabilities, but would still confront an attacker with an unacceptable risk of failure. This is a concept which is very much in line with the traditional preference for "nonprovocation" of the Danish Social Democrats, and may be used to underpin their skepticism towards large naval units and submarines. In fact, this argument was advanced in the discussions in 1984, but not carried to such lengths as to exclude a demand for an increase in F-16s, unquestionably the most offensive weapons system in the Danish arsenal. Next time the political parties meet to discuss a new defense settlement, that is in 1987 at the latest, the concept of defensive defense may very well come to play a significant role, however.

The future of the Danish armed forces will not be decided solely on political criteria; structural factors will also make their influence felt and perhaps increasingly so. Probably most important is the rising cost of modern armaments, that is, the problem of technological inflation, which places small countries in a special jeopardy and which may very well soon force them out of the market for sophisticated, state-of-the-art weapons systems. Since the mid-1970s Denmark has procured a modest force of F-16s, but at the price of a near depletion of its meager materiel investment budget. It is highly unlikely that it will be possible to procure a replacement for the F-16 when that time comes, and the same problem applies to the renewal of other major weapons systems. The problem is perhaps particularly acute for Denmark because the level of materiel investment is traditionally very low, but in principle all small countries are up against it. Defense Minister Hans Engell has recently raised the problem in the NATO Council and advocated a joint NATO solution to it.

Several possible solutions can be thought of, but each holds certain political or economic liabilities. An expansion of the investment budget would of course attenuate but not solve the problem, and may not be politically feasible. A second alternative would be increased integration in NATO involving a more pronounced division of labor between small and large nations with its unpleasant implications of increased dependence on the part of the smaller countries. Third, the smaller countries might consciously opt for a less technologically sophisticated defense posture which might allow for the preservation of at least some quantitative volume in the defense force, but which on the other hand might create difficulties for defense cooperation in NATO between large and small countries. Whatever alternative is chosen, this is a problem which will have to be addressed in earnest before the turn of the century by all small countries in the alliance, not just by Denmark, and also, by implication, by the larger members of NATO. For Denmark, it may mean the end of the practice of incremental changes of the status quo as far as the organization, strength, and armaments of the armed forces are concerned.

Notes

1. See Eric S. Einhorn, *National Security and Domestic Politics in Post-War Denmark: Some Principal Issues, 1945–49* (Odense: Odense University Press, 1975).

2. See Barbara G. Haskel, *The Scandinavian Option: Opportunity Costs in Postwar Scandinavian Politics* (Oslo: Universitetsforlaget, 1976).

3. This point is elaborated in Ole Karup Petersen, "From Neutrality to NATO," *Working Paper 1980* (Copenhagen: Institute of Political Studies, 1980).

4. On the consequences for Denmark of participation in European Political Cooperation, see Neils Jørgen Haagerup & Christian Thune, "Denmark: The European Pragmatic," in *National Foreign Policies and European Political Cooperation*, C. Hill, ed. (London: Allen & Unwin, 1983), 106–120.

5. See Ib Faurby, "Challenges to Nordic Security in the 1980s," in *Security in the North*, Report from a seminar in Iceland (Norwegian National Defense College, April 1982), 31–40.

6. See *Warsaw Pact Aggression Possibilities Against Denmark* (Danish Defense Intelligence Service, May 1983).

7. This point is argued in Michael Clemmsen, "Problemer i Dansk Forsvarspolitik," in *Nedrustning og sikkerhed*, vol. 1 (Copenhagen: Commission for Security and Disarmament Affairs, 1984), 137.

8. On the development of the INF issue in Danish politics, see Hans-Henrik Holm and Nikolaj Petersen, "Dansk INF-politik," in *Slaget om Missilerne: Dobbeltbeslutningen og Sikkerheden i Europa* Hans-Henrik Holm and Nikolaj Peterson, eds. (Århus: Forlaget Politica, 1983), 211–48.

9. The issue of a Nordic Nuclear Free Zone is treated extensively in the first major study of the Danish government-appointed Commission on Security and Disarmament, "Dansk Sikkerhedspolitik og Forslagene om Norden som Kernevabenfri zone," *Det Sikkerheds og Nedrustningspolitiske Udvalg* (Copenhagen: Forlaget Europa, 1982).

10. See Bjarne Lindhardt, "Allierede Forstærkninger til Danmark," (Dansk Udenrigspolitisk Institut: Samfundsvidenskabeligt Forlag, 1981).

11. Presentations of recent developments in Danish Security policies may be

found in Erling Bjol, "Nordic Security," Adelphi Paper no. 181 (London: International Institute for Strategic Studies, 1983) and in Bertel Heurlin, "Danish Security Policy," in *Cooperation and Conflict* vol. 17, no. 4, 1982, 237–55. See also note 21.

12. On the role of experts in the formulation of Danish security policy, see Bertel Heurlin, "Sikkerhedspolitisk expertise i den danske politiske process," in *Økonomi og Politik* vol. 55, no. 3, 1981, 272–289.

13. The official title of the "Seidenfaden Report," is *Problemer omkring dansk sikkerhedspolitik* (Copenhagen: En redegørelse fra det sagkyndige udvalg under regeringsudvalget vedrørende Danmarks sikkerhedspolitik, 1970).

14. A discussion of the role of political parties can be found in Ib Faurby, "Party System and Foreign Policy in Denmark," in *Cooperation and Conflict* vol. 14, no. 4, 1979.

15. The relevant debates of the Folketing are printed in *Dansk Udenrigspolitisk Arbog* (Danish Yearbook on Foreign Affairs), Christian Thune and Nikolaj Petersen, eds. (Copenhagen: Dansk Udenrigspolitisk Institut, 1983).

16. For a discussion on the background and importance of the peace movement see W. Christian Møller, "Fredsbevægelsen og Europas Sikkerhed," in *Dansk Udenrigspolitisk Årbog 1981,* 56–81.

17. The results of the more interesting polls have been published since 1979 in *Dansk Udenrigspolitisk Årbog.*

18. For the texts of these letters and the replies of the Danish Defense Minister, see *Dansk Udenrigspolitisk Årbog 1980,* 261–65. In the autumn of 1984 several official and semi-official statements from sources in the United States and the United Kingdom contained heavy criticism of the implications both of the Danish 1984 defense settlement for NATO strategy and NATO reinforcements to Denmark, and of an eventual further "radicalization" of Danish policy toward nuclear weapons.

19. See Nikolaj Petersen, "The Scandilux Experiment: Towards a Transnational Social Democratic Security Perspective?" in *Cooperation and Conflict,* vol. 20, no. 1 (forthcoming 1985).

20. Cf. Nikolaj Petersen, "Danish Security Policy in the Seventies: Continuity or Change?", in *Five Roads to Nordic Security,* Johan Jørgen Holst ed. (Oslo: Universitetsforlaget, 1973), 7–38, 155–169, 229–230.

21. The following analysis of the genesis of the 1981 defense settlement is based on two articles by Nikolaj Petersen: "Den lange vej mod en ny forsvarsordning: Planlægning, lovforberedelse og politiske sonderinger 1977–1981" ("The Long Way Towards a New Defense Organization: Planning, Law Preparation, and Political Discussions 1977–1981"), in *Dansk Udenrigspolitisk Årbog 1980,* Christian Thune, ed. (Copenhagen: Dansk Udenrigspolitisk Institut, 1981), 41–74; and "Konsensus eller konflikt? Dansk sikkerhedspolitik 1979–83" ("Consensus or Conflict? Danish Security Policy 1979–83"), in *Dansk Udenrigspolitisk Årbog 1982,* Christian Thune & Nikolaj Petersen, eds. (Copenhagen: Dansk Udenrigspolitisk Institut, 1983), 34–62. These articles were mainly based on interviews with politicians and planners, as well as on classified material in the Defense Department and the Defense Command.

22. Final directive, issued November 15, 1978 (Skr. 1. kt. 230–11).

23. Ibid.

24. Notice dated November 1978.

25. See ch. 11 of unclassified version of the Phase 3 report, *Oplæg til forsvar-*

sordning efter 1, april 1981. Fase 3: Alternativer til 1973-ordningen (Defense Command, October 1979).

26. This was in some disagreement with Defense Minister Poul Søgaard who mentioned these tasks as priority tasks in a speech at the Danish Defense College in September 1979.

27. Unclassified Phase 3 report, ch. 11.

28. This position was also argued by the Social Democratic left wing.

29. In 1982 Danish development aid amounted to 0.77 percent of GNP while military expenditures were at 2.5 percent. Corresponding figures for the United States were 0.27 and 6.6 percent. See table in Hans-Henrik Holm, *Peace and Development: Aid and Conflict:* Paper for EADI IVth General Conference, Madrid, September 3–7, 1984, 15.

30. The following analysis is mainly based on interviews with participants. A fuller account will be published in a forthcoming article by Michael H. Clemmesen and Nikolaj Petersen in *Dansk Udenrigspolitisk Årbog 1984.*

31. On Danish INF policy, see Hans-Henrik Holm and Nikolaj Petersen, "Dansk INF-politik," in *Slaget om missilerne. Dobbeltbeslutningen og sikkerheden i Europa,* Hans-Henrik Holm and Nikolaj Petersen, eds. (Århus: Forlaget Politica, 1983), 211–248.

32. *Forsvarschefens skitse til forsvarets udvikling 1985–1989* (Defense Command, February 1984).

33. *Aftale om forsvarets ordning i perioden 1985–87* (Ministry of Defense, June 29, 1984).

34. Michael H. Clemmesen, "Problemet i dansk forsvarspolitik", in *Nedrustning og sikkerhed,* Commission for Security and Disarmament Affairs, vol. 1, 1984, 137.

35. Ibid., 139.

2
Finland

Trond Gilberg

Finnish decision making for defense takes place in several environments, each of which possesses its own special characteristics. Each is tied inextricably to the others. In addition, the institutional and procedural peculiarities of the Finnish decision-making system itself help set the parameters for defense policy. A real understanding of Finnish decision making for defense therefore can be gained only after all of these environments and procedural restraints are examined.

The Setting

Finland's position in the global system is something of an anomaly, as has been pointed out by several writers.[1] During World War II, Finland twice fought the Soviet Union and twice lost against overwhelming odds. After the war, Helsinki was compelled to sign a treaty with the Soviets which limited Finland's ability to make sovereign decisions about its foreign policy, its defense establishment, and its military posture. In addition, important elements of general Finnish foreign policy were established by treaties that were concluded in 1940 and 1947, with recent renewals.

The Paris Peace Treaty of 1947 established specific limits on the size of the Finnish armed forces. According to the treaty, the following restrictions were established: the total size of the army cannot exceed 34,400 personnel; the navy is limited to 3,400; and the air force cannot exceed 3,000. There are also limitations on *equipment:* the total tonnage of the navy is not to exceed 10,000 tons; the air force can acquire a maximum of 60 combat aircraft; and the equipment used must be strictly defensive, thus excluding bombers, missiles, submarines, and the possession and testing of nuclear weapons.[2] On the other hand, a joint interpretation of the treaty, undertaken by the Soviet Union and Finland in 1963, allows Finnish possession of strictly *defensive* missiles.[3]

In addition to the military clauses contained in the Paris Peace treaty, there is a political prohibition against fascist groups and parties in Finland. The treaty also forbids the existence and activity of any other organization engaged in hostile propaganda against the Soviet Union.[4]

The formal agreements of the war settlements have been further enhanced by the codification of other relationships between the Soviet Union and Finland, as exemplified by the Treaty of Friendship, Cooperation, and Mutual Assistance of 1948. This treaty has been extended twice, first in 1955 and then in 1970; the current extension is valid until 1990.[5] Some Finnish political figures have even argued for its extension *now,* several years prior to expiration, as a political gesture to the Soviets.[6] The most important parts of the Friendship Treaty are as follows:

1. Any armed attack on Finland (or the Soviet Union through Finland) by Germany or any of its allies will require Finnish resistance and, if necessary, armed assistance by the Soviet Union.
2. The pact requires consultation between the high commands of both countries in the case of a threat of such an attack.
3. Finland is prohibited from entering into any alliance directed against the Soviet Union (this obligation is also assumed in reciprocity by the Soviets).
4. The contracting parties pledge to respect the sovereignty and integrity of each other.[7]

Formal agreements represent only some of the parameters within which Finnish decision making for defense takes place. It has now become commonplace for Finnish leaders to consult with the Kremlin on most important foreign policy matters, and this type of consultation in turn feeds back into defense policy decisions. For example, the first visit, though only an "unofficial working trip," of the new president, Mauno Koivisto, shortly after his election, was to the Kremlin.[8] Finland, in short, is severely constrained in its policy-making process by informal agreements and practice. One of the most important of these constraints is the long-standing tradition of Finnish neutrality and bridge-building between East and West in Europe. The choice of Helsinki as the site of the final meeting of the European Security Conference, and the subsequent signing of an agreement which effectively ratified the political status quo in this region, mark the special position of Finland in the European politico-military arena. While the Finnish position is at least partly determined by voluntary choice, it is not an exaggeration to say that the Helsinki-Moscow relationship has a considerable effect on Finnish defense decision making.

Soviet Strategy, Tactics, and the Position of Finland in the 1980s

Since the end of World War II, Finland has existed in the shadow of Soviet power which is expressed and exhibited both formally and informally. This relationship has been based upon treaty obligations undertaken by Finland after the defeat of 1944. It has been further strengthened by a tradition of close consultations between Finland and the Soviet Union in matters of foreign and security policy. At the same time, skillful Finnish policy, and especially the personal diplomacy of Presidents Urho Kekkonen and Mauno Koivisto, have secured for Finland a position of national sovereignty and considerable autonomy in foreign affairs. This autonomy is reflected in Finland's national political system, which has remained pluralistic and democratic, and also in the economic field, where private enterprise remains the predominant force. Finally, Finnish culture and public attitudes are staunchly Western and nationalistic—a fact of life which becomes part of the context in which Finland's security policy is produced.

For Finland, a continued peaceful relationship with the Soviet Union remains a cornerstone and a sine qua non. Good foreign-policy relationships with Moscow ensure the relative security of Finland's long and vulnerable eastern border. The acceptance by Moscow of a neutral, politically and socioeconomically pluralistic Finland ensures the continuity and sovereignty of the Finnish nation and state despite the exposed position of this Nordic country.

Finland attaches great importance to its relationship with the other Nordic countries, particularly Sweden and Norway. Through active participation in the Nordic Council and in a variety of bilateral relationships, the Finns have maintained excellent relations with Stockholm and Oslo. Public opinion in these three countries remains very favorably disposed toward the citizens of the other countries in the area. This acceptance and friendship is undergirded by a strong sense of common cultural heritage, "Westernness," and a distinct "Nordic" culture. Even occasional disagreements between Finland and the other Nordic countries, such as the controversy between Oslo and Helsinki over prepositioning of war materiel in Norway, have not seriously threatened this close relationship.[9]

Given this kind of multilateral friendship, Finnish defense policy makers can assume, with considerable equanimity, that no perceptible threat exists to Finland from the other Nordic countries; such a realization helps simplify defense policy making. But while the security of the western frontier and seaboard is thus assured, Finland must take into consideration the security policies of Sweden and Norway, their impact upon the Nordic scene, and their relationship with the Soviet Union. Seen in this context, Nordic relations are not quite as placid and trouble-free as bilateral ties with Stockholm and Oslo would suggest.

The key to a thorough understanding of this complex relationship is the Soviet Union and its policies toward the "northern theater," which includes all the Scandinavian countries, Poland, Finland, and, in a certain sense, even the Baltic republics of the Soviet Union itself. Finland plays an important role in the Soviet approach to the other Nordic countries as well. Because of the strong ties between Finland and its western neighbors, Sweden and Norway, Soviet relations with leaders in Helsinki may have policy effects beyond Finland and into the Nordic countries and also the so-called Nordic Cap, which includes the northernmost parts of the USSR. Kremlin leaders have been persistent in their attempts to cultivate a sense of special relationships between the countries in the Arctic zone, presumably because this geographic location carries with it special problems and hence the need for solutions based on cooperation and cooperative measures.[10] The Soviet approach is clearly designed to reduce the foreign policy ties between the Nordic countries and their traditional Western partners. This is especially true in the case of Norway, a member of NATO and a strategically placed country in the regional and overall military balance between East and West.

Finland is a small regional power in two areas: Nordic and Baltic. As one of the countries with an extensive coastline on the Baltic Sea, Finland shares a geographic and strategic position with parts of the USSR, namely the Baltic Soviet republics of Estonia, Latvia, and Lithuania. The Finnish side of the Gulf of Finland guards one side of the entrance to the Port of Leningrad, which has traditionally been the primary Russian outlet to the West and its most important harbor. Strong cultural and historical ties exist between Finland and the Baltic Soviet republics. In the case of Estonia, this relationship is also linguistic, as exemplified by the popular Estonian habit of watching Finnish television beamed from across the Gulf of Finland. The Soviet leadership clearly considers a good relationship with Finland, because it is a Baltic power, to be a major regional advantage. The Kremlin is likely to remain dedicated to the preservation of this relationship in the future.

Important as Finland is to the Soviet Union in bilateral and regional terms, Moscow's northwestern neighbor also plays a part in the global strategy of the Kremlin leaders. Until recently, the Soviet Union lacked the ability to become a truly global power because it had only limited access to the high seas, hence insufficient capability to project power and influence events on a global scale. This deficiency has been remedied, in considerable measure, through the rapid build-up of Soviet naval forces in the Murmansk region, coupled with an expansion of air power and ground troops in the area. Murmansk now represents one of the most powerful concentrations of military force anywhere in the world. The proximity of this mighty force to the northern regions of Norway, Sweden, and Finland has created considerable problems for political and military leaders in the Nordic countries. Military experts in the West are casting a worried eye on potential Soviet deployment of military force into the territory of any one of the three Nordic countries, especially Norway, whose membership in the NATO alliance and whose important strategic location would make it a major early target in a confrontation or conflict between East and West on a regional or global scale. Occupation of northern Norway would enable Soviet naval and air forces to gain control over areas of the Norwegian Sea and subsequently threaten the vital resupply lines for U.S. troops in Europe.[11]

From the Finnish vantage point, a potential conflict involving northern Norway looks extremely worrisome. Soviet attempts to occupy part of a NATO country would, presumably, lead to a wider conflict. In such a case, it might become necessary for the Soviets to resupply their forces in Norway via Finland. Demands for such transit rights would be hard to resist. Few planners and analysts in the West assume that the Norwegians would be able to hold out very long against a massive Soviet invasion, and even allied help may not be sufficient to remove the Soviet forces from the area. What would Soviet policy toward Finland be in such an event? It seems unlikely that a neutral Finland, when surrounded in part by Soviet-occupied northern Norway, would be allowed to exist without drastic changes in its political system. And if such changes were enforced in Finland, Sweden would find itself equally surrounded. This possibility is one of the most worrisome contingencies being examined by Swedish foreign policy makers in the 1980s.[12]

It is not necessary to hypothesize *actual* warfare to realize the importance of Finland in the Soviet Union's Nordic and global strategy in the 1980s. If the Nordic Cap is important for the Kremlin in its pursuit of a *global* strategy, the message can be brought home to Norway and Sweden via Finland, as it were. Specifically, the Soviets may use the status of Finland as an attractive model for exposed countries such as Sweden and Norway, especially the latter. The Kremlin occasionally (and with increasing frequency in recent years) hints to Oslo that Norwegian security interests may be better served in a status of neutrality, a more "natural" state of affairs given the legitimate rights of the USSR as another Nordic power. After all, both Sweden and Finland are neutral, and their socioeconomic and political systems have flourished.[13] Given the tradition of neutralism which still survives in Norway, the "Finnish example" may yet become a Soviet foreign policy weapon against Oslo if the East-West confrontation continues to heat up in the 1980s. Given the close relations between Norway and Finland, and the understanding which exists in the former country of the *imposed* plight of the Finns, this Soviet approach is likely to have only limited success.

Soviet emphasis on the "realistic" and "peace-loving" policy of Finland as a possible example for Norway (and, to a lesser extent, Denmark) was highlighted by the Kremlin's campaign to prevent prepositioning of NATO materiel in northern Norway in the early 1980s and also Moscow's attempts to induce Norwegian rejection of Pershing II and cruise missiles which are an integral part of NATO policy in Europe. A number of important Finnish officials (most notably President Urho Kekkonen) did, in fact, criticize Norwegian policy in these fields, but the initial controversy between these two close neighbors has since died down.[14]

Finland's position vis-á-vis the Soviet Union will also be influenced by developments in communist-dominated Eastern Europe in the 1980s. As events in Poland have clearly indicated, the Kremlin leadership can expect increased trouble in this vital region during the coming decade. These problems will be multifaceted: they will be economic, as the sluggish, centralized economies of the area become less and less capable of satisfying the growing consumer demands of the modernizing populations; they will be social, as the conflict between privileged elites and the common people intensifies in the face of growing social stratification, and as the demands of the various socioeconomic classes in these societies begin to compete for the attention of leaders whose economic base is shrinking in relative, if not in total, terms; they will be political, as increasingly well-educated citizenries question more forcefully the lack of political choice and opportunity, thus further jeopardizing the very foundation of power upon which the local Communist parties have hitherto ruled. In short, the communist-dominated systems of Eastern Europe will face more societal crises during the coming decade. The Soviet Union, as the hegemonic power in the area, will face increasing political, economic, and psychological costs in its efforts to maintain that hegemony.

Seen against this backdrop of fundamental problems in a vital region, the relative stability of Finland, which is economically solvent and politically legitimate, must be a very attractive feature to the Soviet leaders. The considerable advantages accruing to the Kremlin leadership from the special relationship with Helsinki are likely to become even more attractive when compared to the massive problems of the rest of Eastern Europe. Under these circumstances, one can expect the Kremlin's policy toward Finland to continue throughout this decade.

But what if the imperial ambitions of the Kremlin, in its quest for full-fledged global-power status, profoundly upset the political and military balance in Europe? This is not empty speculation but rather a distinct probability. As the Soviets assess their present strategic advantage vis-á-vis the United States (and since the United States has begun a process of reassertion in the military and strategic fields, this advantage must be considered ephemeral at best) they may decide that the time to advance politically is surely now, or soon, before the internal problems of the USSR and its grudging allies in Eastern Europe, and the rearming of the United States, make such ventures improbable or very impractical. If the Soviet leaders harbor any ideas of political expansion at all, countries such as Finland, which exist in the "gray zone," become extremely vulnerable to political pressure. This is not to say that the current Soviet leadership will attempt to take over Finland politically; such a move would simply cost too much, politically and perhaps even militarily. Rather, the Soviet effort would aim to further restrict the autonomy of Finnish foreign policy, while seeking greater influence in Finland's domestic political life. If this were to occur, one could indeed talk about the real "Finlandization" of Finland. The prevention of such an eventuality, and the preservation of *real* neutrality and sovereignty, remain the primary goals of Finnish defense and security policy in the 1980s.

Domestic Constraints on Finnish Decision Making for Defense

While the global and regional environments and the special relationship between Finland and the Soviet Union set important external parameters for Finnish defense policy, internal constraints are of no less significance. These constraints include geographic location; climate and terrain; economic resources; and political conditions.

The location of Finland with its severe climate, which includes snow cover from October to April or May in the northern part, and from November or December to early April in the rest of the country, has profound effects on defense policy. This long winter has placed special requirements on training and equipment, a fact of considerable importance in a country with a small population, large territory, and a modest economic base.

In Finland there are approximately 75,000 lakes, several of them large, which create both opportunities and liabilities in defense planning. Of primary importance is the need to maintain an adequate road and railroad network for regional deployment of forces in a country of Finland's size (337,032 square kilometers, making Finland the fourth largest country in Europe, after France, Spain, and Sweden). Since fully one-third of the country is located north of the Arctic Circle, further communications problems are encountered due to severe climatic conditions.[15]

The economic conditions of Finland place further restrictions on defense decision making. Originally very dependent on the forest industry for employment and revenue, since World War II the Finnish economy has become diversified, especially in the fields of machine building, ship construction, and metal working. In the period 1944–1952, much of the national economic effort was devoted to paying off the war reparations demanded by the Soviet Union (the Paris Peace Treaty stipulated that this debt was to be fixed at $300 million). Since the successful retirement of this debt, the Finnish economy has been capable of rapid expansion, ensuring a high standard of living and an extensive system of social services. Particularly impressive has been the development of a strong machine-building sector. Thus, the higher economic base has also produced more claimants upon existing resources, and the defense effort must be considered in this context. Over the postwar period, defense expenditures have ranged from 1.3 to 2.0 percent of the GNP; in 1978 it reached the lowest level in this era.[16]

While geographic, climatic, and economic conditions represent important constraints on defense decision making, the internal political scene sets parameters which significantly influence the defense decision-making process. Finland has a pluralistic political system with considerable ideological differences among the many contending groups and parties. All of these participants operate under the formal restraints of the Paris Peace Treaty concerning "anti-Soviet propaganda," and this factor has tended to dampen the overt differences in the debate over foreign and security policy and national defense. Certain agreements simply are considered too controversial, given Finland's exposed position and special relationship with its giant eastern neighbor. Thus the various factions of the political spectrum have reached tacit agreements on the limits of security policy debate. In addition to this, there is a powerful Finnish Communist party (Suomen Kommunistinen Puolue—SKP) which is a leading force in the Finnish People's Democratic League (Suomen Kansan Demokraattinen Liitto—SKDL), an electoral organization. Through the SKDL, the SKP has been represented in the national government in 1944–1948, 1966–1971, 1975–1976, 1977–1979, and throughout much of the 1980s. An ideological split, which occurred in the party in the late 1960s, produced a "moderate" and an "orthodox" faction, thus reducing somewhat the importance of the Communists in decision making. But this fission has had limited effect in the field of foreign and security policy, since both communist groups agree on the need for close consultation and cooperation with the Soviet Union in this field.[17]

The complexity of the Finnish political system is shown by table 2–1. The political pluralism of the Finnish party system produces lively discussion and controversy over matters of economic and social policy, as well as the distribution of wealth and relations among the socioeconomic classes and the various regions of this country. In this concept, then, it is noteworthy that a consensus has developed among the leaderships of the major parties that the foreign and security policy of Finland is set on a course of neutralism and continued good relationships with the mighty neighbor to the east. This relative consensus among political elites simplifies defense policy decision making, insofar as the options are limited by treaty and by political agreement, but it complicates matters greatly for any individual or group who would wish to alter this long-standing status quo. This approach to defense policy decision making limits the range of potential options, a condition that has been given the pejorative label "Finlandization" by certain observers.[18]

Table 2-1. Political Strength and Policy Positions of the Principal Finnish Political Parties in Recent Years

Party	Representatives in Parliament		Percent of Seats		Policy Positions
	1979	1983	1979	1983	
Social Democrats (SDP)	52	57	26	28.5	Mixed economy; some central planning; political pluralism; welfare state orientation; neutrality.
Center Party (KES) (former Agrarians)	36		18		Located in the ideological center; emphasis on agricultural and regional development; neutrality.
National Coalition (KOK) (Conservatives)	47	44	23.5	22	Conservative; emphasis on private enterprise coupled with elements of welfare state social policy; strong national defense; since 1957, more moderate economic program; neutrality in foreign policy.
Swedish People's Party (SFP)	10	11	5	5.5	Ideologically heterogeneous; mixed economy; Swedish language rights; welfare state emphasis; neutrality.
Finnish Rural Party (SMP)	7	17	3.5	8.5	Populist; emphasis on agrarianism; integrates several protest groups; accepts some state ownership and aspects of the welfare state; accepts neutrality.
Liberal People's Party (LKP)	4		2		Located in ideological center; propounds classical liberalism infused with values of social welfare state; accepts neutrality.
Finnish Christian League	9	3	4.5	1.5	
Election Coalition: Democratic League (SKDL), Communist Party (SKP), and Socialists	35	27	17.5	13.5	Emphasis on public ownership of important elements of industry; welfare state policies in social sector; foreign policy neutrality with emphasis on good relations with the Soviet Union and foreign policy consultations with Moscow. The doctrinal wing of the SKP is orthodox Marxist, both in foreign and domestic policy matters. Recently, there has been internal strife between the pragmatic and orthodox factions of the SKP.
Other Parties		3		1.5	
Total Seats	200				
Working Coalition: Center-Liberal Alliance		8			See description of Center and Liberal Parties

Source: Political positions of the parties derived from a variety of sources: Nordic Council, *Yearbook of Nordic Statistics, 1979*; A.F. Upton, *Communism in Scandinavia and Finland* (Garden City: Anchor Press/Doubleday); Jaako Nousiainen, *The Finnish Political System*; and *Facts on File* (New York), April 1, 1983. Also: the Embassy of Finland, Washington, D.C.

Note: Minor parties include: Finnish Christian League (SKL) which emphasizes Christian values; liberal in outlook but rather heterogeneous ideologically; devoted to neutralism in foreign policy. The SKL had 9 representatives in the Eduskunta in 1979 but dropped to 3 in 1983. Furthermore, in 1983 the environmental Green Party had 2 representatives and the Constitutional Party had one representative.

The concept of "Finlandization" may have some limited value as a description of certain aspects of Finnish defense and security decision making. It falls wide of the mark, however, as a description of the functions of the political system in areas not related to external affairs and is an inaccurate portrayal of Finland's relations with the Soviet Union. The very complexity of the Finnish political system; the existence of numerous political parties whose economic and political philosophies are clearly in the capitalist tradition; the Western orientation of much of Finnish culture, music, art, literature, and cinema; and the close economic contacts between the Finns and non-communist Europe—all these belie the notion that Finland is somehow "inside" the Soviet sphere of interest in political and economic terms. Finnish public opinion is also solidly Western in orientation, with a good deal of anti-Russianism in it. The Finns are avid nationalists, and recognize the need for a credible defense that can protect the nation's vigorous pluralism which hangs in a precarious international position. Since few believe that this hard fought independence is threatened from the West, the relative consensus on national defense takes on a special character and a special direction.[19] In this context, the Finns, both at the elite and mass levels, attempt to make it abundantly clear that they are ready, willing, and able to defend their country against *any* enemy. Public opinion polls have documented this attitude, and the outcry in Helsinki after General Bernard Rogers questioned the defense capability of the Finns represents another element in this determination to defend the hard-won autonomy of Finland.[20]

Decision Making for National Defense: Structures and Processes

The president is the supreme commander of the Finnish armed forces. This function is executed in conjunction with the Council of State (the cabinet) and the Finnish parliament (Eduskunta). The Defense Council is the primary deliberative body on national defense, but it lacks executive power. Such power is exercised through the supreme commander, the executive functions of the individual members of the Defense Council, and the military chain of command (the commander-in-chief and the general headquarters). In the field, military activities are further decentralized into seven military districts, where commanding generals are in charge of operations within their jurisdictions. Civilian defense is under the jurisdiction of the minister of defense, and in the field it is under the supervision of county and local executives and boards. The Frontier Guards may be fused with the regular armed forces in the case of conflict. In peacetime they are under the control of the Ministry of the Interior.[21]

Appropriations for the national defense effort are deliberated on and completed in the parliament. There are also several important parliamentary committees which concern themselves with matters of strategy, tactics, equipment, and mission. One of the most important of these is the Parliament Defense Commission, which has been formed twice in the last decade (1971 and 1976).[22] A third commission is currently being set up. The actual appropriations for defense are debated both in the plenum of the Eduskunta and in the so-called Supply Committee, whose deliberations and recommendations have tended to be decisive. Party representation in this crucial committee is proportional to the strength of the parties in the Eduskunta as a whole, thus allowing basic debate and a recommendation which is likely to receive the acceptance of the plenum. Finnish parliamentary committees, like committees in the other Nordic parliamentary systems, are crucial institutions in the decision-making process. Their deliberations often become centers of political activity for interest groups and other claimants. The Supply Committee frequently holds hearings involving outside experts, representatives of the government and the bureaucracy, and occasionally members of other committees. This dynamic process of interaction has a fundamental bearing on Finnish defense policy.[23]

While the deliberative functions of the parliament (eventually resulting in an appropriation for national defense) are crucial for the decision-making process, it should be emphasized that the legislative initiative remains in the hands of the political executive, the president and the State Council. The government proposes legislation after a lengthy process of fact finding and listening to expert advice. This process, which becomes increasingly complicated as Finnish society modernizes, eventually produces a defense budget which relates to other parts of the national budget in a complex web of mutual dependencies. Parliamentary committees do not have the staff necessary to question the proposed budget in a fundamental way. Rather, they tend to nibble away at the fringes of the appropriations request without basically altering it. This tendency is well known in all modern societies, and Finland thus represents no deviation from a common trend. However, in the Finnish case there is one additional element which strengthens the legislative initiative of the executive branch, namely the unique stature and power of the former president, Urho Kekkonen, and his successor, Mauno Koivisto. Kekkonen's influence on national policies, especially foreign and security policy, was of such a magnitude that it warrants more detailed examination.

Institutionally, the president is a major power in the Finnish political system. The president is elected for a six-year term and may be reelected. The nomination process is informal, normally dominated by the executive committees of the major political parties. The legislative powers of the president include the following:

1. Introduction of legislation in the parliament.

2. Suspensive veto (which can be overridden by the parliament)—the right to halt legislation until the Eduskunta reviews it. Although the parliamentary body may override this veto, it has in fact exercised this option only a few times, thus rendering the presidential veto all but absolute.
3. Extensive decree power, including the power to make rules concerning the execution of laws.
4. Power to direct and administer bureaucratic agencies and the use of state property.
5. The right to dissolve the parliament and order new elections.
6. Leadership of foreign policy.
7. Supreme command of the armed forces.
8. Civil service appointments and supervision of the administration.
9. Power to grant pardons, immunity, and naturalization.[24]

These constitutional powers have combined to give the Finnish president an independent base of power which exceeds that of parliamentary leaders in the other Nordic countries. Through forceful exercise of these powers, a succession of Finnish presidents has managed to combine the powers of head of state, legislative leader, and supreme military command in such a way that they enjoyed both popular prestige and real power of decision making. Such individuals as P.E. Svinhufvud and J.K. Paasikivi have done much to solidify presidential power in Finland. The most forceful and successful of them all was Urho Kekkonen.[25]

Kekkonen achieved a very special position in the Finnish political system. First elected in 1956, he was reelected several times. There were earnest attempts to persuade him to stand for reelection in 1984 despite his advanced age (eighty-four). The proposed reelection had wide political support in a political system which otherwise has often been characterized by its divisiveness. The demands for Kekkonen's retention reflected the prestige of the man and the respect in which the nation and most of its political and socioeconomic elites held him. The source of this admiration was first and foremost Kekkonen's skill as a mediator in international affairs and his personal stature in the Kremlin, which made it feasible for Finland to maintain both its special relationship with the Soviet Union in defense and security matters and its Western orientation in culture, economic affairs, and domestic political conditions.

The primary reasons for Kekkonen's foreign policy success were his genuine commitment to neutrality, his desire to promote closer relationships between East and West, especially in Europe, and his ability to establish strong and favorable personal relationships with Soviet leaders as diverse as Nikita Krushchev and Leonid Brezhnev. Through frequent trips to Moscow, with careful consultations preceding any important foreign policy decision taken by Finland, President Kekkonen won the trust of the Soviet leadership.

Under these circumstances, close relations with the Kremlin at the personal level enabled the Finnish leader to retain foreign and domestic political flexibility unknown in other countries tied to the Soviet Union by means of mutual defense and assistance pacts. This is a feat of personal statesmanship which will be hard to duplicate. It is understandable why the Finns were anxious to retain the services of Urho Kekkonen as long as possible.

After Kekkonen's illness and resignation in 1981, the head of the National Bank and a prominent Social Democrat, Mauno Koivisto, was elected president. Koivisto has continued the policies of his predecessor, albeit with less personal flair and with more attention to political consultation with other political leaders at home. Koivisto, who was not the Kremlin's first choice for the position of president (this "honor" was bestowed upon a member of the Agrarian party, Ahti Karjalainen), has nevertheless succeeded in establishing a good relationship with the Kremlin through a series of meetings with Soviet leaders and a faithful continuation of the general foreign policy of Finland known as the "Paasikivi-Kekkonen line." Thus, under the new leadership, the policies of Helsinki in foreign and defense matters continue with concurrent approval in Moscow.[26]

The defense community, in a broader sense, includes a host of noninstitutional actors as well; some of them are as influential as the institutional actors described above. Chief among these noninstitutional elements are interest groups, weapons manufacturers, and certain academics who have expertise on national defense and foreign policy.

The Finnish interest group system is strong, with large, cohesive units which in many cases have more influence on decision making than the smaller political parties. Interest groups also contribute money, expertise, and manpower to the larger parties, thereby helping to control the functions of the parties in the political system.

Among the main Finnish interest groups with an impact upon defense and security policy can be found the Confederation of Finnish Wood Processing Industries (Suomen Puunjalostusteollisuuden Keskusliitto), which represents one of the main export industries of Finland. Since a considerable amount of the production emanating from the paper and pulp industry is exported to the Soviet Union, this confederation has a vested interest in cordial relations with the giant eastern neighbor. By the same token, elements inside the Federation of Finnish Industries (Suomen Teollisuusliitto) occasionally act as spokesmen for closer cooperation with Soviet authorities and economic organizations; this pertains especially to the Association of Finnish Metal Industries. This association represents the employees of the metal industries whose activities aim at stable economic relationships with an economic partner of considerable magnitude. The employees' associations are affiliated with the Confederation of Finnish Employers (STK-Suomen Työnantajain Keskusliitto).

In the trade-union movement ideological splits have prevailed since independence in 1917. There are also splits along functional lines, predominantly between blue-collar workers and salaried employees. These splits have produced a complicated situation in which some unions have become spokesmen for the strongest possible relations with the Soviet Union, within the parameters of national independence, while others decry the tendency toward foreign policy dependence which they perceive in the Helsinki-Moscow relationship. There are three major trade-union confederations, the most important of which is the SAK (Suomen Ammattiliittojen Keskusjärjestö—the Confederation of Finnish Trade Unions) whose membership is approximately 465,000. There are several independent unions, however, and even a small confederation of rural groups named SAJ (Suomen Ammattijärjestö—Finland's Trade Union Organization). Even though most of the unions (as well as the SAK) are under Social Democratic control, there is significant Communist influence at many levels. This has resulted in considerable pressure from this end of the trade-union spectrum for good relations with the Soviet Union.

Due to the functional and ideological splits in the Finnish trade-union movements, these groups generally have less influence than their counterparts in the Scandinavian countries. Finnish soldiers remain unattached to unions, although there is an extensive ombudsman system.[27]

A significant input mechanism in Finnish defense policy is the armaments industry, which has grown considerably and now carries a great deal of political influence. The defense industries are important employers which help reduce the problem of unemployment in Finland. Furthermore, the neutralist position of the country in foreign and defense policy demands that the armed forces remain independent of foreign weapons suppliers, or at least rely upon domestic sources for some of their equipment needs. Finland produces most of its small arms, such as the army rifle (which is based on the Soviet AK47, but with some improved features). Furthermore, one of the main artillery pieces in the Finnish army, the 122-millimeter cannon known as the 122D60, is produced in Finland (at Tampere). Even imported arms are serviced in Finland (e.g., the 130mm cannon, imported from the Soviet Union, the Bofors 44mm, imported from Sweden, and the 21MF and Draken aircraft, imported from the Soviet Union and Sweden, respectively),[28] thus producing a good many places of employment and a considerable pressure group. Since one of the main aspects of the Finnish neutrality policy is an even-handed armaments policy, based on procurement in both the East and the West as well as on considerable domestic production, it is fully consistent that the domestic arms industry should be an active participant in national security policy formation.[29]

The most important companies in the Finnish armaments industry are the Valmet group, the Wärtsilä group, and Oy Tampella AB (primarily weapons producers); Kemuri Oy and Lapuan Patruunatehdas (munitions); Oy Sisu-Auto AB (vehicles); the Nokia group (communications equipment); and Oy Sako-Tikka AB (rifles and ammunitions).[30]

The academic community in Finland is rather small, which is to be expected from a country of four and one-half million inhabitants. In this community, there are some scholars who concern themselves with defense and foreign policy matters; some of them are advisors to the government, and many of these scholars are housed in the Foreign Policy Institute, which publishes the foreign policy yearbook—the most authoritative and informed publication on this subject in Finland.[31]

Finnish defense policy making takes place in a *presidential* system interspersed with elements of parliamentarism. The president is constitutionally empowered to conduct foreign policy, and this has been supported by practice as well during the period of independence. The president and the cabinet are required to consult the Eduskunta for parliamentary approval of foreign and security policy in three instances, namely: (1) matters pertaining to war and peace; (2) specific foreign policy measures needing legislative action to be implemented (often foreign policy is conducted by means of executive order, which requires no direct parliamentary approval); and (3) budgetary matters. It is in this last category that the Eduskunta exercises the greatest power over foreign policy.[32]

The Foreign Affairs Committee of the Eduskunta is formally the most important body in the parliament dealing with foreign policy. There is no constitutional provision requiring governmental reports to that committee, however, and this has meant that the committee receives reports on foreign policy rather sporadically, at times after the fact. Such a practice is not conducive to a high profile for the Foreign Affairs Committee, and there have been complaints by committee members of the "high-handedness" of the executive in these matters.[33]

Parliamentary influence thus is limited primarily to the budgetary process. The yearly budget is produced by the government; in foreign policy matters, the president has a great deal of influence in the budgetary proposal. The bill containing the budget proposal goes through a formal procedure of hearings in the budget committee of the Eduskunta and a formal debate on the floor. But due to the external constraints on Finnish foreign policy, the parliamentary debate must of necessity remain rather limited in scope. The Eduskunta cannot decide on a sudden increase in the defense budget, since the size of the Finnish armed forces on land, at sea, and in the air, as well as their equipment, has been established by treaty. By the same token, one of the underpinnings of Finnish neutrality is a credible defense, which precludes drastic reductions in the budget. The arms procurement process, based on the domestic arms industry as well as suppliers from both East and West, has broad political agreement in the country. Furthermore, trade agreements with the Soviet Union postulate a balance in the exchange between the two countries. The structure and level of the Soviet economy are such that the Kremlin can only deliver oil and weaponry to meet genuine Finnish needs. Thus, external constraints reassert themselves even in the budgeting process. In the end, the predominant influence of the president and the government in foreign policy formation and execution asserts itself even in the budgetary process.[34]

The clear predominance of the executive branch, and particularly the president, in foreign policy matters has also tended to focus interest-group activity on these institutions and on the person inhabiting the presidential office. Some interest-group activity does center around the work of the budgetary and foreign-affairs committees and the political parties themselves, but this is less the case than in truly parliamentary systems, such as the Scandinavian states. The president, and especially the personality of Urho Kekkonen, has remained the focal point for foreign policy formation and execution.[35] His successor has established a similar, if less mercurial, position on these issues.[36]

Economic and Technological Constraints

The external and domestic political constraints which impinge upon the Finnish defense decision-making process are enhanced by economic and technological problems. The Finnish economy is clearly too small to maintain a defense establishment solely on the basis of domestic production (which has been Swedish policy), and this means that the Finns must import weaponry. The scientific establishment is too small for the needs of a modern army, navy, and air force (even the Swedes are finding this out in the 1980s), and technology from external sources must be obtained. As discussed above, the Finns have acquired such technology primarily from Sweden and the Soviet Union, with scattered purchases in Western Europe and the United States. This creates a dangerous dependency. The Swedish defense establishment is almost swamped by the costs of building new planes and weapons systems to replace the aging arsenal of armed neutrality. If the Swedes should decide to scale down their defense industries significantly and instead join a West European consortium for the procurement of aircraft, for example, Finland may not be able to obtain the Draken plane or other weapons systems so urgently needed. There will always be, of course, a Soviet airplane industry, and the Kremlin will be all too happy to supply Finnish needs in toto. Such a development would run counter to the carefully established principle of rough equivalence in arms procurement, however, and it would produce extreme difficulties for Finnish decision makers and planners. This may indeed become one of the main issues of Finnish politics in this decade.[37]

The problems discussed above do not apply to small-arms production. Here, Finnish technology is superior, and the productive capacity of the country, together with Swedish imports, will most likely maintain the needed balance with Soviet imports.

The Goals and Objectives of Finnish Defense Policy

The elaborate mechanism for defense decision making has produced a set of fundamental tasks for the Finnish military forces and the elements of civilian defense. These tasks are presumably an integral part of general Finnish foreign policy and are subsumed under several fundamental goals and objectives. These general goals are as follows:

1. The preservation of the territorial integrity of Finland in peacetime and in war.
2. Denial of Finnish territory to any would-be aggressor whose purpose may focus either on the subjugation of Finland proper or on the utilization of Finnish land, sea, or air space for aggression against third parties.
3. Preservation of the political, socioeconomic, and legal systems of Finland.

In order to execute these fundamental tasks, the defense forces and the political authorities immediately responsible for them have established a number of more specific functions, the most important of which are the following:

1. Maintenance of the forces authorized under existing treaties and proper training of personnel.
2. Production, procurement, and maintenance of equipment needed by the defense forces.
3. Enhancement of the population's support for the defense effort, and development of physical education and sports, thereby improving the ability of all Finns to participate in this national effort.[38]

In addition to these fundamental goals and their implementing tasks, Finnish authorities have increasingly involved the country in a variety of international peace-keeping missions, especially those carried out under the auspices of the United Nations.[39]

This brief review of the primary tasks of the Finnish defense forces indicates the importance of these goals in the total foreign policy of Finland. Of greatest importance is the emphasis on the preservation of the existing political and socioeconomic order and the cultural tradition of the country. Such emphasis clearly underlines Finland's determination to remain outside the Soviet political and economic sphere, while still making adjustments to the Kremlin's special demands. At the same time, Finland is determined to prevent the possible involvement of the country in any major move designed to weaken or actually attack the Soviet Union. These defense tasks are therefore directed both against Soviet efforts (should they be forthcoming) to undermine the nature of the Finnish societal system while, at the same time, scrupulously adhering to a neutral status in any East-West confrontation in northern Europe or the Baltic. Western analysts, who have often emphasized the degree to which Finland subordinates its interests to the Kremlin, believe that it is worth studying Finland's defense policy as it applies both to the Soviet Union and the Western alliance.

Finnish defense planners and civilian authorities charged with military preparations clearly base their predictions and assumptions on the dedication of the general population to Finnish independence, territorial integrity, and the inviolability of the political system and its institutions. Public opinion polls have shown consistently high levels of public support for Finnish foreign and security policy and the socioeconomic and political systems of the country. Given this kind of support, and given the organizational measures undertaken for rapid implementation of defense plans in cases of emergency or war, Finland appears prepared for a "people's war" against any potential or actual invader. This is a formidable commitment indeed for a country with a small resource base and a relatively small population.

Execution of Finnish Defense Policy: Forces and Training

Force Structure and Conscript Training

The complicated decision-making process described above is designed to ensure both political consensus about defense at home and external acceptance of the policies produced. As stated repeatedly in both publications and interviews, the Finns clearly are concerned that *all* external powers realize the dedication of the Helsinki leadership to true neutrality; in other words, Finnish decision making is designed to be credible to all interested parties, be they from East or West. Such a position of armed neutrality requires the wherewithal in manpower and materiel to ensure continued inviolability of Finnish territory. To this end, the Finnish armed forces consist of three subdivisions: general forces, local forces, and support troops.

The general forces constitute the primary war-making capacity of Finland. They are organized into brigade-level units and their subunits in the army, air force, and navy. In the army, the following branches are represented: infantry, field artillery, coastal artillery, antiaircraft units, engineering troops, the signal corps, and logistics units. In the infantry units there are also armored forces and some airborne troops.

In peacetime, the Finnish defense forces are stationed as follows:

1. *Army:* Seven military districts, with at least one brigade in each:
   Southwestern District (3 brigades, 3 battalions)
   Osterbotten District (3 battalions)
   Interior District (1 brigade, 3 battalions)
   Southern District (5 brigades, 2 battalions)
   Savolaks-Karelian District (1 brigade, 1 battalion)
   Northern District (3 brigades, 1 battalion)
2. *Navy:* Total forces:
   2 corvettes
   6 fast-attack craft equipped with missiles
   10 fast-attack craft equipped with guns
   1 coastal patrol craft of the Hurja class (experimental)
   5 larger (and older) patrol craft
   3 minelayers
   1 log ship
   25 landing craft
   The activities of the navy, which include occasional inspections of the demilitarized Åland Islands, are coordinated from navy headquarters in Helsinki.
3. *Air Force:* Two combat squadrons, including 21 Soviet MiG-21s and 12 Swedish Draken interceptors, stationed in three air defense districts, at Satakunta (southwest and central Finland), Karjala (southeastern and central Finland) and Lappi (northern Finland); defended by radar networks and antiaircraft artillery and some defensive missiles.[40]

The most important element of the Finnish defense forces is the army.[41] In the army, the most important operational unit is the brigade.

Local forces by contrast have limited functions; primarily surveillance, guard duty, and various other operations of a localized nature. These forces can operate in the rear or in the frontline areas depending on the situation at hand. In the former case, they are subdivided into one of the seven military district commands; in the latter case, they fall under the jurisdiction of the appropriate brigade-level unit.[42] The Frontier Guards are technically subordinate to the Ministry of the Interior and are charged with the task of patrolling the borders of Finland as well as all territorial waters. These forces have a military organization and are trained by military officers. In times of crisis and in actual warfare they may be joined with regular military forces.

Finland has universal conscription (ages 17–60), a fact which is of the utmost importance for the defense strategy and tactics established as well as for the nature of the force structure. Under such a policy, the Finnish armed forces can train up to 40,000 conscripts annually and, over time, this produces a sizable reserve which can be mobilized with relative ease and speed. Total mobilization in Finland in 1983 would have resulted in a combined defense force of over 700,000 men—a considerable number. Refresher training for reservists also helps maintain a basic level of skill for those who have served their minimum obligation and should help shorten the delay between call-up and combat readiness for such personnel.

Training of Finnish military personnel is an obligatory 240 days for lower-ranking enlisted people and 330 days for NCOs and reserve officers. Every year, approximately 30,000 reservists are given refresher courses. Through a variety of activities such as basic training (eight to ten weeks), special training (seventeen weeks), and maneuvers (seven to nine weeks), it is generally held that Finnish troops are well prepared for their tasks. These inductees provide the backbone of the standing Finnish Army, which numbers approximately 30,000 in peacetime.[43]

Officer Training

The basic training path for reserve officers is the three-year cadet course. After graduation from this course, the officer is given the rank of senior lieutenant and serves in a basic unit as an instructor (or as a commander of a basic unit in wartime). This type of field experience usually lasts three or four years, whereupon the senior lieutenant may enter a course of eight to ten months in duration, qualifying him for the captain's examination, and, if successful in the test, commission to the rank of captain.

The rank of captain usually involves service as a basic unit commander in peacetime (and battalion commander in time of war). Advancement from this position may proceed along one of two basic tracks. The first track involves a period of study of two or three years at the War College, provided the captain seeking such admission passes an entrance examination. Successful completion of the War College course leads to promotion to the grades of colonel and general in the armed forces. The navy follows a similar path in the training of its general officers. The second promotion track from the position of captain proceeds through a "senior staff officer course," lasting seven to eight months, followed by an examination. After successful completion of this examination, the candidates are eligible for promotion to the ranks of major and lieutenant colonel.[44]

For noncommissioned officers, there are also several paths to promotion. After the completion of junior secondary school in the general school system, the NCO is trained for one year (phase I) and completes an examination qualifying him for the rank of staff sergeant or warrant officer. The normal term of service after attainment of this rank is three years. A one-year course (phase II) at a noncommissioned officers' school may follow upon application, and successful completion of this course establishes eligibility for the rank of chief warrant officer. A "suitable" period of training and service with active units will follow before possible admission to phase III, which is the "lieutenants' course" (six months duration). The highest rank obtainable after completion of this course is senior lieutenant.[45] Staff sergeants may branch out from phase I to take a four-month staff sergeant course. This track leads to the position of senior staff sergeant.

The principles underlying the training of Finnish officers are fairly simple. These procedures are designed to provide continuous training and a high state of readiness, thereby increasing the efficiency of available manpower. The training of enlisted personnel is aimed in the same direction. Together, these procedures have established a level of readiness which is commendable in a small nation. At the same time, the staying power of such a force becomes questionable, since so much of the available resources are brought to bear early in a conflict. The problem of staying power becomes especially important in a neutral country whose leaders cannot depend upon reinforcement from allies. All in all, then, the Finnish force structure and the training of its personnel are well suited for a short confrontation, but may be less appropriate for protracted conflicts. Finnish defense planners, realizing this potential problem, nevertheless argue that there is no meaningful alternative to this approach, given the political constraints on Finland's defense policy. In this respect, they may be right.

Defense Strategy

Finnish defense strategy is based on a few crucial premises. First, the defense forces are designed to offer such resistance that an easy and early victory for any invader is prevented, thereby increasing both the costs of the action itself and the unpredictability of the political and military consequences thereof. Because Finland is a neutral country, the prepositioning of the standing air, land, and sea forces must reflect this evenhandedness, thus potentially reducing the ability of the forces to deal effectively with an incursion or full-fledged invasion in a particular area along the extended borders and territorial waters of Finland.

Second, Finnish defense is predicated upon rapid mobilization of the large reserves discussed earlier and swift deployment of these forces to the active fronts. In this manner the active fighting force can be increased several times in a matter of a few days.

Third, Finland's defense planners are committed to the concept of *total defense*. This concept involves the combination of: the civilian economy; psychological warfare and information; civil defense, especially aimed at reducing the loss to the civilian population; rapid drafting of women into auxiliary military units, industrial production, and other defense-related economic activity; and the utilization of diplomatic and other political channels for rapid conclusion of hostilities. This total defense, therefore, is dedicated to the maintenance of Finnish sovereignty and territorial integrity until practical diplomatic solutions to the conflict can be found. At the same time, total defense is considered vital to the survival of Finland as a viable economic, political, and social entity after the conclusion of hostilities.

Fourth, there is a deep realization in Finland that military conflicts may take place in a series of localized clashes, rather than on a national scale, due to breakdowns in communication and enemy attempts at reducing or destroying relief efforts and mobilization plans. For this reason Finnish regional and local defense forces as well as the border guards are designed as self-contained units which can carry out their tasks in relative isolation for a limited time. Toward this end there exists a close cooperation between regional military commanders and the county and community civilian authorities for emergency planning. The emergency plan is designed to use existing administrative personnel, augmented with experts in various fields related to defense, thereby creating almost instantaneously a capable crisis staff. Once again, the principle of rapid mobilization of existing manpower and expertise permeates Finnish administrative thinking.[46]

This coordinated effort is designed to accomplish several military objectives. Territorial violations and minor incursions are to be repelled by the standing forces and the border guards. A more important incursion, considered a "violation of neutrality," requires the action of standing forces plus reinforcements called up from the pool of reservists. An actual invasion will be met with the totality of wartime defense forces, numbering over 700,000 men. As stated in the pamphlet, "Finnish National Defense":

> The military operations are based on the principle of strategic territorial defense, according to which, in a deep area, starting from the frontiers and the sea, tactics of delay and attrition are used against the attacker to prevent him from reaching vital areas. In decisive combat, action is focused on striking at and destroying the attacker through concentrated, extensive counterattacks. In areas possibly seized by the attacker, fighting is continued by resorting to means of regional combatting, i.e., barriers, surprise, and limited attacks.
>
> This defensive system is marked by the fact that its effect can be stepped up flexibly, when necessary, as required by each particular situation of threat. In normal times the forces in services are peacetime forces carrying out surveillance of their respective areas and training conscripts while being prepared for defensive action.[47]

The mobilization of civil defense and the economy rapidly focuses the total war effort on the whole nation to repel the invader or to deal with more limited incursions. Emergency stockpiling, which is undertaken under normal conditions, can now be utilized for the war effort. Emergency shelters are available for over 2 million people. A total of 400,000 individuals currently participate in training designed to integrate them quickly into the civil defense effort. Finland also boasts the capacity to increase its hospital beds by 75 percent in emergency situations.[48]

Conclusion

Finnish defense decision making takes place in a more complex and difficult environment than is the case in the four Scandinavian countries. The special relationship with the Soviet Union, which is closely monitored in Moscow, produces extreme difficulties in foreign policy formulation and execution. The need to maintain a good relationship with Finland's giant eastern neighbor, while safeguarding the traditional friendly ties with the West, represents problems of such magnitude that only highly skilled diplomats can successfully conduct foreign relations. It is a monument to this skill that Finland has maintained real neutrality in a world increasingly dominated by power blocs.

Helsinki has not only succeeded in maintaining a meaningful neutrality, the Finnish leaders have also managed to safeguard the democratic and pluralistic nature of their political system, despite the close scrutiny of the local political scene by Soviet observers, and despite the existence of a strong Finnish Communist party and considerable leftist influence in many of the working-class mass movements, notably the trade unions. In fact, Soviet pressure on Helsinki in recent years has resulted in a swing to the right in Finnish public opinion, as exemplified by the elections of 1979 and 1983 (see table 2–1). Thus, the concept "Finlandization," which has been utilized to describe a gradual trend toward increased Soviet influence over the foreign and security policies of a country and its domestic politics as well, is only partly correct in the case of Finland itself.

The successful Finnish balancing act depends to a considerable extent upon restraints in Soviet policy toward Helsinki. To what extent can one expect that such restraint will continue in the 1980s? Analysts in Washington and Helsinki alike are casting a wary eye on the increasing assertiveness in Soviet foreign policy which has accompanied the massive build-up of military might in the Warsaw Pact. The aging leaders in the Kremlin are apparently committed to the achievement of full global-power status, on a par with the United States. Such an elevated status is likely to carry with it increased assertiveness in relations with the states on the Soviet borders, of which Finland represents an exposed "vanguard" of Western attitudes, lifestyles, and socioeconomic and political systems. One should therefore expect increased Soviet pressure on Finland, both in terms of Helsinki's conformity to established agreements, and also in domestic politics, where Moscow will emphasize the need for "progressive" leadership and safeguards against "reactionary" and "anti-Soviet" behavior.

Finnish developments along the lines described above would have considerable effects in the other Nordic countries as well, especially Sweden and Norway. Swedish neutrality has been buttressed by the existence of a stable, neutral, and reasonably strong Finnish state. By the same token, Sweden's position outside of any military blocs has made Finnish neutrality less odious, indeed acceptable, in the Kremlin. Should the Soviets press for greater influence on Finnish foreign policy, Stockholm would become increasingly vulnerable to pressure from the East as well. Norway, which shares a common border with the Soviet Union, nervously examines the strident statements emanating from the Kremlin in matters pertaining to security and military policy. In the Norwegian case, membership in NATO is an important safeguard, but the present problems in the alliance produce an aura of hesitance and internal friction in the West which bode ill for the 1980s. In short, Finnish defense policy and Finnish national security are intimately related to the security of Sweden and Norway. No one in Washington, Helsinki, Stockholm, or Oslo would like to see a Nordic version of the domino theory in practice.

Notes

1. See, for example, G.A. Gripenberg, *Finland and the Great Powers,* (Lincoln: University of Nebraska Press, 1965).

2. General Headquarters' Information Section, *Finnish National Defense,* (Helsinki: SKK oy 1978), 9–13.

3. Ibid., 10.

4. For the complete text of the peace treaty, see Anatole G. Mazour, *Finland Between East and West,* (Princeton: D. Van Nostrand, 1956), 260–279.

5. The complete text of the agreement can be found in: General Headquarters, Educational Section, *Uppgifter om Försvaret* (Information about Defense), (Helsinki: 1978), Appendix 3, 197–199.

6. This point was made by the social democrat Kalevi Sorsa after he became prime minister in one of the many cabinet reformulations conducted in Finland during the last few years. For details, see *Frankfurter Allgemeine* (Frankfurt), March 7–8, 1982.

7. *Uppgifter om Försvaret,* Appendix 3.

8. *Neue Zuercher Zeitung* (Zurich), March 7–8, 1982.

9. This controversy was carried on in part by Kekkonen himself, who criticized

the Norwegians for their defense policy. See, for example, *Neue Zuercher Zeitung*, April 2, 1977. Subsequently, this criticism was tempered, and a Finnish general who had denounced Norwegian policy in sharp language was administratively punished (Ibid., March 1-2, 1981). Kekkonen also stated that Norwegian policy would not upset the balance of power in the Nordic region (*Frankfurter Allgemeine Zeitung*, September 9, 1980). Koivisto, Kekkonen's successor as president, has tried to improve relations with Oslo. For a discussion of these ties, see the Norwegian daily, *Arbeiderbladet* (Oslo), March 9, 1983.

10. The Finns exhibit a keen sense of the main Soviet perception of this issue. See, for example, Ministry of Defense, *Extract from the Report by the Second Parliamentary Defense Committee submitted June 3, 1976,* (Helsinki: N.D.), esp. 2-3.

11. For a detailed discussion of the Soviet military threat in the area, see R.D.M. Furlong, "The Threat to Northern Europe," *International Defense Review*, April 1979, 521-523, and "The Strategic Situation in Northern Europe: Improvements Vital for NATO," Ibid., June 1979, 900-903.

12. See, for example, chapter 5 (Sweden), pp. 127-186, in this book.

13. This point has been made repeatedly, both directly and indirectly, e.g., during the meeting between Norwegian officials and Soviet leaders in Moscow in December 1980, as reported in *Dagbladet* (Oslo), December 22, 1980.

14. This Soviet campaign was further enhanced by Brezhnev's statements that Nordic accommodations on this issue, such as willingness to establish a formal nuclear-free zone in the area, might lead to Soviet accommodations also (e.g., *Frankfurter Allgemeine Zeitung,* June 2, 1981). This idea was subsequently altered, so that no Soviet installations would be included (*Neue Zuercher Zeitung,* July 28, 1981).

15. *Finnish National Defense,* 14-15.

16. Ibid., 18.

17. For a thorough discussion of Finnish communism, see John H. Hodgson, "Finland: The SKP and Electoral Politics," in David E. Albright (ed.), *Communism and Political Systems in Western Europe,* (Boulder: Westview Press, 1979), 243-267.

18. The Finns reject this concept. For a definition of Finnish security policy, see Keijo Korhonen, "Finlands Utrikespolitik som Del av Säkerhetspolitiken" (Finnish Foreign Policy as a Part of Security Policy), *Uppgifter om Försvaret,* 13-19.

19. For a discussion of Finnish public opinion on foreign and security policy, see Markku Haranne, "Opinion Polls on Security and Foreign Policy and the Related Debate," *Yearbook of Finnish Foreign Policy,* 1979, 48-52.

20. *Die Welt* (Hamburg), January 6, 1983.

21. *Finnish National Defense,* 16.

22. The Second Committee on defense submitted a highly influential review on security policy in 1976. See *Extract from the Report by the Second Parliamentary Defense Committee Submitted June 3, 1976.*

23. Jaakko Nousiainen, *The Finnish Political System,* (Cambridge: Harvard University Press, 1971), esp. 191-209.

24. Ibid., esp. chapter 7.

25. Ibid.

26. For an excellent analysis of this, see *Die Zeit* (Hamburg), February 5, 1982.

27. *The Finnish Political System,* esp. chapter 3.

28. For a report on Finnish procurement of Soviet weaponry, especially aircraft, see *Helsingin Sanomat* (Helsinki), November 25, 1978.

29. On Finnish domestic armaments production, see *Finnish National Defense,* esp. 38-40.
30. *International Defense Review,* No. 3/1984, 277-281.
31. Finnish foreign policy has also been discussed in considerable detail elsewhere, e.g., Max Jakobson, *Aspects of Finnish Foreign Policy Since the Second World War,* (London: Hugh Evelyn, 1968).
32. *The Finnish Political System,* esp. 195-209.
33. Ibid., 361-362.
34. *Finnish National Defense,* 16-18.
35. Ibid.
36. E.g., *Die Zeit,* February 5, 1982.
37. A detailed study of these problems can be found in Ingemar Dörfer, *System 37 Viggen: Arms, Technology, and the Domestication of Glory,* (Oslo: Scandinavian University Books, 1973).
38. For example, Seppo Räisänen, "Försvarets Ledning and Förberedelser" (The Leadership and Preparation of Defense), *Uppgifter om Försvaret,* esp. 55-59.
39. Tauno Tuominen, "Förenta Nationernas Verksamhet för att Trygga Freden och Finlands Deltagande i Den" (The Activity of the U.N. to Safeguard Peace and Finland's Participation in It), Ibid., 35-42.
40. *The Military Balance 1983-1984,* (London: The International Institute for Strategic Studies), p. 46. See also Finland, General Headquarters Information Section, *Finnish National Defense,* (Helsinki: SKK oy 1978), 26-34.
41. *Finnish National Defense,* 26-27.
42. *Finnish National Defense,* 33-34.
43. Ibid., 22-23.
44. Ibid.
45. Ibid.
46. Lauri Relander, "Kommunalförvaltningens Organisation under Kristid" (The Organization of Local Administration in Times of Crisis), *Uppgifter om Försvaret,* 91-100.
47. *Finnish National Defense,* 27.
48. Ibid., 39.

3
Iceland

John Fairlamb

Outside of the Nordic countries, the average person knows very little about Iceland. Iceland's climate is dominated by the intemperate weather of the North Atlantic and its landscape is unusually harsh. Today roughly 82 percent of the land area is uninhabited wasteland: glaciers, lakes, lava fields, desertlike sands, and marshes. As a nation with a homogenous population of 238,000 living on an island of only 103,000 square kilometers (39,698 square miles or slightly smaller than the state of Kentucky) in the middle of the forbidding North Atlantic, Iceland's isolation has been psychological as well as physical. Until recently, even those studying the NATO alliance in detail devoted little effort to analysis of Icelandic defense policy. The changing nature of the Soviet naval threat to NATO's defensive strategy, and realization of the crucial and periodically precarious dependence of NATO on Iceland's strategic location to counter that threat, have generated renewed interest in the northern theater as a whole.

Iceland was uninhabited until late in the ninth century A.D. The first settler, a Norseman named Ingólfur Arnarson, came to Iceland in the year 874. The original site of his homestead is the present capital, Reykjavík. In the next sixty years, Viking settlers from Scandinavia spread their homesteads over the habitable areas. In 930 A.D. a parliamentary body met for the first time at Thingvellir. The present parliament, the Althing, composed of sixty elected members, is a direct descendent of that first consultative body. As a result, Iceland boasts the oldest parliamentary governmental system in the world.

Iceland was originally claimed by Norway. In 1380, Norway and Iceland joined the Kalmar Union, which recognized the king of Denmark as the supreme head of all the Scandinavian countries. From this point, the history of Iceland was characterized by economic exploitation and brutal neglect by Denmark, until the spirit of nationalism and liberalism which swept Europe in the nineteenth century spilled over to Iceland. The ensuing nationalist spirit in Iceland led to the restoration of the old Althing (which had been suspended during Danish rule) as a consultative parliament in 1845, followed by the abolition of the Danish monopoly in 1855, and the establishment of a constitution in 1874 which secured legislative powers. Iceland won home rule in 1904 and obtained complete domestic sovereignty in 1918 when the Union Act ended all official ties to Denmark except for the king's continued control of foreign affairs. During the tumult of World War II, Iceland was able to sever the remaining ties with Denmark and proclaim complete sovereignty in 1944 as the independent Republic of Iceland.

Icelanders typically describe their country as the "land of ice and fire." This characterization is derived from the juxtaposition of giant glaciers with frequently active volcanoes which together have molded and dominated the rugged natural setting of the island. This aura of contrasts and contradictions is descriptive of the environment in which defense policy is formulated as well. The Union Act of 1918, by which Iceland negotiated an arrangement of limited sovereignty with Denmark, proclaimed a policy of perpetual neutrality in international affairs. Yet, when Great Britain occupied Iceland in 1940, the British were treated more as unexpected guests than as invaders. In 1949, Iceland declared its intention neither to raise an army nor maintain military forces of any type. In the same year, Iceland became a founding member of NATO, a collective security organization clearly dedicated to the military defense of Western Europe.

In the 16th Century, the Danish king preferred to disarm Iceland rather than accept the costs of defending a marginally productive subject.[1] As a result, strands of pacifism run long and deep in Icelandic culture. Yet, in a culture that has never known armed conflict, modern Icelanders proudly proclaim the fact that they have "gone to war with Britain" (in 1952, 1958, 1972 and 1975) over fishing rights in the North Atlantic, in a series of confrontations collectively known as the Cod Wars. Because of these and other apparent contradictions, Iceland is frequently perceived as a "reluctant ally"[2] by some NATO observers and as a "troubled ally" by others.[3] The important fact is that these crosscurrents run deep and form the complex societal and governmental milieu in which defense policy must be debated and defended.

An inescapable conclusion from this brief review of Icelandic history is the extent to which Icelanders have been continuously absorbed in a struggle for national identity. Unlike its alliance partners, Iceland has a short history of national sovereignty. Most Icelanders trace their independence to the Act of Union in 1918, by which Denmark ceded significant political autonomy. Actually, Iceland was unable to gain formal control over foreign and defense policy or achieve full sovereignty as an independent state until 1944. Thus, the eleven centuries of Icelandic history are characterized by economic, political, and military domination from external sources. The result has been the slow maturation of a deep vein of nationalistic spirit which runs through the modern Icelandic polity. External domination has contributed to the development of an Icelandic psyche which tends to equate national security with freedom from outside influence regardless of the source. Undue Western influence is rejected as readily as is undue Eastern influence. Given Iceland's history of domination by Western countries and cultures, the modern threat perception is oriented more toward Western cultures than those of the East.

Of greater significance is the fact that, with the exception of a very brief period in the late 1940s, since achieving complete sovereignty in 1944 Iceland has endured the presence of large concentrations of foreign troops on its territory—British followed by Americans. The current U.S. presence, while at a historic low, is to the Icelandic population what a comparable foreign presence of five million people 47 kilometers (29.2 miles) from Washington, D.C. would be to the United States. The Icelanders are extremely ambivalent about the presence of foreign troops. On the one hand, they understand the realities of their strategic but exposed geographical location. On the other hand, they are concerned with the inherent conflict between the continuous presence of foreign troops and true national sovereignty. Thus, like the basic conflicts of nature which dominate the geographical landscape, cross-cutting cultural forces dominate the defense policy environment.

Current Defense Policy

As this introductory review of Icelandic history clearly shows, until 1944 politics in Iceland focused on independence as the primary issue. Since 1944, the policy spectrum can be divided into two main areas: domestic and foreign policy. With respect to foreign policy, issues have clustered around two primary issues: physical security and resource constraints. Icelanders have tended to view national security more in terms of resource constraints than in the politico-military context. Resource interests have conflicted frequently with physical security interests. Such conflicts have influenced defense policy significantly because questions connected with resources have a more immediate impact on domestic politics than those connected with physical security. Faced with such conflicts in the past, the Icelandic government has tended to give priority to securing resource interests. On the other hand, most of the inputs to Icelandic defense policy emanating from its membership in NATO concern issues of physical security. Frequently, the result has been a direct conflict between internal and external inputs to defense policy. Consequently, the defense policy environment in 1984 reflects a degree of paralysis.

The broad outlines of Icelandic defense policy were established between 1949 and 1951. Tradition, history, and culture favor neutrality as the basic approach to Icelandic defense policy. Iceland's exposed position in the Cold War environment which quickly followed the end of World War II imposed on Iceland the requirement to tilt from a policy of neutrality toward the developing framework of collective security.[4] In a politically agonizing and highly contested decision, Iceland joined NATO in 1949. Simultaneously Iceland declared its intention not to raise a military force and never to accept the presence of foreign troops during peacetime. Amidst the deepening Cold War and the deteriorating international climate, Iceland signed the Bilateral Defense Agreement with the United States in 1951 which remains the basic contractual relationship with the United States. Under the terms of the 1951 agreement, Iceland temporarily accepted the presence of an U.S.-manned NATO Defense Force known as the Iceland Defense Force (IDF) based at Keflavík, which lies 47 kilometers from the capital, Reykjavík.

These key decisions, acceptance of NATO membership and the signing of the Bilateral Defense Agreement with the United States, define present Icelandic defense policy. All discussion in the Icelandic polity is focused on issues which are directly related to these two policy decisions. It is conventional wisdom that a greater involvement in NATO is politically unacceptable. The trend from 1951 to the present has been toward lessening the foreign presence in Iceland. Conflicts arising from the clash of defense interests with the more visible perception of resource threats have periodically strained the NATO connection, sometimes to the point of suggesting Iceland's withdrawal from NATO, the Bilateral Agreement, or both.

For a number of reasons, the populace has never totally accepted these broad outlines of Icelandic defense policy. As a result, defense policy has become a very important and divisive political issue. While present defense policy is defined by the same contractual agreements established in 1949–1951, the drift away from neutrality is still contested. The present environment can best be described as one of policy stagnation aggravated by high issue orientation. Specifically, the government is more concerned with resolving issues than with forming policy. This situation is largely due to the ambiguous nature of Icelanders' threat perception.

Icelandic Perceptions of Threat

What do Icelanders perceive as real or potential threats to their national security? From the NATO perspective, most recent analysis cites the growing Soviet deep-water naval capability as the primary threat to security of U.S./NATO interests in the Nordic region. On the other hand, nothing in the public domain has come to grips with the host of issues, perhaps central for the future, concerning Icelandic perceptions of the security of their nation. These perceptions are best understood through an examination of the environment in which defense issues are debated and policy is decided.

Icelandic threat perceptions deserve to be analyzed in depth; however, even a brief examination is illuminating. If the question is posed as the perception of a Soviet threat, Icelanders demonstrate a general awareness of the fact that the Soviet navy has grown in recent years and that Iceland's geography is consequently strategically important to NATO and to the Soviets as well. This awareness is not accompanied by any real sense of urgency concerning Icelandic national security. However, bearing in mind that in Iceland political opinion on any issue runs the ideological spectrum from left to right, it is possible to detect a consensus on the Soviet Union.

There is a pronounced tendency among Icelanders to underestimate the Soviets. Some analysts have made much of the fact that the Soviet diplomatic mission is by far the largest in Reykjavík. The most common response to this by the average Icelander is to refer to well-known stereotypes of Russian bureaucratic inefficiency and the Soviet need to ensure political reliability by overlapping functions and redundancy of personnel. There are other contributing factors, for example, Russians perform all functions in the Soviet mission, whereas in Western embassies the bulk of nonrepresentative functions are performed by Icelandic employees. Nevertheless, these reasons are those most frequently cited by Icelanders.

While informed Icelanders are generally aware that the Soviet navy has been growing in size over recent years, there is little understanding that it has also changed in capability and is now able to threaten vital sea lines of communications between North American and European ports. Icelanders tend to separate the concept of a land war in central Europe from the idea of a simultaneous naval war in the Atlantic. Many believe it entirely possible for NATO and the Warsaw Pact to fight a central European land war without necessarily involving Iceland.

Generally speaking, the Icelandic threat perception of the Soviet Union in peacetime has been at a very low level. Icelanders tend to view the USSR more than anything else as a large and potentially larger market for Icelandic fish products. However, it is true historically that specific acts of aggression traceable to the Soviet Union have generated increased interest and awareness of the potential threat to Icelandic security. It has been at these points that key Icelandic defense decisions typically have been made. (See table 3–1.)

Thus, although the perception of the Soviet threat is routinely low, there is strong evidence that indicates specific acts of Soviet aggression or breaches of peace are perceived frequently as threats to Icelandic security.

In order to gain a fuller appreciation of the much wider range of Icelandic threat perception, the question should not be posed only in terms of Soviet threats to security. If threat perception is approached from a more neutral direction, that is, "What do you see as possible threats to the independence and well-being of Iceland?," some interesting responses result. In the majority of responses to such an open-ended question, the Soviet Union is not mentioned. When the Soviets are mentioned, it is almost never as a first consideration. The consensus on perception of threat seems to contain several widely held elements: cultural, economic, foreign investment and a desire to maintain freedom of action and independence from both superpowers.

Table 3-1
Icelandic Responses to Soviet Aggression

	Events Involving Overt Soviet Action		Key Icelandic Defense Decisions
1948	Fall of Czechoslovakia and subversion of other Eastern European states by the USSR	1949	Iceland joins NATO
1950	North Korea invades South Korea	1951	Iceland signs the Bilateral Defense Agreement with the United States
1955	Soviet "peace offensive": USSR withdraws from Austria and relinquishes naval base at Porkkala, Finland	1955	Government of Iceland demands evacuation of Iceland Defense Force (IDF)
1956	Soviet invasion of Hungary	1956	Iceland drops call for evacuation of IDF
1968	Soviet invasion of Czechoslovakia	1968–69	Increased threat perception measured in opinion poll
1973	Middle East war U.S./Soviet confrontation	1974	Public opinion petition shows over 50 percent of voters favor retaining the IDF. A second proposal for withdrawing the IDF dropped
1979	Soviet invasion of Afghanistan	1980	Public opinion poll records 54 percent of Icelanders support retention of IDF

According to a former political officer at the U.S. Embassy in Reykjavík

> ... Probably the gravest long-term problem facing the U.S. presence in Iceland is our ability to deal with the Icelandic perception that the American presence, even as restricted as it is, is damaging to Icelandic culture.[5]

The majority of Icelanders are deeply concerned with the culture issue. In addition to the political parties which express concerns, various intellectual groups outside of the political process keep the issue before the public constantly. Even many of those who support NATO membership and the U.S. presence are concerned about cultural erosion.[6] National pride has centered around the homogeneous character of the population and the resistance to cultural change in customs and language. Icelanders perceive a major threat to their national well-being from the possibility that American values, some of which are inconsistent with Icelandic values, may supplant their own.

Except for a very brief period after World War II, Iceland has had to deal with the presence of foreign troops from the first days of formal national sovereignty. Initially a very large and visible presence, over the years the number of U.S. forces stationed in Iceland has decreased steadily so that the total number of U.S. nationals resident in Keflavík in 1984 was only approximately five-thousand. Yet the litany of cultural threats from the foreign presence has been heard for so long that the average Icelander regards it as a clear and present danger.

For most Icelanders the clearest threat to individual and national security is economic. Icelanders have become used to a very high standard of living based on the ready availability of imported consumer products and a government dedication to social welfare programs. Throughout the 1970s, this resulted in a relentlessly increasing inflation rate which topped 100 percent on an annual basis in April and May 1983.[7] Virtually all of the consumer goods required to support the lifestyle of high mass consumption to which Icelanders have grown accustomed must be imported due to a dearth of native industry. Thus, Iceland imports a good portion of the inflation generated in the Western industrial nations.

It is still accurate to refer to Iceland as a single industry economy.[8] In 1981, 78.3 percent of the dollar value of all Icelandic exports consisted of fish products.[9] Approximately 14.4 percent of the total labor force is involved in the fishing industry.[10] These figures alone explain why the dominant concern of Icelandic foreign policy since 1944 has been to secure the stock of fish in the North Atlantic and to insure Iceland's access to these stocks. Three times the fishing industry has faced external threats severe enough to warrant extreme responses by the Icelandic government. The bottom line is that any threat to either Icelandic fish stocks or export markets is in fact, as well as perception, a direct threat to the Icelandic standard of living.

The obvious answer would appear to lie in diversification of the economy. There was some sympathy for this in the previous coalition government, but no one wants to move too far too fast.[11] Iceland is a land bereft of raw materials and most natural resources. Only in the area of hydroelectric power and geothermal energy does there appear to be a potential solution. Until recently, the approach of the government has been to proceed slowly for fear of economic domination from abroad. Icelanders are suspicious of multinational companies which either seem to honor no flag or to be insensitive to Icelandic concerns or immune to Icelandic influence. Because of the relatively small size of the Icelandic economy (1981 GNP = $2.8 billion), a very real risk to the Icelandic economy exists. If contracts are not carefully managed, the economy could be dominated easily by foreign interests. As an example, in the late 1960s the Icelandic government entered a cooperative agreement with Alusuisse, (a Swiss-based multinational corporation) to build an aluminum plant (completed in 1969) south of Reykjavík.[12] By 1981, this single industry accounted for 14.2 percent of total Icelandic exports.[13] Although a success story for the Icelandic economy, this illustrates how easily a foreign investment can achieve a commanding place in the Icelandic economy. Many Icelanders perceive the threat from direct foreign investment to be a major challenge to national freedom of action. Thus diversification, including direct foreign investment, has become a political issue.

Finally, a general goal of Icelandic foreign policy (supported by the average Icelander) since World War II, has been to chart a course of independence and freedom of action designed to remain clear of external domination. In this context, Icelanders perceive both the United States and the Soviet Union as threats. The Soviets generally are perceived as a distant threat. Ironically, since 1945 some of Iceland's NATO allies have figured as more direct threats. Britain and Iceland have clashed seriously over fishing rights on four occasions. Norway is perceived by many Icelanders as attempting to expand its territory in the North Sea. Negotiations on fishing rights and the control of Jan Mayen Island are ongoing. With its past history of economic exploitation of Iceland, Denmark is still viewed, in a subtle way, with suspicion by some in the business community. This suspicion surfaces when Icelandic businessmen object to dealing with U.S. companies through Danish subsidiaries.[14]

In sum, there are many facets to Icelandic security threat perceptions. The Soviet threat is not likely to be dominant in Icelandic defense policy making in the 1980s.

The Defense Community

As this comparative study demonstrates, there is much similarity among the Nordic nations regarding defense community infrastructure. A cabinet-level ministry devoted to defense management; a military and civilian defense bureaucracy; a minimum range of standing armed forces covering land, sea, and air; a budgetary process which allocates a share for defense-related spending; a portion of civilian industry devoted to defense production; independent civilian organizations based either on the "think tank" model or centered around university departments providing independent analysis: all prove to be common features of defense communities in the Nordic nations. This is true whether the country is a member of NATO or a declared neutral. However, in most of these respects Iceland is clearly the divergent case.

Iceland has not and does not maintain armed forces. It is one of few existing societies without experience in domestic military forces, including raising militias. Iceland's geographic isolation provided its physical security for centuries. As improved travel and other communications eroded this isolation, Iceland's security was maintained by the British and U.S. navies. Today, despite heavy reliance on the fishing industry and foreign imports, which makes water rights and sea lines of communication vital interests for Icelandic security, the nation maintains only a small coast-guard constabulary force of five modern gunboats and approximately 160 men whose primary mission is to police Iceland's fishing zones.[15] Thus, the only funds allocated by Iceland for anything remotely related to national defense is for this tiny coast guard which is organized as a separate government agency.[16]

Unlike other Nordic countries, Iceland's governmental structure does not include a minister of defense who presides over a large military and civilian bureaucracy charged with managing the national defense. The civilian sector exhibits no Icelandic equivalent of the Rand Corporation or the Norwegian Institute of International Relations which might conduct independent analysis of defense issues. The University of Reykjavík does not have a section of the faculty or students engaged in analysis of defense issues or policy.[17] Icelandic industry does not manufacture weapons of any kind. In the absence of features which have come to be regarded as the infrastructure of a defense community, many have concluded that no such community exists in Iceland.

This comparative study poses a framework for analysis in which a defense community consists of all the public and private participants, individuals, interest groups, and sectors that are attentive to and that seek to influence defense policy at any stage from conceptual planning to execution. Such a definition does not imply a typical structure which must exist in order for the policy-making function to exist. Rather, given the assumption that national defense is a consideration for every sovereign state, the framework suggests a need to discover where in the governmental structure and by whom defense policy is conceived and executed.

Compared to the vast governmental structure and byzantine personal and role relationships which influence U.S. defense policy, Iceland is clearly a small-scale operation. Even in relation to its Nordic neighbors the Icelandic defense community lacks structural maturity. On the other hand, to conclude that such a structure does not exist or that Iceland does not formulate defense policy is incorrect. Important actors in the defense policy formulation process in Iceland include: the governing coalition, the cabinet, the foreign minister, the Ministry for Foreign Affairs, and a new Committee for Defense Studies.

The Icelandic polity is best described as fragmented and politically polarized. As the diagram (figure 3–1) of the political spectrum indicates, the organized political parties range ideologically from left (People's Alliance) to right (Independence party). The political parties typically are divided into factions by differences on particular issues. Party splinter groups are a common feature stemming from differences over specific issue orientations. The 1984 governing coalition is composed of the parties of the center and right (see table 3–2). The coalition leadership is provided by the smaller centrist Progressive party which holds three cabinet posts in addition to the prime minister's post. The larger Independence party holds six government posts, including those of foreign affairs and finance.

Radical Left		Center			Conservative Right
People's Alliance	Women's League	Social Democratic Alliance	Social Democrats	Progressive Party[a]	Independence Party

[a]Politically the Progressives are a centrist group. On the issue of NATO and the defense agreement with the U.S. they are to the right of the center.

Figure 3-1. Icelandic Political Spectrum

All of the major Icelandic political parties have established positions on the key issues of national defense. When such an issue surfaces in the defense policy debate, the parties take predictably opposing stands which are derived from their historical party positions. In most pluralistic political systems, the United States for example, the political parties exhibit a range of positions on defense issues such that cross-party coalitions on specific issues become possible. In the Icelandic case, party positions on basic questions of defense policy, for example, NATO membership and the U.S. presence, have hardened, which make cross-party coalitions unlikely. The extent to which this "politicization" of defense policy has developed in Iceland serves as a major constraint on the policy formulation process. The high political visibility accorded to any defense-related issue is reflected in the organization and procedures of Icelandic coalition governments. Icelandic governments have always been coalitions. They typically include political parties with widely divergent views on defense matters. Coalition partners will agree frequently to disagree on basic defense policy in order to form a *modus vivendi*. In such

Table 3-2
The Icelandic Parliament in May 1984: Based on Results of Elections in April 1983

Party	Seats	Change
Independence Party (IP)[a]	23	+1
Progressive Party (PP)[a]	14	−3
People's Alliance (PA)	10	−1
Social Democratic Party (SD)	6	−4
Social Democratic Alliance[b]	4	
Women's League[b]	3	
Total	60	

[a]The governing coalition formed of the Independence party and the Progressive party held a total of 37 seats.
[b]The April 1983 election saw two new parties enter parliament for the first time.

cases, the program of the governing coalition will specify that basic defense policy will remain unchanged for the life of the coalition.

The fact that the 1980 coalition embraced the entire range of the political spectrum made defense issues particularly divisive. In the published political program of Gunnar Thoroddsen's 1980 coalition, defense policy was conspicuously absent. The twenty-five-page document detailing the coalition's political program and basic policy positions devoted only eight sentences to issues of foreign and defense policy under the subheading "Foreign Affairs, etc."[18] No mention was made in the entire document of either NATO membership or the U.S. base at Keflavík.

The primary concern of the coalition was to strengthen the Icelandic economy.[19] As has been the case with past coalitions, the agreement of all coalition members with the published program was taken as tacit consent that the basic outlines of Icelandic defense policy would remain intact for the life of the coalition.

The Cabinet

According to the Constitution of the Republic of Iceland, the legislative power is jointly vested in the parliament (Althing) and the president of the Republic of Iceland.[20] Article 13, however, specifies that effective legislative power is exercised through the cabinet.[21] In practice, the president decides, based on electoral results, who shall form a working government coalition and serve as prime minister.

The number of cabinet posts is not fixed. In recent governments membership has ranged around seven to ten ministries. Table 3–3 shows that the 1984 cabinet was composed of a prime minister and nine ministers with portfolio. Icelandic conventional political wisdom holds that there is an unwritten political understanding that when the People's Alliance (PA) serves in a government coalition, as in the 1980 coalition, it will not get the Ministry of Foreign Affairs as one of its cabinet posts. Over the course of the last several coalition governments the PA seems to have acquiesced in this format.

Thus, two features of Icelandic political culture tend to work against significant leftist influence in defense policy formulation. First, the negotiation process by which coalitions are formed has effectively precluded defense policy from serious policy debate. Second, the Left will not head the Ministry for Foreign Affairs, the ministry where the primary responsibility for defense-related issues is vested in the governmental structure.

The Ministry for Foreign Affairs

Since 1954, primary responsibility for defense policy formulation in Iceland has been with the Ministry for Foreign Affairs.[22] This linkage of foreign

Table 3-3
The 1984 Icelandic Cabinet

Ministry	Name	Political Party
Prime Minister	Steingrímur Hermannsson	PP
Foreign Affairs	Geir Hallgrímsson	IP
Fisheries	Halldór Asgrimsson	PP
Health, Social Security, and Communication	Matthías Bjarnason	IP
Commerce and Banking	Matthías Mathesen	IP
Agriculture, Justice, and Ecclesiastical Affairs	Jón Helgason	PP
Power and Industries	Sverrir Hermannsson	IP
Finance	Albert Gudmundsson	IP
Culture and Education	Mrs. Ragnhildur Helgadottir	IP
Social Affairs	Alexander Stefánsson	PP

policy and defense policy in the Icelandic political culture began as custom and is now institutionalized by Icelandic law.[23] Gaining control over foreign policy only in 1944, Iceland did not have a defense policy as such until joining NATO in 1949. According to Hörtur Helgason, former permanent undersecretary in the Ministry for Foreign Affairs, this first experience with defense policy was linked intimately to the decision to join NATO and was viewed by the Icelandic leadership as a major feature of Icelandic foreign policy.[24]

After signing the Bilateral Defense Treaty with the United States in 1951, Iceland began to experience policy coordination problems. Initally, problems involving the U.S. base at Keflavík and other issues generated in implementing the treaty provisions were handled by whichever ministry seemed to have natural jurisdiction. For example, money issues were addressed by the Finance Ministry, whose decisions from a domestic budgetary perspective conflicted with the more international perspective of the Ministry for Foreign Affairs. The result was confusion bred by too many decision points and overlapping functions and responsibilities. For this reason, it was determined in 1954 that all issues dealing with defense policy would be the sole responsibility of the Ministry for Foreign Affairs.[25]

The Defense Division is one of four administrative divisions. It is staffed by two Icelandic foreign service officers who handle all defense-related issue for the Icelandic government. Those who work in Defense Division clearly view themselves as performing an administrative function. They conduct issue analyses, provide advice, and carry out the policy and tasks of the government in day-to-day operations.[26] There is widespread agreement within the ministry that the Defense Division does not perform a policy-making function. It was also widely recognized in 1984 that the two members authorized in the Defense Division could not keep pace with the growing workload. The Foreign Ministry has sought for some time to expand the Defense Division, but this is a political issue per se. Requests were made to the Finance Ministry for funds to hire additional staff. However, in the distribution of governmental functions among the previous governing coalition partners, the People's Alliance generally controlled the Ministry for Finance and thus was in a position to block funds for expansion. Even so, there was general agreement on the need for additional expertise on defense-related issues and some funds in the new budget to hire an additional staffer.

The Minister for Foreign Affairs appoints seven committees which are organized functionally to deal with specific issue areas. Five of these committees perform functions directly related to defense policy. The bulk of their work is related to issues which arise as a result of the 1951 Defense Agreement and the U.S. base at Keflavík. The Claims Committee, for example, is charged by Icelandic Law Number 110/1951 to settle all monetary claims which may arise from the defense agreement with the United States.[27]

Of the five committees dealing with defense-related issues, clearly the most significant for policy formulation is the Defense Committee. The Defense Committee of the Ministry for Foreign Affairs is composed of five Icelanders appointed by the minister to represent Iceland in negotiations with U.S. personnel based at Keflavík. Membership in 1984 was a mix of ministry employees and prominent civilians.

When the five Icelandic members of this committee meet with three senior U.S. military officers assigned to the Defense Force commander's Staff, the Iceland-United States Defense Council is formed. U.S. membership has been guided by the desire to appoint people of sufficient stature to ensure that they can speak authoritatively concerning U.S. interests. Thus, the staff judge advocate and the base commander have usually been members. The Defense Council dates from 1951 when the defense agreement was signed with the United States. Its purpose has always been to serve as a liaison body between the Icelandic government and the Keflavík base. The Defense Council is viewed as the ". . . point of official working contact between the Government of Iceland and the Defense Forces."[28] The Council attempts to deal with specific problems which might arise between U.S. servicemen and Icelandic civilians and with the various impacts which the base has on local Icelandic citizens. The Council meets every two weeks. Its role as a policy-making body varies with the level of analysis. It deals with the day-to-day problems associated with a foreign military base in Iceland, rather than issues of grand policy such as whether the U.S. base should remain in Iceland. On issues such as the deployment of new U.S. weapon systems in Iceland the Defense Council would act in a communications role only.

There is, however, some feeling that since the Council meets frequently, resolves problems, and keeps minutes which form an official record, over time a policy routine has been established. Both Icelanders and Americans consider the Defense Council to be an important forum for the discussion of defense-related issues.

The consensus seems to be that the actors most influential in defense policy formulation are the civil servants in the Ministry for Foreign Affairs and the foreign minister. The enhanced role of the civil servants can be traced to the manner in which coalitions have led to negotiated settlements between parties with widely divergent positions on the basic defense policy. Such an arrangement has had two results. First, it insures that basic policy trends will be maintained. Second, it means that the civil servants in the Foreign Ministry enjoy a certain amount of leeway to conduct policy within well-defined parameters.

Of those closely associated with defense policy in Iceland, the clear consensus is that the minister for foreign affairs is the dominant actor in the formulation of defense policy. There are two primary reasons why this is so. The first concerns the nature of the ministerial system in Icelandic political culture. In the Icelandic system, both by law and custom, ministers tend to be supreme in their own functional areas.[29] The negotiation process by which the coalition is formed sets the tone of the government concerning major policy lines. The prime minister publishes a written program which establishes the broad outlines of policy for his government. The program serves as a guide for the duration of the coalition. However, policy implementation related to particular issues is the province of individual ministers. This is true especially in the case of defense policy since the typical coalition negotiation has tended to avoid defense policy because it is a potentially contentious issue. The prime minister cannot fire a subordinate minister if the latter does not agree with a particular policy decision. The Constitution provides for a degree of ministerial autonomy by specifying that only the Althing can impeach a minister.[30] Foreign ministers have been particularly aggressive about maintaining their prerogatives in the area of defense policy.[31]

The Icelandic Commission on Security and International Affairs

The Icelandic Commission on Security and International Affairs (CSIA) is the newest structural actor in the Icelandic defense community. The CSIA concept originated in February 1979, under a left-coalition government. The foreign minister in that coalition, Benedikt Gröndal (the Social Democratic party leader in 1980), decided that a major problem facing decision makers in the area of defense policy formulation was the lack of information available on which to base informed judgment. Looking to Norway which had a similar defense committee, Mr. Gröndal decided to appoint a special committee with the mandate to function as a defense information institute.[32]

In discussion of defense policy with Icelanders, one hears this commission referred to frequently as the Parliamentary Defense Committee. This is an inappropriate description and the distinction is an important one. As originally conceived, the commission is appointed by the prime minister and reports directly to him rather than to parliament.[33] This commission has nothing to do with debating or formulating defense policy. In fact, the intention in making the commission directly subordinate to the prime minister was to demonstrate that it had nothing to do with current policy.[34] Ideally, the commission serves as an agency within the governmental structure where research and study of defense issues can be accomplished to facilitate the development of a body of informed, factual analysis available to decision makers.

All political parties were represented on the commission. It should be pointed out that only two of the eight members were members of parliament. The other six were former members of parliament, government employees, or private citizens who have interests in defense issues. The consensus of outside observers and members of the commission alike is that by 1983 the CSIA had accomplished very little. Clearly, the fact that there is only one part-time staffer allocated to the commission automatically limits the scope of its ability to perform research and analysis of complex defense issues.

The commission has yet to establish itself within the defense community, and it is not yet clear whether it will fulfill its mandate as a research institute or will be used for political purposes.[35] The possibility for political exploitation stems from the exclusion of some coalition partners from defense decision making. One or more of the parties might use the official status of the commission as an in-house organ to challenge the government's positions on defense questions. Because all political parties are represented on the commission, the potential exists for it to become a forum for airing political views rather than accomplishing much concrete research and analysis. This

Table 3–4
Icelandic Commission on Security and International Affairs

Party Affiliation	Commissioner
Independence Party	Björn Bjarnason
	Matthías Mathiesen
Progressive Party	Haraldur Olafsson
	Þorarinn Þorarinnsson
Social Democratic Party	Bjorgvin Vilmundarson (Chairman)
	Sigurdur Gudmundsson
People's Alliance	Olafur Ragnar Grímsson
	Jónas Árnason
Research Staffer	Gunnar Gunnarsson

possibility will increase when the new commission is formed based on the results of the April 1983 election. That election saw two new parties joining parliament, which will make reaching a consensus on defense issues even more difficult.

The timing of the commission's appointment has led to some suspicion concerning its true purpose. Conventional political wisdom in Iceland has focused on the domestic political circumstances which existed at the time. The political program of the 1980 coalition represented the first time the People's Alliance had participated in a coalition without demanding as government policy the withdrawal of the U.S. base and the termination in one way or another of NATO membership.[36] There was speculation that the existence of this commission would allow the PA leadership to participate in the government coalition while assuring the party membership that these issues were being studied by the Defense Committee.

The News Media

As previously mentioned, defense policy in Iceland is totally politicized. To some extent this politicization is reflected in the news media because there are close political party associations with most of the daily newspapers. Iceland has six nationally circulated papers all of which appear six times per week. In order of size they are *Morgunbladid, Dagbladid Vísir* (D.V.) (both with links to the Independence party but not party controlled), *N.T.* (Nu Tíminn) Progressive party controlled), *þjoðviljinn* (People's Alliance controlled), and *Alþydubladid* (controlled by the Social Democratic party).

All the Icelandic political parties have sought to advance party policy through editorials and feature articles which routinely follow the established political affiliation of the paper. Extracts of these newspaper editorials and features are broadcast daily by the State Radio which increases their impact.[37] Since all the political parties are concerned with defense-related issues, defense policy is frequently the subject of many of these editorials and features. It should not be inferred from this that as a result the public is well informed on defense issues. With the possible exception of *Morgunbladid*, the nature of these editorials and features is more that of party propaganda than sound, objective analysis. The overwhelming focus of the printed news media is toward domestic concerns such as quality of life and the economy. Foreign news and informed defense reporting are marginal.

Given the reality of politically linked printed media, it is perhaps significant that repeated surveys indicate that the average Icelandic family sees 2.6 daily papers.[38] There is some reason to believe that the average Icelander is exposed to at least two or more editorial points of view. Although this is not a guarantee of objectivity, at least most Icelanders are exposed to different interpretations.

In the case of the broadcast media, the story is vastly different. Radio and television are state owned and operated. The Iceland State Broadcasting Service is an umbrella organization which oversees both operations. Surveys suggest that the most popular items on both services are news and current events. Department heads have considerable editorial freedom, but an oversight body, the Broadcasting Council, is charged with ensuring that political bias is not permitted to develop.[39]

As a general characteristic, the news media do not really perform the function of educating the population on defense issues. The interest level among the population for defense problems is extremely low. To an even greater extent than the average American, the average Icelander is largely unconcerned with defense policy. Further, there are historical and cultural reasons why there are no Icelandic defense authorities who can explain complex defense issues. Since Iceland has no military tradition, few Icelanders have become familiar with the technical aspects of national defense. The media's role is reduced to reporting the ongoing political debate between political parties and visible political leaders.

Public Opinion and Civil-Military Relations

Public opinion is not systematically measured in Iceland. The call in 1974 by a left-coalition government for removal of the U.S. base resulted in a probase petition which eventually obtained the signatures of over 50 percent of the registered voters in Iceland.[40] Given historically tepid support for the base by all political parties in Iceland, and in view of the outright hostility of the PA, this was taken at the time as a major show of support for a much-contested aspect of Icelandic defense policy. Two of the daily newspapers have conducted random public opinion surveys dealing generally with election issues. The scientific rigor of these surveys is questionable by U.S. standards and they rarely deal with defense issues.

Assessing the tenor of civil-military relations in Iceland can be either a very easy or a very difficult task, depending on the perspective of analysis. Superficially, the lack of a domestic military establishment, defense industry, or defense budget cycle leads some to conclude that there is nothing to analyze. Alternatively, one might focus, as have some writers, on the relationship between Icelandic civilians and the foreign military presence embodied in the U.S.-manned Iceland Defense Force (IDF).[41]

From the perspective of defense policy formulation, however, there is a very important feature of public opinion and civil-military relations which is vital to understanding the process of defense policy formulation in Iceland. There is virtually a total absence of nongovernmental actors in the Icelandic defense community. With the exception of issues focused on the IDF base, there is no public interest for issues of national defense. In coverage of defense, the media do not educate the public so much as preach the point of view of an affiliated political party. Since there are no independent defense analysts publishing in Iceland or working in civilian institutions such as the University of Reykjavík, the public does not have access to informed and independent debate. This has resulted in public opinions on defense matters derived from an exclusively emotional foundation. Across the political spectrum, Icelandic officials concerned with defense policy decry the lack of information available to the public and upon which informed opinion might be based. One result of the absence of an informed public has been the creation of a major constraint for defense policy makers.

Decision-Making Constraints

It becomes obvious that the defense policy formulation process in Iceland is highly constrained. In most Western democracies, constraints on defense policy formulation tend to fall into three general categories: formal-institutional constraints, informal-societal constraints, and resource constraints. Formal-institutional constraints derive from laws, regulations, or constitutional provisions which tend to establish formal parameters which restrain the range of choice open to decision makers. For example, the Basic Law (Constitution) of West Germany places restraints on the manufacture of weapons and makes the waging of aggressive war illegal.[42]

Despite Iceland's basic hostility to the very principle of foreign and domestic armed forces, there are no real institutional constraints on defense decision making. Neutralism is an important element in Icelandic thinking and opinion. In 1918 Iceland declared perpetual neutrality as a basic defense orientation. Many mistakenly believe that this government proclamation currently has the force of law. Article 75 of the Constitution of Iceland states clearly that ". . . every person able to carry arms shall be obliged to take part in the defense of the country according to provisions which may be detailed by law."[43] Although no such provisions have ever been made, the reasons are cultural rather than institutional.

Although the policy process is not subject to formal-institutional constraints, there are three classes of informal-societal and resource constraints which define the freedom of choice for defense policy decision makers in Iceland.

Social and Cultural Constraints

Because Iceland has never had a national army, there is no native military tradition. Consequently, regular armed forces are regarded as alien—as "un-Icelandic." There is no appreciation among the population for the role of armed forces in society and no frame of reference from which to judge the value or functions of military forces. These are issues considered irrelevant to Icelandic lifestyle and therefore rarely thought about. A major reason the news media do not focus on military issues is this very pronounced lack of interest in the target audience.

Several outcomes of this social/cultural phenomenon directly constrain the policy-making process. Probably the most important constraint is the absence of a factual basis for the debate of defense issues. As noted previously, Icelanders are very poorly prepared to engage in objective, informed discussions of defense policy. This lack of preparation is so basic as to include the absence of vocabulary to describe modern defense issues. The Icelandic language is viewed as a national treasure. Foreign words are not incorporated into the formal language. A national linguistics board constantly monitors the language to preserve its purity.[44] It is a myth, however, that the language is the same today as it was a thousand years ago. While modern Icelanders can read the ancient sagas in the original text of the Old Norse, the vocabulary has greatly expanded over the years. Once a need to expand vocabulary is perceived, the technique used is to return to the original linguistic base and construct an Icelandic word which conveys the desired meaning. Given the absence of a military tradition, the original linguistic base lacks a diverse military vocabulary.

A popular vignette sums up the problem. In the spring of 1980, Norway was debating the wisdom of prestocking U.S. equipment in northern Norway to facilitate rapid reinforcement in a crisis. This was an issue of some interest in Iceland. However, before the issue could be explained, a word had to be found to describe the concept of prestocking military supplies. The Icelanders settled on a word which had been used by the Vikings to denote a hut behind the house where spears were kept.[45]

From this most basic problem, the information gap rapidly widens for two additional reasons. First, because there is low interest in military strategy and policy in general, there is no market for independent defense experts in Iceland. Lacking a domestic market for the product, bright students do not focus their studies on defense policy processes or military studies. Thus, there are no think-tank operations to conduct independent analysis of defense issues and perform an information function. A second reason can be traced directly to the fact that Iceland does not have a defense budget process. Since there is no defense budgeting cycle to generate a continuing debate, the natural impetus for factual information and analysis is totally absent.[46]

This general lack of expertise in military affairs also characterizes those who serve in the government. As the description of the Ministry for Foreign Affairs demonstrated, there are few individuals dealing directly with defense issues. Those who do are not trained in the technicalities which characterize defense issues. This problem is widely recognized among the Icelandic policy elite. There is a perceived need and some movement toward improving the capability of the Icelandic government for independent analysis of defense problems.[47] This was the major intent of Mr. Gröndal's decision to appoint a defense committee when he was foreign minister in a previous coalition government.[48] In the early 1980s, Iceland sent several young men to study in Norway at the Norwegian Military Academy.[49] There is some thought of educating these individuals further, perhaps in Canada, the United States, and the United Kingdom. Since they are starting from a zero base so far as awareness of security issues is concerned, these new "experts" are going to require training and seasoning. Mr Hörtur Helgason of the Ministry for Foreign Affairs envisioned a regimen of seasoning for these selected young people, possibly to include field service with the United Nations as members of a peace-keeping force to provide an opportunity for field experience.[50] The foreign minister in 1980 expressed his intention to hire one or more of these young Icelanders to serve as an adviser on defense policy.[51] Though obviously a long-term proposition, this demonstrates that the problem has been officially acknowledged.

Political Constraints

A second set of informal-societal constraints with direct impact on defense policy formulation are political. In many obvious ways the nature of these political constraints is closely related to the social and cultural milieu. In any society where cleavages exist over basic policy orientation and where a degree of free political expression is ensured, political party orientation will incorporate and in some cases institutionalize those cleavages. This has clearly happened in the Icelandic polity with respect to defense policy. The cause can be traced to the decision to abandon neutrality.

Because defense policy in Iceland is totally politicized, on any given defense issue, each of the political parties can be expected to take a position based on its approach to three policy orientations: neutrality, the NATO connection, and the U.S. presence. This has been true since the initial decision in 1949 to join NATO. That decision was hotly disputed and resulted in protest riots in Reykjavík.[52] Iceland has no tradition of comprehensive, cross-party cooperation in the formulation of defense policy corresponding to the U.S. period of bipartisanship in the late 1940s and 1950s. A split resulted from the decision to tilt from neutrality and has been perpetuated by the major political parties. Although the split is over core issues, there are discernable limits. No political party advocates a tilt toward the Soviets. What passes for the Communist party in Iceland takes a strong nationalistic position in favor of neutrality. All four of the major political parties have well-defined stands on defense policy and routinely enter the policy debate.

Independence Party (IP). Since 1946 the IP has been the largest party in the Althing. As it normally polls 35–40 percent of the vote, this party is the natural and most frequent coalition leader. Although the May 1983 coalition was led by members of the Progressive party, the Independence Party held six of ten ministerial portfolios including the prestigious Ministries of Foreign Affairs and Finance. The party is ideologically conservative and is considered the party of business interests. On the key issues of defense policy, the IP supports both NATO membership and continuation of the U.S. military presence.

Progressive Party (PP). The second largest party, the PP, represents the interests of fishermen and farmers. Iceland boasts a large and active cooperative movement centered in the north and this movement provides the base of support for the PP. On economic policy the PP represents the center of the Icelandic political spectrum. However, on defense policy it is slightly to the right of center. The PP supports NATO membership, but maintains that NATO and the U.S. presence are separate issues. The party believes that in peacetime no military presence is required and has periodically supported moves to renounce the 1951 Bilateral Agreement.

The People's Alliance (PA). The PA consistently polls approximately 20 percent of the vote. The party has participated in coalitions with all of the other parties at one time or another. It was formed in 1956 when a number of factions and interests groups opposed to the U.S. presence and NATO membership joined with the old Icelandic Communist party. Although they are commonly referred to as communists, it is important to recognize that many of the supporters are not communists.[53] The party remains a coalition of political factions held together by common views on defense policy and an extremely nationalistic orientation. The true communists in the party are a minority and run the gamut from Marxists to Stalinists. Ties to the Soviet Union are both weak and deemphasized. The average party supporter does not consider himself to be a communist. Party views on foreign policy stem from a nationalistic, almost chauvinistic, conception of Iceland's relationship to other nations. In 1983 their platform did not include the prospect of tilting away from the West and toward the East. Rather, they are propelled by an arrogant nationalism in the direction of virtual isolationism in foreign affairs.

In defense policy the party is both anti-NATO and anti–U.S. presence. Two key characteristics account for the adversarial nature of the party's positions on defense policy. First, the bulk of the membership is not imbued with Marxist or any other brand of communist ideology. Therefore, ideology cannot bind the party together. Secondly, as explained above, the party was formed from a conglomeration of interest groups opposed to the basic outlines of Icelandic defense policy. Largely as a result of these characteristics, the party perpetuates a highly visible protest on defense policy as a means of holding the membership together. The leadership of the PA will seize any opportunity to focus attention on defense issues, particularly when they are serving in coalition governments which force them to compromise on core party principles.

Social Democratic Party (SDP). The smallest of the four major Icelandic parties, the SDP clings to a narrow base of support centered on the urban trade unions. The SDP has always offered firm support for the NATO commitment and, after 1956, has also supported the U.S. presence.

Social Democratic Alliance and Women's League. The 1983 election saw two new parties join the parliament. The Social Democratic Alliance is a breakaway group of the SDP, and the Women's League is a militant feminist organization. Although it is too early to discern a party orientation on defense issues, the basis of support for these two parties predicts they will oppose the NATO base and U.S. presence. Their addition to the Icelandic political spectrum ensures further diffusion of opinion on defense issues.

The four major parties in Iceland have firmly entrenched positions on key defense issues. Roughly 80 percent of the electorate supports the NATO connection.[54] Only one of the parties is unequivocally opposed to NATO membership. On the other hand, none of the parties view the presence of foreign troops as a permanent or desirable condition. The average Icelander considers the presence of foreign troops to be a distasteful necessity resulting from a temporary condition of international instability and superpower conflict.[55]

In summation, the demonstrated concern of Icelandic political parties with defense policy has led to some discernible constraints on the policy process. The highly politicized nature of defense issues has encouraged the gradual structuring of governmental processes which effectively isolate defense policy from direct political impact. There are some clear examples which illustrate this point. The negotiation process by which coalitions decide in advance the broad outlines of government policy has been especially important in the area of defense policy. In the absence of such a procedure, basic defense orientation would be at issue with each election. The firm adherence to principles of ministerial control has had the effect of compartmentalizing policy in general and is vital to the longevity of coalition governments frequently composed of parties strongly opposed to the traditional defense policy. Finally, the informal practice of excluding members of the People's Alliance from the key offices of prime minister and foreign minister has made a tenuous political equilibrium possible.[56] The net result in 1983 was a policy environment which sought a virtual freeze on defense policy so that progress might be made on domestic economic policy.

Resource Constraints

In the European context, the mini-state is not as remarkable an entity as in the American perspective which tends to equate sovereignty with size. Luxembourg and Monaco, other European mini-states, derive a measure of security from their common borders with powerful, friendly states. Iceland, in addition to being small, is geographically isolated in an area of extreme strategic interest both to the United States and the Soviet Union. To understand the Icelandic security perspective, one must become comfortable with the issue of scale because, to a large extent, Iceland's approach to security has been dictated by size.

Since Iceland maintains no military forces and therefore has no requirement for a defense budget, resource constraints have affected defense decision making in Iceland in a way different from other Nordic countries. Iceland is practically bereft of natural resources. Geothermal heat, hydroelectric power, and access to bountiful fishing grounds are virtually the only exploitable resources. Iceland depends totally on foreign trade for economic viability. In 1981, 78 percent of Iceland's exports were in fish products.[57] It is clear why Icelanders view national security in terms of economic rather than military threats.

There are Icelanders who believe it is an affront to sovereignty to rely on others completely for basic security. Even those who advocate some type of militia structure for self-defense readily acknowledge that the population base of 238,000 could not sustain a credible force. Only around 50,000 would even be capable of military service. Thus, after eleven centuries of struggle for national identity, the pragmatic requirements of survival in a hostile international environment have forced the Icelanders to rely on others for physical security—but they have never liked it.

Conclusion

The negotiation of broad policy outlines by governing coalitions, the evolution of ministerial autonomy, and the political character of defense issues have all had a major impact on the defense decision-making channels in Iceland. There is no effective input to policy making from interest groups or policy elites outside the governmental structure. The People's Alliance, effectively excluded from the defense policy process, periodically has sought to bring defense issues to the cabinet for discussion. Under the principle of ministerial autonomy, issues conceptualized as defense-related fall under the exclusive purview of the Ministry for Foreign Affairs, thus excluding the People's Alliance from the deliberative process. For this reason, when it participates in government the P.A. tries to cast defense issues in other than defense terms so that ministries they direct might become involved in defense decision making.

A clear example which illustrates each of these conclusions was the August and September 1980 issue of construction of new fuel storage tanks for the Defense Force at Keflavík.[58] The PA is convinced that NATO intends for Keflavík to function as an advanced supply and staging area in the event of conflict with the Soviet Union. They argue that this role is provocative to the Soviets and makes Iceland a high-value target early in any crisis situation. The PA raised questions about the increased capacity of the new storage tanks which they consider to be far in excess of base requirements, and therefore confirmation of their suspicions concerning the true role of the NATO base. To enter the policy debate, the leadership of the PA surfaced issues concerning the environmental impact and health considerations of the positioning of these new storage tanks, questions which might be explored by the Ministry of Health, Social Security, and Social Affairs which they controlled. The foreign minister, Ólafur Jóhannesson, actively opposed this attempt to dilute his decision-making authority in the face of a wavering prime minister.[59] The resolution of this challenge reiterated that within the well-established parameters of basic policy, the Ministry of Foreign Affairs handles defense issues and the foreign minister generally makes the final decisions. Defense policy is rarely debated in the cabinet.

The policy process has adapted to the constant background noise of politically motivated defense policy debate. Under certain conditions the political pressure can dominate the decision-making process. In 1979 the foreign minister attempted to lift some of the restrictions which prevent Americans assigned to the Defense Force from moving freely outside the limits of the Keflavík base. The political pressure across the spectrum was such that he was left completely isolated, and forced to rescind the policy change.[60]

The major outcome of this politically charged decision-making environment is a policy process which relegates most defense decision making to the bureaucracy. Decisions affecting grand defense policy, such as leaving NATO or terminating the Bilateral Agreement with the United States, would have to be decided by the Althing.[61]

In the scant writings available on Icelandic defense policy, it is normal to find speculation as to whether or not Iceland will remain a member of NATO. These basically shallow articles on Iceland impart a clear feeling of the precariousness of the U.S. presence there. On the contrary, there is every reason to believe that fundamental changes in Icelandic defense decision making will not be forthcoming in the late 1980s for several reasons. First, and of greatest importance, is the clear understanding across the political spectrum that the government must give priority to solving increasingly severe economic problems. In 1983 inflation was well over 100 percent on an annual basis. The 1983 election signalled that the electorate clearly expected a new economic program. The fishing industry was suffering from overmechanization and a downturn in demand from traditional markets, both of which were causing unemployment where there was none previously. The new coalition formed in May 1983 immediately launched an economic austerity program featuring a major devaluation of the króna by 14.5 percent against a basket of currencies, and reduction of expected increases of 20-25 percent in wages and farm prices to increases of 8 percent. With such a full plate of domestic economic problems, the last item on the Icelandic government's agenda would be an agonizing and fractious reappraisal of basic defense policy.

Secondly, since the mid-1970s there has been a growing understanding among politically aware Icelanders of the added leverage Iceland exerts in international negotiations as a result of the NATO connection. In the final negotiated settlement of the Cod Wars, the preliminary agreements on Jan Mayen Island with Norway in May 1980, and continuing negotiations with Denmark, Norway, and the European Community over fishing rights, Iceland is finding the NATO connection useful in strengthening its bargaining position. Consequently, the NATO connection may be seen by Icelanders as furthering Icelandic security interests beyond mere physical security.

Finally, the U.S. presence has declined to such an extent that the cultural-erosion argument has been greatly undermined. Due to a gradual but steady decrease in the number of facilities and the number of Americans manning remaining facilities, the U.S. presence and influence are seen as declining rather than expanding. In 1984 both the Americans at the defense base and the Icelanders seemed to exhibit a live-and-let-live attitude.

The issue of U.S. nuclear weapons at the defense base is one which could upset the balance. However, the United States is bound by treaty to consult with the Icelandic government before introducing any new weapons systems and, through 1984, the Icelandic government seemed satisfied with U.S. guarantees. Barring any new revelations of a dramatic nature, the delicate equilibrium should continue at least for the remainder of the 1980s.

Notes

1. Benedikt Gröndal, *Iceland From Neutrality to NATO Membership,* (Oslo: Universitetsforlaget, 1971), 14.
2. Donald E. Nuechterlein, *Iceland, Reluctant Ally,* (Ithaca, New York: Cornell University Press, 1961).
3. CDR Neil F. O'Connor, USN, *Iceland—Troubled Ally,* (Norfolk: The Naval War College, 1975), ii.
4. *Iceland From Neutrality to NATO Membership,* 47.
5. Interview in the U.S. Embassy in Reykjavík, June 24, 1980.

6. Interview with leadership of the Social Democratic Party in Reykjavík, July 11, 1980.
7. *Facts on File, World News Digest with Index,* (New York, 6 May 1983), 435.
8. Ibid.
9. *The Europa Year Book 1983, Volume I,* (London: Europa Publications Limited, 1983), 794.
10. Economic Statistics Quarterly, (Reykjavík: Central Bank of Iceland, 1983 Vol. 4), 1.
11. Interview in the economic/commercial section of the American Embassy in Reykjavík, June 20, 1980.
12. Ibid.
13. *The Europa Year Book 1983, Volume I,* (London: Europa Publications Limited, 1983), 795.
14. Interview in the economic/commercial section of the U.S. Embassy in Reykjavík, June 20, 1980.
15. "Iceland," *Janes Fighting Ships 1980–1981,* 218.
16. *Who's Who in Iceland,* a directory of the Icelandic government prepared by the U.S. Embassy in Reykjavík, 1980 version.
17. Interview with members of the Public Affairs Office of the Iceland Defense Force, June 16, 1980.
18. *Political Program of Gunnar Thoroddsen's Government* (Reykjavík: Gutenberg, February 1980), 19–20.
19. Ibid.
20. *The Constitution of Iceland* (Reykjavík: Gutenberg, 1974), 3.
21. Ibid., 5.
22. Interview in Ministry for Foreign Affairs, July 14, 1980.
23. Ibid.
24. Ibid.
25. Ibid.
26. Ibid.
27. *Manual of the Ministry of Foreign Affairs of Iceland,* (Reykjavík: Gutenberg, May 1980), 11.
28. *Keflavík, Iceland: Information Brochure,* (Keflavík: PAO, Iceland Defense Force, 1979), 6.
29. *The Constitution of Iceland,* 5.
30. Ibid.
31. "Ólafur Jóhannesson on the Helguvík Project," Translation from *Morgunbladid,* Reykjavík, August 12, 1980, p. 3.
32. Notes from interview with leadership of the Social Democratic Party in Reykjavík, July 11, 1980.
33. Ibid.
34. Ibid.
35. Notes from interview with a member of the Committee for Defense Studies, July 7, 1980.
36. Björn Bjarnason, "View from Reykjavík," in *NATO's Fifteen Nations,* (April–May 1980) 55.

37. Interview with members of the Public Affairs Office of the Iceland Defense Force, June 16, 1980.
38. Ibid.
39. Ibid.
40. Ibid.
41. O'Connor, "Iceland—Troubled Ally", 20–26 and Nils Ørvik, "NATO and the Northern Rim," in *NATO Review,* Number 2, April 1980, 10–13.
42. Guide Goldman, *The German Political System,* (New York: Random House, 1974), 165.
43. *The Constitution of Iceland,* 18.
44. Interview in the United States International Communications Agency Center in Reykjavík, July 5, 1980.
45. Interview in the economic/commercial section of the Embassy in Reykjavík, June 20, 1980.
46. Interview in the U.S. Embassy, June 24, 1980.
47. Interview in the Defense Division of the Ministry for Foreign Affairs, July 14, 1980.
48. Interview with leadership of the Social Democratic Party, July 11, 1980.
49. Ibid.
50. Interview in the Ministry for Foreign Affairs, July 14, 1980.
51. Interview in the J2 Section Iceland Defense Force, July 15, 1980.
52. *Iceland From Neutrality to NATO Membership,* 44.
53. Ibid., 45.
54. Ibid., 95.
55. Interview with leadership of the Social Democratic Party, July 11, 1980.
56. *Iceland From Neutrality to NATO Membership,* 40.
57. *The Europa Year Book 1983, Volume I,* 794.
58. "Ólafur Jóhannesson on the Helguvík Project," 3.
59. Ibid.
60. Interview with leadership of the Social Democratic Party, July 11, 1980.
61. Interview in the Ministry for Foreign Affairs, July 14, 1980.

4
Norway

James Stark

The Kingdom of Norway is the key to the northern theater. Occupying the western part of the Scandinavian peninsula, it is bounded on the east by Sweden except in the far north where it shares common borders with both the Soviet Union and Finland. Its western boundaries are the North Sea and the Atlantic Ocean, and the north is bounded by the Arctic Ocean. Norway's immediate economic, security, and legal jurisdiction has grown dramatically; first by the adoption of a 200-mile Exclusive Economic Zone (EEZ) and second by the rapidly growing ability to exploit longstanding claims to its continental shelf. Economic expansion into coastal waters has brought vast new oil, gas, and fisheries resources, new wealth, renewed national self-confidence, and intensified bilateral contacts with the Soviet Union over control of these economic resources.

For reasons outlined in the introduction, Norway is strategically important to both NATO and the Warsaw Pact. For U.S. and other NATO strategists, an understanding of how and why Norwegian defense policy is made will be important in the 1980s. This chapter seeks to enhance that understanding by examining the communities, channels, constraints, and functions inherent in the Norwegian national security decision-making process.

The Actors

In most open societies, the national security policy community is comprised of practically any organization interested in a particular issue. The interests of these actors differ in scope and permanence, and the nature and extent of their ability to influence the process varies.

In Norway three major categories of actors participate in the defense decision-making process: the executive branch of the national government[1], the Storting or legislative branch, and a third group which includes all nongovernmental actors. The lines dividing these three categories are indistinct and, as will be shown, individuals often belong to more than one of these groups.

Executive Branch

The Norwegian Eidsvold Constitution of 1814 established Norway as a constitutional monarchy.[2] Although the constitution itself refers to either the king or the king in council, the actual role of Norway's king is that of chief of state rather than head of government. In reality, the term "king" as employed in the constitution is used to define the role and powers of the prime minister and his cabinet.

The prime minister has ultimate responsibility for the policies of the Norwegian government. Within the cabinet he sets the tone, arbitrates differences among his ministers, and ensures that due consideration is given to domestic political factors before any policy is announced or forwarded for legislative approval. The prime minister's staff is surprisingly small, consisting of three senior advisors supported by a small number of administrative and secretarial personnel. The prime minister is able to function effectively by relying on individual cabinet members and their respective ministries to perform the bulk of the required staff work. Invariably, major decisions involve the prime minister, and in general one or two of his ministers, and a small nucleus of party and parliamentary leaders.

Within the cabinet, the most obvious participants in national security issues are the ministers of foreign affairs and defense. The Ministry of Foreign Affairs has primary responsibility for Norway's relations with other states and is the preeminent agency in setting national security policy. It is usually, but not always, the principal actor in the negotiation of treaties and other international agreements. The Ministry of Foreign Affairs carries out routine interactions with other governments. Thus it has a major impact upon Norway's security policy, determining both the tenor and specifics of relations with NATO allies, the Soviet Union, the other Nordic states, and the Third World. The Ministry of Defense has responsibility for the protection of Norway and the execution or support of any decision requiring the actual employment of military force. As a result, the Defense Ministry is the primary implementer of security policy and often plays a key role in its formation.

Other ministries also participate in the national security policy process. Significant roles are played by the minister of justice in internal security, the minister of commerce in decisions concerning the role of Norwegian shipping for NATO contingencies, and the minister of finance in the formulation of the defense budget. Occasionally these ministries (or others) are the principal actors in security-related issues. One example is Mr. Jens Evensen, the minister for the Law of the Sea during the late 1970s, who had the principal responsibility for negotiations with the Soviet Union over the disputed "gray zone" offshore fisheries in the Barents Sea.[3]

This explains in part why national security issues are not easily compartmentalized between ministries. Issues which may seem to be defense related may in fact have broader implications in other areas. For example, the Foreign Ministry played an important role in a decision to place a ceiling on West German (FRG) troop participation in NATO exercises in Norway.[4] Although the Foreign Ministry was not alone in raising objections to the FRG troop levels proposed by the Ministry of Defense, its position was a significant factor in the ultimate policy decision. The position of the Foreign Ministry emphasized the role of FRG exercise participation in the normalization of relations between the two countries. At the same time, both the USSR and Finland had expressed criticism and concern about the Norwegian decision. In light of these various foreign policy considerations, the foreign minister supported the more modest position which was eventually adopted by the government.[5]

Within the Defense Ministry there are several key actors involved in defense decision making. The minister of defense is a political appointee, for whom experience in the area is a desirable qualification but not necessarily a prerequisite. He is supported by a defense staff (comparable to the Office of the Secretary of Defense in the United States) which reviews policy, develops options, and presents recommendations to the minister. This staff is comprised of both civilian professionals and military officers. The minister of defense is also supported by Norway's senior military officer, the chief of defense, who is responsible for the operation and administration of Norway's armed forces in peacetime. The chief of defense functions in policy matters as the senior military advisor to the minister of defense. Although his recommendations are theoretically based upon purely military considerations, the chief of defense certainly recognizes and accounts for political factors.

Figure 4-1 depicts the peacetime organization of Norway's defense establishment.[6] Actual operational command of Norway's military forces belongs to the commander, South Norway, and the commander, North Norway. During peacetime and in the transition to war, they are responsible to the chief of defense. However, during a major conflict, they would report directly to the NATO commander in Northern Europe. It should be noted, however, that this shift of operational control does not occur automatically. Any decision to transfer Norwegian forces to NATO is the responsibility of the prime minister and his cabinet.[7] The administrative staffs of all four services (Norway includes its Home Guard together with the army, navy, and air force) report to the chief of defense through the individual service chiefs. In addition, the chief of defense has his own support staff for personnel, operations, intelligence, logistics, and program planning. The organization of the Norwegian Defense Staff is shown in figure 4-2. This is comparable to the Joint Staff in the U.S. military organization.

Unlike U.S. intelligence agencies, Norway's national intelligence organization is part of the military staff and reports to the prime minister through

94 • Nordic Defense: Comparative Decision Making

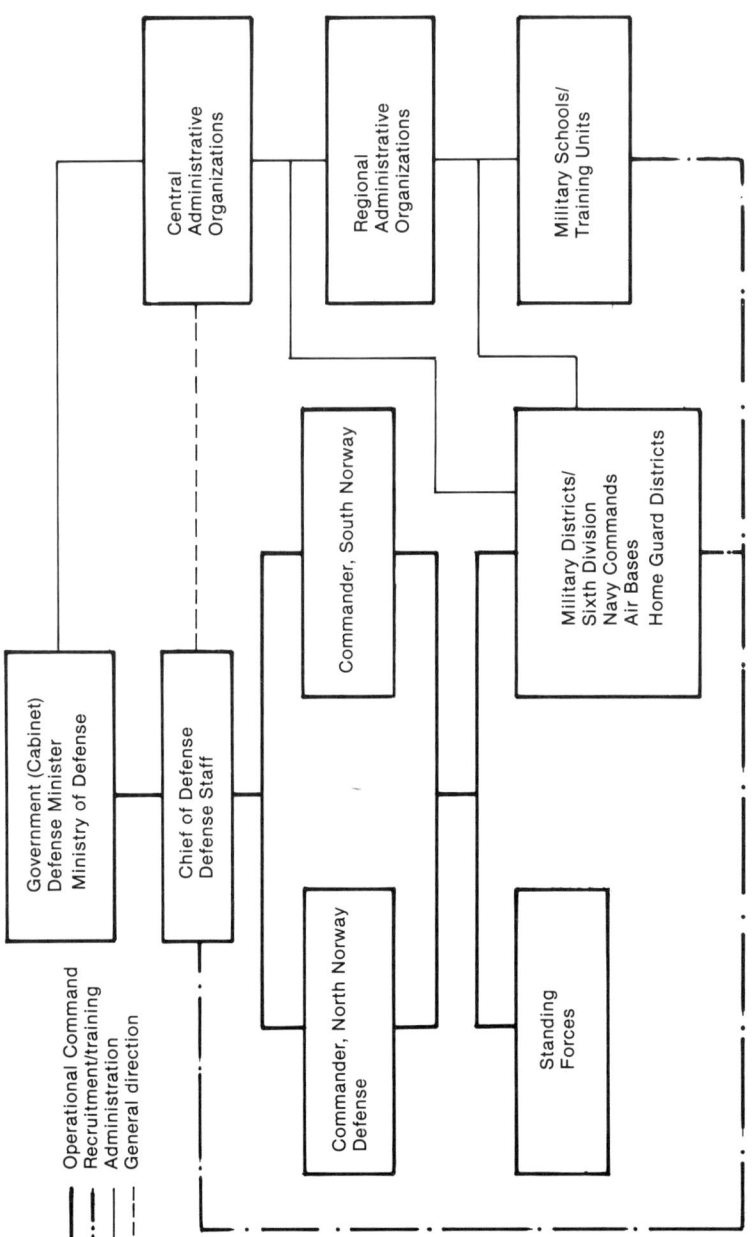

Figure 4-1. Norway's Peacetime Defense Organization

Norway • 95

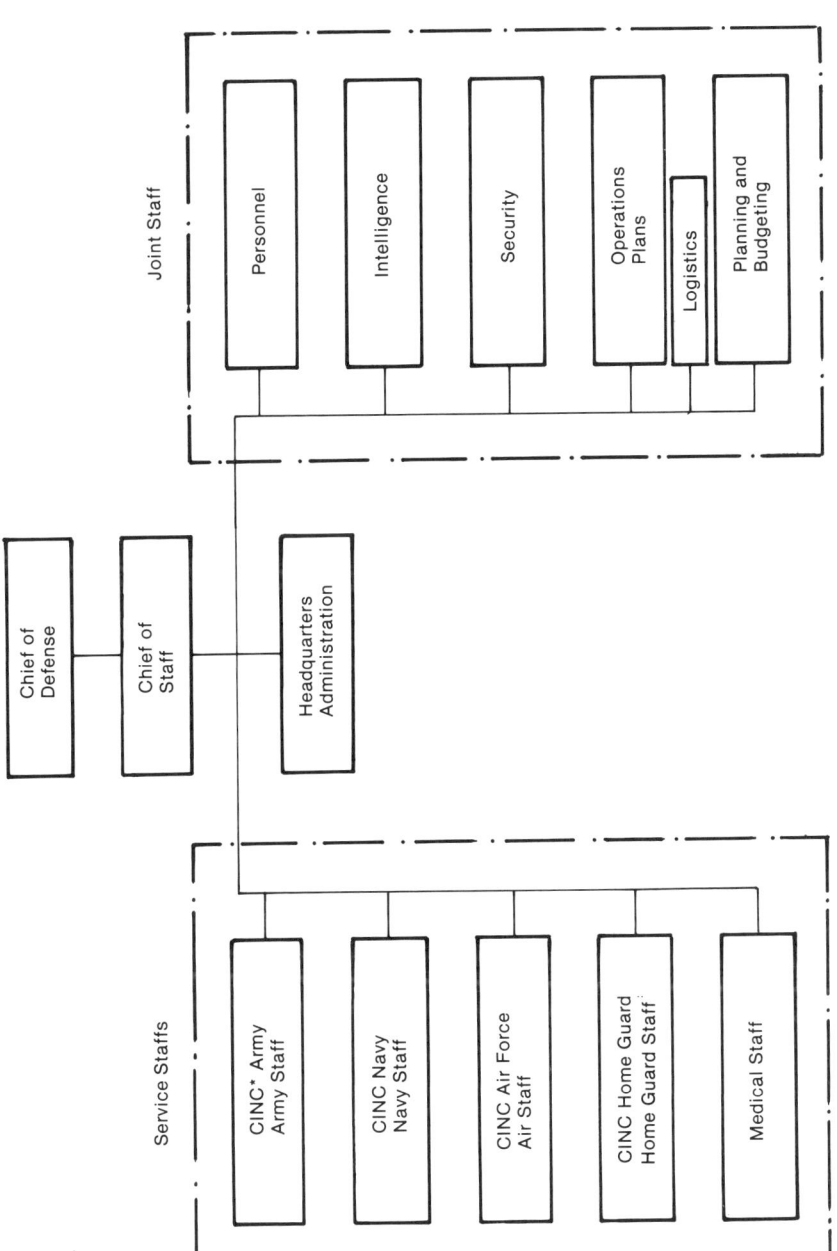

Figure 4–2. Norwegian Defense Staff

*CINC = Commander-in-Chief.

both the minister of defense and chief of defense. Certainly, an intelligence organization does not make policy. However, information is an essential part of any decision-making process and can be critical in a crisis. Even though the intelligence service is a military organization, intelligence policy guidance is provided by the minister of defense, a civilian. He is assisted in this by an Intelligence Steering Group of civilian and military officials chosen for their familiarity and experience in the field to provide a general review of intelligence operations.[8]

Two other important organizations within the Ministry of Defense are the Norwegian Defense Research Establishment (NDRE) and the Kongsberg Weapons Factory. NDRE is the premier scientific and analytic institute of the Norwegian defense organization. Kongsberg is the leading Norwegian developer and manufacturer of high-technology weaponry. Both Kongsberg and the NDRE had major roles in the Norwegian decision to purchase the U.S. F-16 fighter. NDRE conducted the initial analysis that compared various modern fighters, while Kongsberg pushed for the F-16 purchase in order to gain access to U.S. technology as part of the F-16 offset agreements. NDRE is under the jurisdiction of the Ministry of Defense and probably has a greater direct influence on various policy and procurement decisions than Kongsberg.[9]

In addition to the actors who occupy discrete positions in the government's bureaucratic structure, several other committees or subgroups exist which cut across these lines. The most important of these is the Government Security Committee, a special group within the cabinet which considers major security issues. It consists of the prime minister, and the ministers of foreign affairs, defense, trade, commerce, finance, and justice. It does not usually discuss broad policy issues, but rather decides on specific defense matters, especially those of a classified nature. It meets every six to eight weeks, or more often if circumstances require. This appears to be a relatively light schedule. However, Norwegian sources indicate that the Security Committee's meetings are more frequent during periods of heightened tension or when major security policy is under consideration. Moreover, this schedule is probably adequate to deal with the relatively small number of really important issues which normally arise.[10]

A second important interagency actor, or more accurately, group of actors, are the senior civil servant committees (Embedsmannskomiteen). These are coordinating groups which deal with a variety of topics. In the area of national security, this group is headed by the senior civil servant in the Foreign Ministry and receives its staff support from that ministry.[11] It does not convene for routine matters; rather, it serves in a crisis as a focal point for gathering information and presenting policy options to the cabinet and as a coordination mechanism for policy execution.

Similar to a committee, but at a higher level, is the Defense Advisory Group (Forsvarsraadet), which is composed of the chief of defense, the head of the Norwegian Defense Research Establishment, and the permanent secretaries from the Ministries of Defense and Foreign Affairs. The advisory group is an ad hoc actor, called together only in the case of a serious national security crisis. This group, made up of very senior officials at the immediate subcabinet level, would appear to have a very high potential importance. However, it apparently is no longer used and was last convened during the 1968 Czechoslovakian crisis.[12]

Another important actor is an informal group consisting of the ministers of defense and foreign affairs and their deputies (known in Norway as Statssekretaer). Originated under the Labor government in January 1976, probably at the initiative of then State Secretary for Defense, Johan Holst, the group meets weekly, usually prior to the full cabinet meetings.[13] The object is to have full informal discussions by the leadership of the two ministries primarily concerned with national security on questions which may become major formal issues within the cabinet.

A final periodic participant within the government is the special blue-ribbon commission, specifically the Defense Review Commission of 1974. This group is sometimes referred to as either the Nordli Commission (after its original chairman, Odvar Nordli, who left to become prime minister) or the Bye Commission after its final chairman, Ronald Bye, a former secretary general of the Norwegian Labor Party. It was formed in 1974 to examine long-range defense and security problems and reported its findings in the spring of 1978.[14] This was only the second time that such a group had been established, the first such instance being the Defense Commission of 1946 which examined Norway's long-term security plans in the postwar era. The Commission's nine "political" members were broadly representative of the major party structure within the Storting. For example, the four Labor party delegates were carefully chosen to represent the older prodefense group, the more leftist Labor Youth, trade unions, and women's groups. The commission also included four representatives from the Defense Ministry: three uniformed officers of various ranks and a delegate from the Norwegian Defense Research Establishment. The Defense Review Commission examined all aspects of Norway's security. Given the "rapid and far-reaching changes" which had taken place in the international environment since the early postwar years, and with a new generation of postwar political leaders coming to the fore, the government wanted to reconstitute and reaffirm the basis for the national consensus in Norway's security policies.[15] In essence, the Commission's report did exactly that; it supported Norway's current defense alignments and strategy.

Parliament

The Norwegian parliament, the Storting, is the primary legislative body of the country. Its 155 members are chosen in national elections every four years. Their duties include enacting laws, approving all budgets, and passing final judgment on treaties which require new legislation or budgeting appropriations or which are considered to be of special importance.[16] Routine executive agreements with other governments do not require Storting approval.

One critical element of Norway's constitution is the stipulation that, except to repel a hostile attack, foreign military forces may not be introduced into the country without the consent of the Storting. Similarly, Storting approval is also required prior to employing any conscripts outside Norway.[17] This latter point has significance today because of Norway's participation in UN peacekeeping operations, as is currently the case in southern Lebanon.

The Storting has seldom been the scene of dramatic national debates on major issues of national security, although recent heated discussion of Intermediate-range Nuclear Forces (INF) negotiations and the nuclear freeze question have been notable exceptions.[18] In large measure, this is due to the general support which exists for Norway's overall national security policy—full membership in NATO with several specific limiting provisions. It also reflects the fact that most of the Storting members, like Norway's population as a whole, are primarily concerned with domestic economic and political issues which have more immediate impact upon their daily lives. Unlike the U.S. Congress, which is composed predominately of lawyers, the Storting is a uniquely representative body comprised of teachers, fishermen, farmers, businessmen, and housewives. Because of their background and need to concentrate on other issues, they are generally content with having the relevant Storting committees, party leaders, and government experts thrash out difficult national security questions. Many observers have noted, however, that this is changing—there is now increased Storting interest and attention given to important international issues. Thus far, this has focused more on general foreign policy matters such as human rights, energy policy, and North-South issues, but has also included such defense matters as disarmament and Norway's base policy. Greater Storting involvement in these questions is due at least as much to deliberate government efforts to consult with and involve the parliament as it is to purely Storting initiative. Moreover, with the exception of a small group of parliamentarians with extensive backgrounds in national security issues, their interest is, at least at present, greater than their expertise.[19]

A final factor is the paucity of staff support in the Storting. In contrast to the United States, where Congress is supported by large individual and committee staffs as well as the expertise of such organizations as the Congressional Research Service and the Congressional Budget Office, Storting members have tiny staffs. Junior members are required to share offices with their colleagues, and even senior members have just a single secretary. It is only natural, therefore, that most Storting delegates must devote the bulk of their attention to a relatively narrow area of concentration, allowing only a very broad view of overall national security issues.[20]

This concentration of resources in the executive branch is an integral part of a parliamentary as opposed to a federal system. The prime minister and his cabinet are selected by the ruling party or coalition within the Storting, and naturally represent their views. As long as they are in office, they will pursue policies which reflect the views of that parliamentary majority. One result of this is that Storting members examine government policies or draft laws on the basis of general principles, rather than specific programmatic details. To do otherwise, in effect mirroring the balance of power which characterizes U.S. federalism, would create tensions and stresses which would be incompatible with a realistic parliamentary system.[21]

As in the United States, the most important decisions concerning national security are arrived at in standing parliamentary committees. The most prominent of these are the Foreign and Constitutional Affairs Committee and the Defense Committee. The Foreign Affairs Committee, in addition to its direct responsibilities to the Foreign Ministry, is also concerned with constitutional and election law, trade policies, and Arctic/Antarctic issues. Any other parliamentary standing committee whose work touches on these areas must submit their reports or proposals to the Foreign Affairs Committee for review prior to sending them to the full Storting.[22] The Defense Committee handles all issues for which the Ministry of Defense is responsible and oversees matters pertaining to readiness.

Of the two, membership in the Foreign Affairs Committee is the more highly regarded, primarily because of the broad responsibilities of the committee, its historic role as the premier Storting group, and, at least in some measure, by the fact that the "defense constituency" in Norway is relatively limited. However, both committees have responsibility to review government policy and budgets in their respective areas. Although proceedings can be closed, decisions and reports are generally unclassified and open to public inspection.

A less well-known but possibly even more influential group is the Expanded Foreign Affairs Committee. In addition to the twelve regular members of the Foreign and Constitution Affairs Committee, it also includes the chairman of the Defense Committee and the parliamentary leaders of all the major parties, a total of about twenty-five members.[23] Although it is a purely consultative body, it serves a very important role in the policy process. It does not give formal advice to the government, thus avoiding any overt responsibility. Instead, it functions as a vital political sounding board for consultations between the executive and legislative branches. One of the most significant aspects of the Expanded Foreign Affairs Committee is its secrecy. The proceedings of the committee, its agenda, and even its meeting schedule are all classified. Because of this, it is a useful forum for the discussion of the most sensitive issues of national security.[24] This is especially true today, since the extreme left wing parties are not large enough to qualify for membership.

Less formal but still very influential actors within the Storting are the parliamentary leaders of the individual parties, party caucuses, and the ad hoc interparty leadership groups which occasionally meet to discuss or decide upon various issues. Despite the fact that each of Norway's political parties contains a range of views on national security, party discipline is fairly strong, with open intraparty breaks being the exception rather than the rule. This is probably due in part to the fact that Norway's political parties allow fair representation of all views in various forums. Because it is about twice as large as any of the other political groups, Norway's Labor (Social Democratic) party is generally considered the most influential single political group. Within each party, the Storting leadership and the party defense experts exert strong influence on the other members in areas of national security policy.

The leaders of the various parties consult with each other, as well as with outside actors, on a fairly regular basis. These small meetings of the Storting's leadership are often called at the behest of the prime minister or another cabinet member. Their informal discussions are probably among the most important factors in policy determination, serving to solidify parliamentary support behind the government and to indicate the political climate from the viewpoint of the party leadership.

Other Actors

Outside the formal structure of the executive and legislative branches of the government, the most active participants in the policy process are the political parties. The parties have a major role since they are, at least indirectly, the means by which the general populace expresses its views. However, other than the fact that the parties are collectively representative of the views of their individual members, party positions on various issues are decided by the leadership. The most important of the party organs are the steering committees, which make major decisions on significant issues. The steering committees are usually supported in this function by two groups: a platform committee and a foreign relations committee. The platform committees provide analysis and recommend positions on major political issues, especially during the period preceding local or national elections. The foreign relations committees deal with issues on a more regular basis. Usually, they function as periodic discussion groups at which party leaders openly discuss current questions of international affairs. These discussions are often attended by the party chairman, the minister of foreign affairs or his deputy, the deputy defense minister, the chairman and party members of the Storting Foreign Affairs Committee, as well as a variety of trade-union, academic and government officials who are party members and who have some responsibility or major interest in the topic. Assessments of the importance of these party foreign relations committees vary. At the very least they indirectly affect policy by exposing officials or Storting members to the views of other actors outside the government.[25]

Another major influence within the party apparatus is the importance of party background and ties that exist between individuals within the government. To varying degrees, most government officials, bureaucrats, and military officers maintain some form of party affiliation or preference. Obviously, this is a sine qua non for Storting members and higher political appointees within the executive branch. A common political outlook and long-term personal and professional relationships among party leaders naturally affect the perceptions and actions of individuals in policy-making positions.

Trade unions play a major role in Norway's domestic politics. In general, Norwegians believe that the direct role of the trade unions on national security policy is overemphasized by Americans. Instead, the trade unions are more accurately characterized as the economic and social arm of the workers' movement in Norway, while the Labor party constitutes its political arm.[26] Although many union members belong to or vote for other parties, the political influence of trade unions is directed mostly at bread and butter economic and social-welfare issues. Nevertheless, the involvement of the trade unions in the formation and support of the national consensus which determines the direction of Norway's postwar foreign and defense policies has been and is significant. Without broad-based agreement from both union leadership and rank-and-file members, such national policies as NATO membership and the current level of defense spending would have been highly improbable. Although the unions do not normally become deeply involved in policy debate of specific lesser issues, union leaders are generally informally consulted and kept advised by the government.[27]

The most powerful organ of the unions is the national trade-union council, Landsorganisasjonen (LO). This organization, working through the Labor party, is able to exert very strong leverage, especially since it is a major source of political funds for the Labor party and the party's newspapers. Most of the LO's interests are centered on the same economic and social issues which concern the unions and their members. However, it is also active in a variety of international endeavors, maintains direct ties with foreign union organizations, and is concerned with those national security policies which have economic impact. Within the LO, the most powerful policy group is the Cooperation Committee (Samarbeidskomiteen), which is comprised of the LO and Labor party leadership, the party's Storting leaders and the Prime Minister (when the Labor party is in power). One Norwegian source considers this "the single most powerful policy group in Norway."[28] On economic issues, this may well be true. However, other component observers consider both the LO and the Cooperation Committee as dormant actors in most security matters.

Military unions are widespread and active within the Norwegian armed forces. They are, in effect, more accurately characterized as organizations of military personnel than as trade unions in the fullest sense of that term. Certainly, they have far less influence than other more traditional unions.[29] There are several military unions and their character, style, and goals vary. Some are composed primarily of enlisted men, others of NCO's and officers. Each differs in its emphasis on political or professional activity. Within the political structure they function as any other interest group that affects the Storting or government.[30] Their political influence, though modest, is growing. Their primary interests are in the areas of pay, working conditions, leave, overtime, and other terms of employment. Though indirect, the effects of military unions upon national security are not inconsequential. For example, military unions have generated requirements that conscripts stationed in remote northern Norway are entitled to a limited number of government-funded trips to their homes in southern Norway each year. Obviously, such trips are paid for by defense funds diverted from other areas of military expenditure. In addition, the temporary loss of these troops on leave affects the immediate combat readiness of the combat brigade in north Norway.[31]

Norway's academic and professional policy and analysis community exerts a far smaller influence upon government decisions that its U.S. counterpart. There are several reasons for this. First, the efforts of these institutions are focused primarily upon domestic economic, social, and political issues, or upon international questions with relatively little national security relevance. This is even more true of purely defense matters than with those areas pertaining to international affairs. As an example, none of the Norwegian academic groups functions as a shadow government or puts out an alternative national budget as some U.S. institutions do. A second important consideration is the absence of personnel movement between the academic and the policy communities—the familiar Washington "revolving door." Norway has very few equivalents to the Kissingers, Brzezinskis, Huntingtons, Rostows, and Bundys who are such a familiar and important part of the Washington policy scene. Johan Holst, who made an international academic reputation as an analyst of Nordic security policy before becoming state secretary for defense, and Anders Sjaastad, the current Conservative minister of defense, are two notable exceptions to this rule. Otherwise, policy makers consist of civil servants and knowledgeable political officials, while academic analysts observe and write for an audience, which, though rather confined, does include the primary actors of the policy-making community. Norwegian civil servants and politicians express deep skepticism about the actual value of pure academicians or political scientists in government.[32]

Norwegian universities are the largest of the academic groups. However, their actual influence upon policy is probably the least of all the actors in this category. Much more important are two policy research groups—the

Norwegian Foreign Policy Institute (NUPI) and the Peace Research Institution of Oslo (PRIO). Neither of these has a significant *direct* influence, although both are active in publishing reports on national security issues. Of the two, NUPI has by far the greater impact, since the views of its analysts are usually much closer to those of the actual policy makers themselves, who may be influenced, at least indirectly by various NUPI reports. NUPI is funded by the Ministry of Education, and until recently, did not have direct institutional contracts with either the foreign affairs or defense ministries. However, several of the NUPI analysts, acting in a purely private capacity, have done studies for the government.[33] This is not true of PRIO, which is generally pacifist and more closely associated with leftist political views. Like NUPI, PRIO is funded by the Ministry of Education. Recently, it has devoted considerable attention to publicizing various "relevations" of previously classified information concerning Norwegian cooperation with NATO.

Both PRIO and NUPI have been instrumental in the public debate of national security issues over the past decade. NUPI has been preeminent in the area of defense matters, while PRIO played a significant role in mobilizing public opposition to Norwegian EEC membership in the early 1970s. However, PRIO's influence in the area of national security affairs may be declining.[34] PRIO, by its own admission, has had very little overt effect upon government decisions.[35] Certainly, its recent efforts to generate a national debate through accusations that Norwegian government cooperation with NATO has violated either the letter or spirit of national policy on foreign bases and nuclear weapons have apparently failed to arouse widespread interest.

The Norwegian media does not play either a major or direct role in most national security decisions. This is partly due to the fact that investigative reporting and publication of any very sensitive or classified issue is a relatively recent phenomenon in Norway. Broad questions which are widely known—U.S. involvement in Vietnam, North-South issues, EEC membership—get a great deal of coverage. Informed, clear editorials and accurate reporting influence public opinion and possibly decision makers. However, unless a policy has already become the object of extended debate, the primary media achievement is straight reporting rather than direct influence.

The final actor is the Norwegian public itself. Usually, its views and concerns are voiced through the normal political process—election of Storting representatives, public expression on an openly debated issue, participation in pressure group activities via parties, unions, trade groups, and so on. However, the public does not get involved to any great extent in specific international security decisions. Norwegian sources state that there has recently been increasing public interest in Norway's foreign affairs. The public's reaction to the proposed deployment of U.S. cruise missiles in Europe illustrates this interest. The Norwegian government supported this deployment, and despite the fact that no missiles were to be based in Norway, the left wing of the Labor party and the public raised a cry of dissent.[36]

Increased tension with the Soviet Union over such issues as boundary delimitations, seaward expansion of exclusive economic zones, and incursions by Soviet ships, submarines, and aircraft into Norwegian territory have combined with a heightened public awareness of the Soviet threat to generate a general increase of interest in and support for national security. In some cases public reaction has been stronger than the government might have liked. This reaction constrained the government's ability to negotiate or act.[37] There is broad general support for Norway's NATO membership as well as its self-imposed limitations on basing foreign troops or nuclear weapons on Norwegian soil. Certainly, any change in these policies would generate a powerful public debate.

An example of the latent power of the Norwegian public in influencing foreign policy is the debate and subsequent decision by Norwegians on EEC membership, which did have some security implications. The labor government originally anticipated that it would not have serious difficulty obtaining public and Storting approval for its decision to join the Common Market. However, for a variety of reasons, public opinion, expressed through a national referendum, went against EEC membership.

Interestingly, although the Norwegian constitution does not specifically provide for public referenda, they have been used in the past to deal with issues in a fashion similar to the use of constitutional amendments in the United States. Examples include: the decision to dissolve the union with Sweden in 1905, the choice between a monarchy or a republic, the choice of the new king, and the establishment and dissolution of Prohibition. Significantly, NATO membership was not subject to a public referendum.

The Process

The process is the means by which the various members of the policy community interact to originate, alter, or support decisions and policies necessary for national security. These interactions take two forms. First, there is the formal process, which is defined in the constitution and explained in any good civics text. Second, and far more interesting, is the informal process. This is based upon subtle changes to the formal process, personal ties, and long-standing practices which are not codified.

The formal process begins within the ministry responsible for a given issue. The origin of a policy may be either external or internal—that is, action may be required in response to international events, an inquiry from the cabinet, or an issue of public concern. Alternatively, policy can be generated by an internally recognized need, either at the working level or from the top ministry officials. One Foreign Ministry official remarked that whatever the origin of the stimulus, the usual first response to a policy question is to review the issue against current policy statements which might be relevant, then "cut and paste" a cogent, compatible policy statement for the new issue, filling in the blank spots where necessary. To a large degree, this is similar to U.S. practice and ensures consistency between established policy and current issues. At the same time, the processes in both the United States and Norway also incorporate consideration and evaluation of alternatives to current policy.

Once a position has been established within the responsible ministry, it is then brought before the cabinet. Naturally, some lower-level or specific policies are formulated and implemented at the ministry level without any need for further review or approval. However, the constitution requires that all questions of importance be put before the cabinet by the responsible minister. For an issue which requires action by the executive branch only, a policy is decided upon within the cabinet, and once a decision is reached, the necessary action to implement the policy is taken. An example of this would be the 1978 Norwegian decision to limit the size of West German troop participation in NATO exercises in Norway. In this instance, the Ministry of Defense formulated a recommended position which would have allowed a substantial increase in West German military participation. After debate and discussion within the cabinet, the previous arbitrary troop ceiling was raised somewhat, but was still kept at a level below that originally put forward by the Defense Ministry.[38] Although this decision was roundly debated in the public forum, this did not occur until after the cabinet decision had been made. Moreover, though there was no formal requirement for parliamentary approval of the government's policy, key Storting leaders were almost certainly kept informed throughout the process.

Most questions of importance such as major agreements, policies requiring new laws for implementation, or decisions requiring budgetary appropriations must go before the Storting. Recently, critics such as PRIO have charged that the government has made and implemented major decisions concerning Norwegian security without consulting the Storting. The specific charges by the PRIO involve the establishment of LORAN C and OMEGA navigation stations in Norway during the 1960s.[39] However, it does not appear that these accusations have elicited any great response, either from the public or the Storting.

Cabinet policy proposals and new legislation which do go to the parliament are sent in draft form to the Storting. National security issues are considered by the appropriate committee, generally either the Foreign Affairs or Defense committee, depending upon the subject and the ministry responsible for the proposal. The government proposal is usually presented by the responsible ministry officials. After the committee has reviewed the proposal it is sent to the Storting floor. There it is voted upon by the whole Storting in joint session for policy decisions, or the lower and upper house in succession for new laws. After passage, laws are returned to the cabinet for royal signature.

The informal policy process for national security issues is built around and augments the formal structure. It utilizes a number of ad hoc groups and brings into play a large array of personal contacts. However, this informal process is also characterized by a small number of actors. To be sure, it does bring in a greater variety of players than the formal process; in many cases, however, these are the same people acting in a different capacity.

In general, policies are made within the executive branch at the ministry or cabinet level. Once this is done, a "trial balloon" is floated among a small group of Storting members. If the policy receives their endorsement, it is sent to the Storting via the formal process. Public debate, media coverage, and pressure by institutional as opposed to individual actors outside the government and Storting does not usually commence until after a government proposal is formally placed before the Storting. Both of these processes are shown very roughly in figure 4–3.

As in the formal process, the impetus for a policy decision usually comes from somewhere within the government. Preliminary investigation, research, working papers, and policy alternatives are drawn up by working-level civil servants or military officers within the cognizant ministry. During this stage, there is usually direct horizontal liaison with working-level counterparts in other ministries. There may also be some informal dialogue with key members of the parliamentary defense or foreign affairs committees. When asked about the existence of such contacts, one Storting member replied that such informal liaison with various government officials would be quite natural. He had gone to the university with half the Foreign Ministry, knew them by their first names, and often saw them socially. However, he cautioned that although he often initiated these contacts, subcabinet officials would be hesitant to call him first without prior permission.

Ministry officials do consider political factors and public attitudes at this stage, even though there has usually been no open debate of the issues. Nevertheless, the cabinet minister and his state secretary, as political appointees, are more attuned to such matters. Together with the prime minister and the rest of the cabinet, they are probably the actors who give greatest consideration to purely political factors.

After an internal decision is reached within a ministry, the minister brings the policy to the cabinet level for a preliminary decision. This could be done at a meeting of the full cabinet or it may first be debated within the smaller forum of the Government Security Committee. Quite often, the decision is taken by the triad of the prime minister, foreign minister, and defense minister.

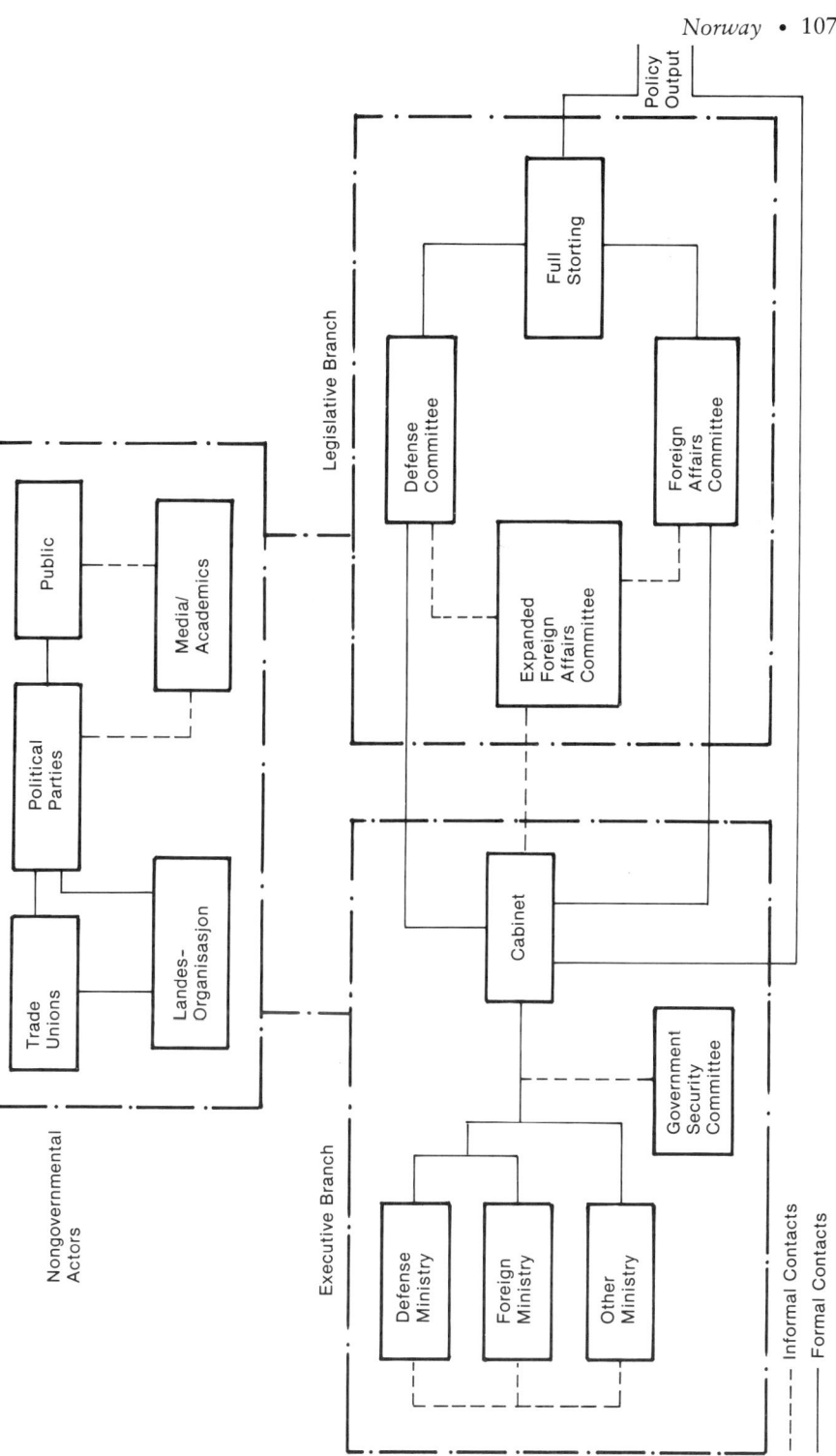

Figure 4-3. The Norwegian Security Policy Process

Note: The relationships among the various nongovernmental actors and between this group and the government are widespread and encompass both formal and informal ties. For the policy process, the importance of the informal ties is emphasized.

Before a law or policy is formally sent to the Storting for consideration, there is usually some less official liaison. In security matters this often entails the presentation of the government position to the Expanded Foreign Affairs Committee. Because its deliberations and minutes are secret, and because its composition brings together many of the Storting's leaders in this area, this committee provides a very accurate reflection of Storting opinion.[40] Another common technique is for the prime minister, defense minister, or foreign minister to meet together with the Storting leaders of all the major parties. Both of these methods keep the deliberations secure and also avoid providing far leftist groups with sensitive information.[41]

There is also opportunity at this stage for informal dialogue with actors outside the official government-Storting community. Usually, this includes the leadership of the ruling party, who naturally have longstanding political relationships with both the prime minister and the Storting leadership. However, these contacts will often include opposition party leaders, the foreign relations committees of the various parties, and the trade unions and trade-union council (LO).[42]

Because the circle of actors at this stage has started to widen somewhat beyond the formal structure, preliminary discussions are sometimes reflected in the media and among the interested public. However, unless the government has seriously miscalculated public attitudes, there is seldom a groundswell of debate. If these informal contacts indicate that a given government proposal will have significant problems, it is retained by the cabinet for reconsideration and possible change; otherwise it is formally submitted to the Storting.

The Constraints

The actual workings of the national security process in Norway and its outputs or decisions are directly affected by a variety of constraints. These set the stage and define the boundaries within which the policy community can realistically operate. For example, Norway has been described as a nation where policy is arrived at by consensus. To a great extent, this is true. Support for NATO membership is solid, broadly based, and is probably stronger today than at any time in the last decade. In a recent national poll, over 80 percent of Norwegians polled favored NATO membership. This is one of the highest ratings since the Atlantic Alliance was formed in 1949. Any serious attempt to measurably alter that policy would almost certainly fail unless a drastic change in attitude could be effected throughout the public as well as the policy community. This chapter divides the various constraints which act upon the process into five broad categories: institutional, social, strategic, technological, and economic. Other categories such as historical or bugetary constraints which might also be logical possibilities will be treated within the five stated groups.

Institutional Constraints

There are a large number of purely institutional constraints which govern Norwegian policy. Foremost is the Eidsvold Constitution itself, which establishes the formal structure and process, defines roles, lines of authority, and relative power. The constitution, together with royal decrees, places formal limitations on the employment of Norwegian armed forces. For example, Norwegian armed forces may not be employed outside Norway—as in a UN peacekeeping role—without the consent of the Storting.[43] However, if Norway is invaded, Norwegian troops also have orders to fight without waiting for instructions from Oslo. Moreover, the prime minister has unilateral authority to declare war if Norway is attacked, although he would almost certainly consult with party and parliamentary leaders if time permitted.

A second institutional consideration, and probably the major facet of Norway's security policy, is NATO membership. All issues of national security are considered against this background, taking into account Norway's own self-imposed constraints upon its alliance participation. These constraints prohibit the permanent basing of foreign troops in Norway or the presence of nuclear weapons upon Norwegian soil, and place limitations on the numbers of troops and the location of NATO exercises in Norway.[44] Although the government would not attempt to change any of these fundamental policies without full national participation, it still faces the problem of translating them into decisions on specific issues. The government has twice published official statements stating what the "base policy" really means, yet it is still subject to debate and differing interpretation.[45]

Just as important, Norwegian membership in NATO has broadened the focus of its security problems, bringing permanent political consultations and participation on various military staffs. This has forced Norway to take positions on issues it might otherwise have avoided or ignored, and has made such questions as the U.S. role in Vietnam, Portuguese colonialism in Africa, and the military junta in Greece important factors in domestic defense debates. Finally, the influx of information available through NATO membership has added depth and sophistication to Norway's defense policy formulations.[46]

A third, more indirect institutional constraint is the allocation of personnel resources among the various governmental actors. The depth of analysis and range of issues which can be focused upon by decision makers in various organizations reflects, at least in part, the manpower and staff support available. For most issues, the executive branch has the edge. Certainly, the lack of analytical staff support within the Storting means that it has to rely almost completely upon figures and analysis furnished by the government.[47]

Norway's membership in the Nordic community is also a consideration in certain defense and foreign relations questions. This reflects a spectrum of social and strategic constraints such as historic ties among the Scandinavian states, political and economic cooperation among the Nordic nations, and the concept of a Nordic balance.[48] At the least, Nordic concerns have meant that before policies are adopted, potential complications for other states, particularly Finland, are considered by Norwegian policy makers. However, such considerations have not meant that Norway would ever go against its own national interests purely for the sake of another Nordic nation.

Social Constraints

Social constraints upon Norwegian decision making are very general in nature. Norway, with its homogeneous population and the unique representation of societal and occupational groups within the Storting itself, does not appear to have strong ethnic or societal pressure groups, although economic pressure groups are important. The country is characterized by broad public consensus for the overall structure of Norway's security policies. This is due largely to the impact of World War II, when the German invasion of 1940 marked the end of neutrality and forced upon Norway the realization that it could not unilaterally opt out of great power politics.

Nevertheless, there has continued to exist an underlying affinity for neutralism, pacifism, and disarmament. Some Norwegian officials feel that this has been overemphasized by foreign observers, maintaining that enthusiasm for these concepts is largely a function of Norway's relatively small size.[49] With fewer assets and global responsibilities, it is much easier for small states to advocate idealistic positions, confident that larger powers will ensure that final decisions are tempered by hard reality. Within Norway, however, these concerns are seldom articulated outside a small sector of the policy community. Most observers agree that these tendencies, especially the affinity for neutralist policies, have declined over time.

A final important consideration is Norwegian nationalism, which is reflected in the idea of "Norway for the Norwegians." Despite their openness and hospitality, Norwegians are content with and proud of their country's traditions and culture and are not anxious to see them changed by outside influences. This was certainly a factor in the 1949 decision against basing foreign troops there under NATO and was also important in the anti-Common Market vote in 1972. It would certainly be a factor today if Norway were to consider changes to its current basing policy.

Strategic Constraints

Strategic realities play a major role in affecting Norway's policy options. This is partially a function of Norway's common border with the Soviet Union. Even more, it demonstrates the continuing strategic importance of Norway for NATO's northern flank.[50] Just as in World War II, it means that Norway can be drawn into conflicts not of its own making. This was a major factor in Norway's decision on NATO membership and continues to involve Norway in broad superpower issues.

Norway's social inclination towards neutralism adds to the strategic pressures. These pressures increased in February 1981 with the resumption of discussions in the United States concerning deployment of neutron warheads in Western Europe. Former Prime Minister Gro Harlem Brundtland summarized the unease of some Norwegians with what is perceived to be increasing pressure (presumably by the United States) in Europe: "People feel the need to be safely inside the Western alliance but not in a provocative or leading role.... We are so closely placed to the Soviet Union, and there is a big ocean between us and the United States."[51]

Strategic constraints are a subtle aspect of many policy decisions, even those not dealing directly with defense policy or national security. Decisions which might appear to be purely economic, such as that on the Common Market issue, must also be evaluated based on their effect upon relations with NATO or the Soviet Union. However, the strategic constraint is a two edged sword. The effects of Soviet pressure on Norway have often been the opposite of what the Soviets intended. As one Norwegian editor has noted, "It is strange that the Soviets still have not learned that by using their big sledgehammer against Norway, they create a determined and negative Norwegian reaction. It is not clear whether they realize the full effects of these verbal and physical attacks."[52]

Technological Constraints

Technological advances tend to create both problems and opportunities for Norwegian security. This is true even for areas which are only indirectly related to national defense. The discovery of oil on the Norwegian continental shelf, combined with the ability to exploit these resources, has created an important source of wealth. But the possibility of a large scale Western presence in the Barents Sea has brought other pressures from the Soviet Union. The Soviets are concerned not only about the rights to oil in the area, but also by the prospects of northward exploration for oil by Western oil companies.[53] Already the expansion of drilling rigs and wells in the north create problems for the maneuver of naval surface and subsurface vessels and the Soviets worry that oil rigs could serve also as listening and detection stations.[54] Similarly, the growing importance of fisheries, together with disputes related to the evolving Law of the Sea, have brought a need to formulate new rules and resolve problems.

Other new technologies are more directly applicable to defense issues. Increasing airlift capabilities are making rapid reinforcement of Norway more plausible, while at the same time increasing the threat from Soviet airborne forces. Precision guided munitions (PGMs) appear well suited to enhance Norway's defensive capabilities against overland or seaborne attack. However, development of long-range cruise missiles which could be launched against the Soviet Union from either Norwegian soil or air space could also create new problems and concerns for Norway's relations with both its allies and neighbors. Finally, the evolution of submarine-launched ballistic missile (SLBM) technology has changed the nature of Norway's strategic security concerns. For the United States, introduction of longer range Poseidon and Trident missiles lessens the need to place ballistic missile submarines in the Norwegian Sea. For the Soviet Union, on the other hand, gradual replacement of its Yankee Class SSBNs with the newer Delta class vessels, whose missiles have a substantially longer range, means that the Norwegian and Barents Seas must be controlled to protect the new patrol areas of their strategic deterrent forces.[55] All of these developments have focused increasing superpower attention upon Norway, which is now feeling that pressure.

Economic Constraints

The final constraints upon Norway's security policies are economic, requiring some form of compromise between desired strategy and available resources. The actual process by which funding is allocated is relatively straightforward. Every five years the government sends a Defense White Paper to the Storting. In keeping with the informal policy process, the prime minister gathers a group of Storting leaders from all parties to review the White Paper prior to its formal presentation to the Storting. The defense minister presents the plan and discusses specific issues, using this forum to get unofficial views which are generally representative of overall parliamentary and party reactions. This Defense White Paper is essentially a declaration of intent and is not binding on subsequent Storting action. It contains overall policy and budgetary guidelines, including the proposed real growth in defense spending.

Although the government as a whole employs a rolling five-year budget which is updated annually, defense budgets are submitted on an annual basis without revising the five-year defense plan. Thus, by the end of a given five-year period, actual defense spending will be significantly different from the original plan.

The annual defense budget originates in a series of planning documents within the Ministry of Defense. The proposed budget is submitted to the Ministry of Finance, which reviews the requests of all the ministries and attempts to make changes necessary to stay within fiscal guidelines. These budgets, together with the proposed Finance Ministry changes, are then submitted to the cabinet for final resolution. A balanced budget proposal is sent to the Storting in the form of two documents: an economic policy statement and a proposal for taxes and expenditures. The Storting usually makes only relatively minor changes to these proposals prior to their approval.[56]

Just as in the United States, there is constant pressure on the defense budget from other claimants within the government. The main competitors for funds are domestic social programs. Additionally, Norway is constrained by NATO agreements which promise to maintain certain funding levels and to support a variety of infrastructure programs. In 1978, the Defense Review Commission took the unusual step of recommending a fifteen-year defense budget program which was comprised of three successive five-year plans. During the first third of the program, defense spending averaged 3 percent annual real growth overall, though the proposal called for about 4 percent annual real growth during the first five-year period.[57] The Norwegian economy did not support the program's target of 4 percent annual real growth. Other sectors of government spending continued to demand support, and actual inflation rates rose higher than predicted, cutting into real funding. In fact, defense spending in real terms (adjusted for inflation) declined from 1978 to 1980. Recently, however, the conservative government has been able to increase the defense budget at an annual rate of 3.5 percent.

Security Guidelines

The broad outlines of Norwegian security are quite distinct and are characterized by several interrelated policies. The most important of these is membership in the North Atlantic Alliance. NATO, like neutrality for Sweden, is the cornerstone of Norwegian security. Although this implies a rejection of bilateral security arrangements in favor of multilateral guarantees, it is also apparent that Norway places its major reliance upon the two major naval powers, the United States and Great Britain.[58]

Because of its small size and limited economic resources, Norway has based its military defenses on peacetime conscription, wartime mobilization, and early NATO reinforcements.[59] This provides a broad base of trained manpower and reduces the operating costs of keeping large standing armed forces. However, it also means that Norway must rely on some form of warning in a crisis. This policy further demands that Norway must be able to respond quickly and correctly to external events, something it was not able to do in 1940. A final concern is the internal transportation problem created during crisis periods, since the manpower mobilization base is in more heavily populated southern Norway, while the primary threat would be in sparsely populated northern Norway.[60]

In order to maintain a credible deterrent, Norway has kept a relatively consistent level of defense spending and maintained a strategy which emphasizes defense of north Norway against a limited attack using forces in place.[61] This not only protects against a possible limited attack with little or no warning, but also provides a delaying force to enable the mobilization and deployment of reserves. Related to this is the strong Norwegian commitment to territorial defense, using both regular forces and Home Guard units. World War II gave evidence of the psychological difficulty of shifting from a commitment to neutrality to an effective wartime defense. Plainly stated, Norway was not mentally prepared for war in 1940. Today, that is no longer the case.

Closely related to this are Norway's unilateral measures for reassurance and nonprovocation of the Soviet Union, which have resulted in various self-imposed restrictions upon its full participation in NATO. Despite the fact that domestic, social, and political considerations are also responsible for these restrictions, Norway has consistently sought to lessen the risk of crisis or conflict, first through its early postwar "bridge-building" and UN policies, and later by seeking to downplay incidents which might lead to confrontation with the USSR. As technological advance expands the potential problem areas between Norway and the Soviets, it is uncertain whether the Norwegians will be able to apply this policy of nonprovocation to new issues with equal success. Certainly, recent events on Svalbard, the negotiations over boundaries and fishing zones, and incidents in north Norway all point to continuing and possibly expanding problems.

A third major policy guideline is the Norwegian rejection of a purely Nordic solution to its problems.[62] This was certainly apparent in Norway's attitude during the 1948 Nordic defense pact negotiations, when Norway was the least enthusiastic of the three participants. Subsequent reviews of a Nordic alternative have continued to support this position. This does not, however, imply any decrease in Norwegian support for Scandinavian cooperation. On the contrary, Norway specifically considers the impact of its own national decisions upon the policies of its Nordic neighbors.

The Policy Process: Two Cases

The F-16 Decision

The translation of these broad policy guidelines to specific decisions is the heart of the Norwegian process. Several recent actions illustrate in varying degrees the roles and interests of the members of the policy community and the nature of the process. The decision to purchase the F-16 aircraft, one of Norway's major postwar military procurement actions, is certainly representative of this interactive process. This decision was ultimately the result of events in three widely separated locations during the early 1970s: Norway, where a new fighter was needed; NATO, where a multinational consortium was set up to examine the purchase of a common aircraft; and the United States, where large-scale procurement of an advanced lightweight fighter was being considered.

The Norwegian F-16 decision had its origins within the Ministry of Defense, where planners foresaw a need to replace Norway's aging F-104 fighter aircraft.[63] As a result, the Norwegian Defense Research Establishment (NDRE), in conjunction with the Norwegian Air Force, conducted a study in 1973–74 to identify future mission requirements, priorities, and candidate aircraft for possible purchase. The choices ranged between the expensive F-14 or F-15 to much more modest designs. The F-16, which at that time was still only a conceptual design, was in the upper middle portion of this range. The study analyzed comparative cost and performance of the various aircraft. But it was an information rather than a decision document, and was meant to support subsequent government investigation of various alternatives.

Norwegian military authorities were already aware of a promising U.S design, the Northrop Cobra, which eventually evolved into the F-17. Norwegian officials had also concluded that several possible candidates, such as the American F-14, F-15, and F-111, and the European Tornado and Jaguar, were either too expensive or operationally unsuited for the potential uses envisioned. At this point, however, the Norwegians knew little more about the General Dynamics F-16 design than that it was a candidate in the lightweight fighter competition then underway in the United States. Soon afterward, recommendations were made in NATO that four of the smaller European members—Norway, Denmark, Belgium, and the Netherlands—which had similar operational requirements for a new aircraft should examine procurement of a common fighter.

Norway took the lead in this effort, offering in January 1974 to examine the requirements of each of the four nations in more detail and submit a report on the feasibility of a joint procurement effort. The final report, which was presented in May 1974, concluded that there was a basis for further multilateral cooperation. It also recommended contacting the United States, France, and Sweden to discuss the availability of aircraft to meet the joint requirements. The four aircraft finally considered were the U.S. F-16 and F-17, the Swedish Viggen, and the French Mirage.

About this time, various actors within the Norwegian policy community began to get involved. In general, the Norwegian military favored a U.S. aircraft. Both the U.S. candidates performed better than their European competitors, would be cheaper to buy and maintain, and more importantly, the two U.S. candidate aircraft employed a significantly higher level of technology than their European counterparts. Norway was interested in gaining access to these technologies through anticipated coproduction and licensing agreements. Moreover, the choice of either of the two European aircraft would have had other ancillary drawbacks. Procurement of the French aircraft would have required major changes in Norway's aircraft maintenance and supply system, which was already compatible with that of the United States. Although the Swedish Viggen performed nearly as well as the U.S. aircraft, it lacked the more advanced technology. Much more important, Norwegian decision makers did not feel they could rely on Sweden in a crisis or major conflict to continue to provide adequate support for a NATO country. A Swedish decision to protect its neutrality by denying spare parts could seriously degrade Norway's defenses. Within the Norwegian military, neither the army nor navy favored such a major aircraft procurement, which they accurately foresaw as cutting into available funds for their own investment programs. They were right: the F-16 program accounted for most of Norway's military procurement for the next five years. Not surprisingly, political leaders were concerned about the effect of their decision upon relations with their European neighbors. They were therefore amenable to choosing a European aircraft if one could be found which was more cost-effective than the U.S. candidates.

Both of the European aircraft manufacturers began to explore ways of building support for their products in Norway. The French aircraft industry, which has close ties with many other European arms manufacturers, had already begun to mobilize support. Soon a variety of European defense contractors with ties to Norway voiced their support for procurement of the Mirage. The Swedes, too, tried their hand at influencing the decision. Saab, the Swedish manufacturer of the Viggen, approached the trade-union leadership of the LO, requesting their support. The Swedes were unsuccessful for a number of reasons. The LO did not want to become too deeply involved in what they viewed as a policy question. And, like the military and political leaders, the LO was uncomfortable about the security implications of choosing a Swedish aircraft. Finally, the LO leadership doubted that Saab could bring in the high technology or generate as many jobs in Norway as the U.S. contenders.[64] Norwegian industry, especially the Kongsberg weapons factory, favored a U.S. aircraft and lobbied actively in its behalf. The media also became involved, and generally favored either of the U.S. fighters. However, those close to the issue emphasized that the media had little or no effect upon the actual decision. Nevertheless, the media were important in identifying and elucidating issues for the Storting and the general public.

The final decision became almost inevitable after two important developments occurred in the United States. The first was an air force decision to buy

650 new lightweight fighters. If they capitalized on this, the Europeans could save major R&D costs. Moreover, a large U.S.–European buy would further reduce the unit cost of each production aircraft. In the second development, the U.S. opted for the F-16, thereby taking the F-17 out of consideration.

The final Norwegian decision was made by Prime Minister Trygve Bratteli, with major inputs from the ministers of defense, foreign affairs, finance, and industry. Odvar Nordli, the head of the blue-ribbon Defense Review Commission at the time and later prime minister, also advised the cabinet. Finally, there were informal discussions between cabinet members and key Storting leaders on the subject. Thus, the operative policy was arrived at after thorough examination within the government, including consideration of legislative, union, industry, and public attitudes.

The only real problem was the requirement that any final decision had to be unanimous, with all four of the NATO consortium partners agreeing. Norway, Denmark, and the Netherlands all favored the F-16. Belgium, however, had historically used French aircraft and was under heavy French pressure to adopt the Mirage. Moreover, Belgium's aircraft maintenance and logistics systems were modeled on those of the French, and would have to be changed if U.S. aircraft were produced. Despite these factors, Belgium agreed in April 1975 to procure the F-16, leaving Norway free to implement a purchase agreement. The formal Storting approval of the decision proceeded in two steps. In the spring of 1975, the government officially reported on the status of the negotiations, stating that it would procure a new fighter, provided that the four-nation consortium reached a unanimous decision and that the Storting provided funding. The Storting approved these guidelines. After the multilateral Memorandum of Understanding and the skeleton procurement contract were complete, the Storting authorized funding for seventy-two F-16 aircraft.

The Prepositioning Question

The Norwegian decision to allow the prepositioning of U.S. military equipment is a second interesting example of a national security issue which reveals many characteristic threads of Norway's policy-making process. The origin of the decision lies in the attempt to resolve the problem of Norway's forward geographic location. One of the greatest dangers to Norwegian security is its distance from the United States and the possibility that without adequate warning and quick, decisive action by the United States and NATO, reinforcing U.S. troops would be unable to reach Norway in time to help defend against a rapid Soviet air, naval, and ground attack. The heart of this problem is the necessity to move the bulk of these U.S. forces, especially their heavy equipment, by sea, making their arrival a matter of weeks rather than days. The answer to this dilemma was seen as prepositioning, and it was the result of Norwegian analysis and initiatives.

Under the prepositioning concept, the heavy equipment and supplies for the first U.S. reinforcements would be stored and maintained in Norway. Specifically, it was envisioned that a Marine Amphibious Brigade (about 13,500 men) would be earmarked for early deployment in Norway. Included in the prestocked equipment for this unit would be heavy artillery, hundreds of trucks and tanks, bridging equipment, ammunition, fuel, and food.[65] Since this materiel, which would otherwise have to go by sea, would already be in place, U.S. troops and their lighter equipment could be airlifted to Norway in a period of several days. In addition to this obvious military advantage, Norwegian supporters pointed out that prepositioning would also signal a higher level of U.S. commitment, serve a deterrent role, and yet would not violate the provisions of Norway's ban on foreign troops in peacetime. Actually, this deterrent argument was refined a bit further. Since U.S. forces could arrive earlier in a crisis, it was hoped that this would signal a level of risk and resolve sufficient to prevent a Soviet attack.

Should deterrence fail, NATO war-fighting capability would be considerably enhanced by U.S. forces which would have powerful air and air-defense capabilities in addition to the standard infantry order of battle. Thus, it was argued that the presence of prestocked equipment actually *supported* the "base and ban" policy, that is, the fact that U.S. troops could be brought in more quickly would further obviate any need for foreign troops based on Norwegian soil. Similarly, the added conventional capability would diminish any presumption that nuclear weapons would be employed early in a conflict to avoid conventional defeat. The idea of prestocking U.S. equipment was a Norwegian initiative, and received its strongest push in the late 1970s from Johan Holst, the state secretary for defense in the Labor government of Odvar Nordli.

The way in which the Norwegians handled this question serves as an excellent example how Norway studies an issue, then proceeds to build consensus within the government, next takes the issue to the public, and finally establishes a formal policy. The first step was to convene a joint study group with representatives from both nations to examine the issue. The Bowman (U.S.)–Holst (Norway) Study of 1979–1980 concluded that the equipment should be prepositioned in north Norway. This made good tactical sense, because it allowed the marines to "marry up" with their equipment close to the potential battle zone. The major military drawback was the vulnerability of prepositioned stocks in forward areas to a preemptive Soviet attack before the marines could be airlifted in. Much more important were the political problems—the risk of heightening tension with the Soviet Union in peacetime and of generating extreme pressures from the Norwegian public over what they might perceive as a provocative policy.

The second Norwegian move was to brief key actors within the government and party organizations in order to gain support for the Bowman-Holst Study recommendations. Evidently, the internal political debate was heated, especially within the ruling Labor party. Nevertheless, in September 1980 the steering committee of the Labor party authorized the Nordli government to open formal negotiations with the United States on prepositioning, but only on the condition that the equipment be stored in the Trondheim area of central Norway, over 500 miles from the Soviet border. The stated reason for this, according to Foreign Minister Knut Frydenlund, was to ensure that prestocking would be seen as a purely defensive measure.[66] Obviously, the Labor party wanted to reassure both its own supporters and the Soviet Union.

In December 1980, the Norwegian media and public became involved as leading newspapers commissioned opinion surveys in the areas where the equipment might be prestocked. The Nordli government reacted by appointing a new study committee headed by Bjørn Bruland of the Defense Ministry. This committee was to consider the political imperatives of ensuring that everyone understood that prestocking was a Norwegian initiative; the Norwegians would control prepositioned stocks; that Norway's base and ban policy would in no way be jeopardized; and that the equipment would be common user stocks which could be used by any NATO military units. With a larger military membership than the previous Bowman-Holst committee, the Bruland Committee was also to provide more extensive analysis of strategic and tactical factors, for example, the advantages of prepositioning in central Norway where units using the equipment could reinforce the industrial, highly populated south as well as the north. Clearly, the eventual decision to preposition in the central Trøndelag area was driven by both domestic politics and considerations of military strategy.[67]

As finally agreed, the Norwegians would allow the prestocking of equipment for a U.S. Marine Amphibious Brigade in the Trondheim area. A vital part of the plan provided for Norway to spend $500 million to preposition the equipment for an additional Norwegian brigade in north Norway, doubling its stocks in that area. The United States found this to be a very favorable solution. It fulfilled the original objectives—enhancing the early defense of north Norway, but with the twist that it was Norway and not the United States which had the prepositioned equipment in the north—and it also satisfied U.S. concern about the vulnerability of prestocking too far forward. Thus the U.S. prepositioned equipment would be in a more defensible area, yet would still be able to support the rapid deployment of U.S. troops to the northern flank, with all the considerable political as well as military implications of such a move.

Not surprisingly, the Soviet Union found all this activity on the northern flank particularly objectionable, and waged a strong campaign in its press as well as official contacts to affect the outcome. At one point, the Soviet ambassador to Norway told the deputy chairman of the ruling Labor party "We would know how to react, how to make trouble for you."[68] Many observers felt the formation of a U.S.–Norwegian study commission on this issue was designed in part to placate the Russians as well as to inform and mollify the Norwegian public.[69] Although Soviet criticism subsequently died down, as late as December 1980, during Soviet-Norwegian discussions in Moscow, the Norwegian foreign minister acknowledged receiving "sharp criticism" over the Norwegian decision.[70] Typically, however, the Norwegians rejected Soviet criticism, reemphasized the defensive nature of the prepositioning question, and went ahead with their plans.

Finally, on January 13, 1981, in an almost anticlimactic denouement and with nine Labor members voting against their party, the Storting approved the government's proposal on prepositioning. Three days later, the agreement was formally signed in Washington.[71] Thus, the policy had come full turn. Initiated within the Defense Ministry, it was studied within the government, privately briefed to important political officials in the party and Storting, debated in public, and lastly, officially approved. Along the way national and international political considerations had been reviewed, local sensitivities accounted for, compromises reached, and a broad consensus formed so that official adoption as policy was almost inevitable by the end of the process.

Conclusion

In summary, Norway's national security policy can be described by two overarching characteristics. First, there exists broad agreement on the general structure of foreign policy and national defense. This consensus is shared by the political leadership, senior civil servants, military leaders, the media, and the Norwegian population. It is therefore unlikely that the leadership would make a policy decision that contradicts this consensus, since to do so would also require significant departure from its own strongly held beliefs. Second, security policy in Norway is formulated by a relatively small group within the government. To be sure, official and unofficial mechanisms exist for conveying inputs from the various members of the wider policy community to the essential actors. But the decisions are nonetheless made by a limited number of actors from within the government prior to any widespread public debate of the issues.

There are three primary reasons for this situation. The first is a function of Norway's historical experience. The latter two are related to Norway's physical characteristics.

The invasion and occupation of Norway during World War II created widespread disillusionment with the policy of isolated neutrality. Support for collective security guarantees was created, making NATO membership a credible policy option. This was reinforced by wartime defense cooperation with Britain and the United States. Moreover, the devastation of the war made it imperative for Norway to receive external economic and military assistance after the onset of the Cold War. All of these combined to create widespread public acceptance of and support for Norway's membership in NATO.

A major reason for the small relative size of the Norwegian decision-making community lies simply in the fact that Norway is a small country. Its population of just over four million approximates the number of people in metropolitan Boston. So it is actually quite natural that national leaders at several levels know one another well. Unlike a large nation, Norway is able to maintain close relationships or bureaucratic links within a major segment of the policy community. Decision makers are less isolated from public and extragovernmental opinion because there are fewer institutional filters.

Finally, Norway's small size and relative isolation have, until recently, enabled it to have limited international interests. To be sure, Norway has long possessed a strategic significance over which it had little control. However, NATO's political and security guarantees have largely covered this in the postwar era and have acted as a buffer to the effects of external pressure upon Norwegian political attitudes. Because of these limited international security concerns, the general public has never generated a high level of interest in the specifics of national security policy, preferring instead to leave debates on technical issues to the experts in government. Again, this made the evolution of the current process in Norway almost inevitable.

To some extent, this may be changing. The world, as far as Norway is concerned, is growing more complex, and is drawing the Norwegians inexorably into issues which they could in past years ignore or avoid. There is an increasing interdependence among various economic, social, and political questions. The discovery of oil, the potential exploitation of Svalbard's economic resources, and the evolving regime of the Law of the Sea are all examples of this. However, whether these will ultimately result in any change to the nature of Norway's policy process remains to be seen.

Notes

1. "Government" will be used throughout the chapter for the executive branch. It is a direct translation of the Norwegian term "Regjering."

2. *The Constitution of Norway of 17 May 1984,* (Oslo: Royal Norwegian Ministry of Foreign Affairs, 1974), pp. 1–4.

3. Interviews at the Norwegian Foreign Policy Institute (NUPI) and with *Aftenposten* staff, Oslo, June 1978.

4. Interview with *Aftenposten* staff, Oslo, June 1978.

5. "Norwegian Security Policy," address by Foreign Minister Knut Frydenlund to the Oslo Military Society, 9 October 1978.

6. *Fakta om Førsvaret*, (Oslo: Førsvarsdepartementets Pressetjeneste, 1978), p. 4, and interviews at the Norwegian Ministry of Defense and Ministry of Foreign Affairs, Oslo, June 1978.

7. Interviews with Norwegian Embassy officials, Washington, D.C., November 1978.

8. Interview at the Norwegian Defense Staff, Oslo, June 1978.

9. Interview with Norwegian Embassy officials, Washington, D.C., November 1978.

10. The importance and role of the Government Security Committee, though not shown formally in any organizational description of the Norwegian policy-making community, was attested to in interviews with virtually all segments of that community, including the Ministries of Foreign Affairs and Defense, the Storting, labor organizations and nongovernmental actors.

11. From discussions at the Norwegian Foreign Ministry and Ministry of Defense, Oslo, June 1978.

12. Interview at the Norwegian Ministry of Defense, Oslo, June 1978.

13. Ibid.

14. *Forsvarskommisjonen av 1974*, Norges offentlige Utredninger, NOU 1978: 9 (Oslo: Universitetsforlaget, 1978), pp. 1–2.

15. Frydenlund, "Norwegian Security Policy" and interview with Ministry of Defense official, June 1978.

16. *Constitution of Norway*, Arts. 49–75, pp. 4–5.

17. *Constitution of Norway*, Art. 25, p. 2.

18. One recent exception was the debate over Norway's position on the U.S. deployment to Europe of enhanced radiation weapons—the neutron bomb. In this case the question was whether Norway would officially oppose U.S. deployment of these weapons to central Europe. However, before any final decision was reached, President Carter announced his decision to delay production of the weapons.

19. Discussions with Norwegian Storting member, Oslo, June 1978 and Norwegian Embassy officials, Washington, D.C., November 1978.

20. Interviews with Storting members and staff, Oslo, June 1978.

21. For this point, I am indebted to the insightful comments of Dr. Mats Bergquist, former political counselor of the Embassy of Sweden, Washington, D.C.

22. *Stortingets Forretningsorden* (Stavanger: Dreyer Aksjeselskap, 1977), pp. 9–10.

23. Ibid., pp. 11–12.

24. Interviews with Storting, Norwegian Foreign Ministry and Defense Ministry officials, Oslo, June 1978.

25. Interviews with Norwegian government officials and Labor party members, Oslo, June 1978.

26. Discussions at the Norwegian Foreign Ministry, Oslo, June 1978.

27. Discussions at the Norwegian Embassy, Washington, D.C., November 1978.

28. Interview at the Landsorganisasjonen, Oslo, June 1978.
29. Interview with Norwegian Embassy officials, Washington, D.C., November 1978.
30. It should be noted that Norwegian military unions are not permitted to discuss defense policy issues, which must be addressed outside the union structure through political organizations.
31. Interviews at the Norwegian Ministry of Defense, Oslo, June 1978.
32. Interviews at the Norwegian Ministry of Foreign Affairs and with members of the academic policy analysis community, Oslo, June 1978.
33. Interview with a Norwegian Foreign Policy Institute analyst, Oslo, June 1978.
34. Interview with Norwegian Embassy officials, Washington, D.C., November 1978.
35. Interview with PRIO official, Oslo, June 1978.
36. Quoted in R.W. Apple, Jr., "Plan to Store U.S. Weapons in Norway Faces Obstacles," *New York Times,* August 14, 1980, p. A3.
37. Frydenlund, "Norwegian Security Policy" and interviews with officials of the Ministry of Foreign Affairs, Oslo, June 1978 and the Norwegian Embassy, Washington, D.C., November 1978.
38. Interviews with Norwegian Foreign Ministry officials and members of the Norwegian press, Oslo, June 1978.
39. Nils Petter Gleditsch, Ingvar Botnen, Sverre Lodgaard, and Owen Wilkes, *Norge i Atomstrategien,* (Oslo: Pax Forlag, 1978), and Nils Petter Gleditsch, *The Schei Report on LORAN-C and OMEGA,* PRIO publication no. p-6/78, 1978.
40. Interviews at the Norwegian Ministry of Foreign Affairs and Ministry of Defense, Oslo, June 1978.
41. Interviews at the Norwegian Foreign Ministry and the Storting, Oslo, June 1978.
42. Ibid.
43. *Constitution of Norway,* Art. 25, p. 2.
44. For a historical treatment of the origins of Norway's base policy and NATO membership, see Magne Skodvin, *Norden eller NATO,* (Oslo: Universitetsforlaget, 1971), and Erik Beukel, *Norway's Base Policy: Historical Interplay Between International Security Policy and Domestic Political Needs,* a monograph for Georgetown University's Center for Strategic and International Studies, January 1977.
45. *Fakta om Førsvaret 1978,* pp. 6–8.
46. Interview at the Norwegian Ministry of Defense, Oslo, June 1978.
47. As discussed earlier, this is a normal and necessary phenomenon for a parliamentary governmental system.
48. For an excellent background on Norway's Nordic ties, see Dagfinn Stenseth, "Forstaar Vi Hverandre?" speech presented at the Foreningen Norden symposium, Helsinki, 4–5 August 1977. For a more detailed treatment of the Nordic balance concept, see Arne Olav Brundtland, "The Nordic Balance" and Johan Jørgen Holst, "Norwegian Security Policy," in *Cooperation and Conflict,* Vol. II, 1966, and Col. Arthur E. Dewey, USA, "The Nordic Balance," *Strategic Review,* Fall 1976.
49. Interviews at the U.S. Embassy and the Norwegian Ministry of Defense, Oslo, June 1978.
50. See John Erickson, "The Northern Theater: Soviet Capabilities and Con-

cepts," *Strategic Review,* Summer 1976, pp. 69–72, and a series of articles on NATO's northern flank which appeared in *NATO's Fifteen Nations,* April–May 1978. Also, see Alvin Z. Rubenstein, *Soviet Foreign Policy Since World War II: Imperial and Global,* (Cambridge, Mass.: Winthrop Publishers, 1981), pp. 103–106.

51. Quoted in Leonard Downie, Jr., "New Arms Pact With U.S. Sparks Debate in Norway," *The Washington Post,* December 8, 1980, p. A19.

52. Quoted in Don Cook, "NATO Testing Forces North of Arctic Circle," *Los Angeles Times,* March 16, 1980, p. 4.

53. The possible existence of large oil and gas fields north of 62 degrees latitude, some of which may fall under Norwegian jurisdiction, certainly is of interest to the Soviets. Some authorities estimate that 40 percent of the world's oil reserves may exist in the Arctic area. See Rubenstein, p. 105. For further information on the Spitzbergen controversy, see Carl Jacobsen, "The Spitzbergen Controversy: A Case Study," in *Soviet Oceans Development,* Committee Print for the Committee on Commerce and National Ocean Policy Study, October 1976, pp. 321–330.

54. See M. Kostikov, "NATO Setting Snares," *Pravda,* August 11, 1980, p. 5; trans. in Foreign Broadcast Information Service, *USSR International Affairs: Western Europe,* August 14, 1980, p. G1.

55. For a more thorough treatment of the maritime strategic issues of this area, see Christoph Bertram and Johan J. Holst, eds., *New Strategic Factors in the North Atlantic,* (Oslo: Universitetsforlaget, 1977).

56. Interview at the Norwegian Ministry of Defense, Oslo, June 1978.

57. *Forsvarskommisjonen av 1974,* p. 114.

58. Knut Frydenlund, "The Security of Norway and the Atlantic Alliance," *NATO Review,* June 1976, p. 3.

59. Interview at the Norwegian Ministry of Defense, Oslo, June 1978.

60. The two northernmost counties of Norway, Troms and Finnmark, comprise about one quarter of Norway's territory but contain only 5 percent of the total populace.

61. Interview at the Norwegian Ministry of Defense, Oslo, June 1978.

62. Ibid.

63. The information on Norway's F-16 procurement decision is based largely on discussions with Norwegian defense officials who actually participated in or had first-hand knowledge of the deliberations. Numerous issues of *Aviation Week and Space Technology* provide a running commentary on these developments. The most comprehensive study of this subject is by Atle Forbord, *Norge og F-16, en Studie av en førsvarspolitisk beslutningsprosess,* (Oslo: Institutt for Fredsforskning, Oslo, og Institutt for Statsvitenskap, Universitetet i Oslo, 1976).

64. Interview at the Norwegian Landsorganisasjonen, Oslo, June 1978.

65. *Keesings Contemporary Archives 1981,* Vol. XXVII, Robert Fraser, ed., (London: Keesings Publications, 1981), p. 30730.

66. *New York Times,* September 8, 1980, p. 7.

67. See Trond Gilberg, "Norwegian Threat Perceptions," a paper presented at the 22nd annual conference of the International Studies Association, Philadelphia, PA, March 18–22, 1981.

68. Quoted in Apple.

69. Ibid.
70. Quoted in "Russians Assail Norway on Arms Stockpile," *New York Times,* December 23, 1980, p. A3.
71. *Keesings Contemporary Archives,* Vol. XXVII, p. 30730.

5
Sweden

William J. Taylor, Jr.

Sweden is a parliamentary democracy which blends socialist traditions with a largely capitalist economy. It is a nation that has not been involved in war for more than 170 years and whose policy of neutrality is designed to perpetuate that tradition. An advanced, industrialized state whose populace has long enjoyed the world's highest standard of living, today Sweden is at a major crossroad in planning for national defense. The domestic situation in the fall of 1984 was characterized by a shift away from a tradition of political compromise toward political confrontation; 8 to 9 percent inflation and a burgeoning foreign debt; a Social Democratic party increasingly isolated from its traditional domestic political allies; mounting public concern over the meaning of violations of Swedish territorial waters; a somewhat more secure but still recovering defense industry; interservice conflicts over roles, missions, and resources; and a defense establishment concerned that the budget was driving strategy in dangerous directions.

The Backdrop of Swedish Defense Decision Making

Sweden has a king as symbolic head of state. The king has no political authority: he does not attend meetings of the government, does not sign laws, and, although he is the titular holder of the highest military rank, he is not the commander-in-chief of the armed forces. With a long tradition of constitutional government, the course of political development in Sweden in recent history is marked by the formation and refinement of the institutions of the welfare state and development of a pragmatic socialism which coexists with a capitalist economy.[1] For a country of 8.5 million, the central government is a large organization indeed, employing more than 350,000 people. Another 155,000 work in public enterprises such as the postal service and the National Telecommunications Administration. In addition, a relatively large percentage of total industrial employment, about 15 percent, can be attributed to the government-owned companies in the industrial sector.[2] The number of public sector jobs increased by 43 percent in the decade 1972–1982, now outnumbering the jobs in Swedish industry. As a percentage of GDP, expenditure in the public sector has risen from 44 percent in 1970 to 68 percent in 1983, the largest GDP share in any Western nation.[3]

Sweden has long been one of the most homogeneous societies in the world. Due partly to this homogeneity, and because of a tradition of consensus building, the Swedish parliament (Riksdag) has legislated over a wide range of social activities from military conscription to environmental health and safety. Yet even though Swedish politics has long enjoyed an extraordinary degree of public consensus, this tradition appears to be eroding. The popular issues of the day for most Swedes center on economic matters such as unemployment and the controversial "wage-earner funds" (löntagar fonder) coupled with an increasing awareness of Sweden's vulnerability to violations of its territorial waters.

Whether the result of historical necessity or rational choice, Sweden has not been involved as a belligerent in war since the Napoleonic era. Through a combination of decisions over the years, Sweden has adopted a foreign policy of "nonalignment (or "freedom of alliance") between power blocs in peace, aiming at neutrality in war."[4] The foreign policy objective is de facto neutrality unsupported by international guarantees or by conventional international law as in the cases of Swiss or Austrian neutrality.

The goals of Swedish security policy were reiterated by Prime Minister Olof Palme at the 1984 congress of the Swedish Social Democratic Party:

> Responsibility for Sweden must characterize the foreign policy of the Social Democratic party. This means the defense of our country's independence, our democratic social order, our right to decide our *own* future. This responsibility is best served by a firm policy of neutrality. We Social Democrats intend to carry out this policy with energy, clarity, and consistency. Responsibility for Sweden requires a strong defense in relation to our situation. This is an expression of our determination to defend our independence and repel all intruders. Our responsibility also includes a commitment to contribute to the work for peace and reconciliation in the world, and to pursue a policy of international solidarity. This is also an important element in our security policy.[5]

To achieve these goals, successive governments and all four major political parties have concluded that Sweden requires a strong, all-round (but nonnuclear) "total defense" to preserve the credibility of the policy of neutrality. They have found no contradiction between defense preparations and deep involvement in international work for disarmament.[6] Swedish defense has traditionally played an important role in maintaining the Nordic balance by preventing instabilities which might result in direct confrontation between the superpowers in the Nordic area. With this goal in mind, Sweden has occasionally advocated a nuclear-free zone encompassing Denmark, Finland, Norway, Sweden, and perhaps parts of the Baltic and the Soviet Union. This zone would prohibit the deployment of nuclear weapons in both war and peace.[7]

Defense doctrine is based fundamentally on the realities of a divided Europe and a strategy of deterrence of "marginal attacks." Swedish strategic planners assume that:

> . . . a power which might threaten or even attack Sweden will always have a substantial part of its resources tied up for other purposes, for example to counter any expected or unexpected confrontation with the other superpower. Thus only a marginal part of the military strength of a superpower could be used in an attack on Sweden.
>
> . . . provided that the goal in Sweden is limited and the country can defend itself, the value of controlling Sweden or part of Sweden will not be worth the cost of conquest.[8]

Swedish doctrine calls for "total defense", including: (1) military defense, (2) civil defense, (3) economic defense, (4) psychological defense, and (5) other defense (e.g. telecommunications and medical care). Military, civil, and psychological defense, as well as the responsibility for coordination of total defense, reside with the Ministry of Defense. The Ministry of Trade is responsible for coordinating economic defense. The programs subsumed by each of the categories of total defense will be discussed below in the context of decision-making constraints.

The military strategy planned for meeting a marginal attack has in reality been a combination of *territorial* defense based on rapid mobilization of ground forces armed with relatively inexpensive weapons and *peripheral* defense based principally on high-technology aircraft and naval forces capable of operating well beyond Sweden's land and sea boundaries. In the late 1960s and early 1970s emphasis was on the latter. However, in times of relatively high inflation since the late 1970s, the essence of a major defense debate has been the cost and wisdom of attempting to carry out both strategies simultaneously.[9] In 1985 the debate is not over, but there appears to be a shift toward territorial defense—protecting Sweden's territorial waters and interior from unconventional non-nuclear warfare threats and absorbing and defeating the marginal conventional attack.

Obviously, current force structure weighs heavily in decisions taken on defense plans and programs for the future. Sweden's current force structure is larger than many think and, depending upon one's assumptions about war scenarios in northern Europe, could weigh significantly in the strategic balance. The active duty strength of the armed forces in 1984 is 65,650,[10] with a total strength of approximately 800,000 which may be mobilized within seventy-two hours to fight on their own territory.[11] Added to this are about 95,000 people in the Home Guard. Active duty strength has been declining for the past several years.

The air force has about 400 combat aircraft, the majority of which are Viggen attack and reconnaissance aircraft, with more due to be phased into the inventory to replace the older Draken aircraft. In numbers, this air capability is almost twice as great as those of Norway and Denmark combined. It should be noted that the total number of combat aircraft in the Swedish inventory is declining as a result of the need to obtain high-technology equipment, rising defense costs, and the replacement of older aircraft by the four Viggen versions (attack AJ37, reconnaissance S37, fighter-interceptor JA37, and trainer SK37).[12]

The army has an active duty strength of 47,000 which includes 37,000 conscripts at any given time serving their required seven-and-a-half months of training (some positions require longer terms of service). Fully mobilized, the army has more than 700,000 men organized in twenty-four brigades (nineteen infantry, one mechanized and four armored) under the command of seven military district commanders reporting in wartime to a military supreme commander.[13] Army units have been declining in numbers and over half the army's tanks are aging British Centurions.

The navy has 12 submarines and about 175 other ships and boats, half of which are landing craft. Torpedo boats with surface-to-surface missiles have taken the place of destroyers. The navy also commands five coast artillery brigades with fixed and mobile batteries which are partially armed with surface-to-surface missiles.[14] Navy units and personnel have been shrinking in numbers for several years.

Swedish defense shares the current manpower cost problems typical of Western Europe and the United States. Attempts at cost reductions have an impact on the number of active duty units available, on how well manpower can be trained and retrained, and on unit morale—all of which raises questions about military capability and readiness.[15] The Swedish armed forces are one of the world's six fully or partially unionized military institutions. The Swedish and Norwegian armed forces have the longest unbroken traditions of military unionism and neither appear to have significant problems with military unions. Almost all working Swedes belong to unions and find nothing unique about membership while in military uniform.[16]

Like the military establishments of the other Western democracies, the Swedish armed forces are not without their problems. In 1984 their military personnel appear professional, well-trained, and motivated to carry out the missions assigned them by the government. However, given aging equipment in some major categories, reductions in reserve training, reductions in required periods for conscript service, unit closures, recent problems in anti-submarine warfare capability, and lack of experience in responding to aggression, it is difficult to assess current military capabilities.[17]

The Fighter Aircraft Controversy

Consideration of the first five-year total defense program (FY 1977/78 to 1981/82), simultaneous with long-range perspective planning for defense fifteen years into the future, raised serious debates in the Swedish defense community. Those debates were over the most fundamental defense matters: threat assessment, budget constraints, strategy, weapons systems, and the future of the aircraft industry.

1. *Threat assessment.* Some have suggested that Swedish defense planners have envisioned a change in the primary threat from naval invasions through the Baltic or on the Norwegian coast to a swift Soviet land invasion across Finland and northern Sweden "to secure the northern Norwegian coastline in order to control the ice-free approaches to the vast military complex at Murmansk."[18] The invasion would be based in part on large tank and mechanized infantry forces. Modernization of Soviet amphibious and land forces on the Kola Peninsula have been taken as evidence to support this view. Recent incidents of Soviet submarine operations in Swedish waters have led some to suggest that the Soviets intend to infiltrate Spetznaz units to operate behind Swedish lines in wartime.

2. *Budget constraints.* Several factors—including the high rate of inflation and rising deficits over the last three years; the pressure of increasing military manpower costs and wage costs of weapons production; significant losses in the purchasing power of the krona due to rising dollar exchange rates; and insistence on a larger share of the budget for welfare programs—have caused the size of the entire defense budget to be called into serious question.[19] The opportunity costs for defense spending, in both resource and international political terms, are seen as extraordinarily high in some quarters.

3. *Strategy.* Due to changes in threat assessment and because of budget constraints, harsh debates over defense strategy have arisen between the advocates of perimeter defense on the one hand and territorial defense on the other. The equipment and manpower requirements for these two strategies have been viewed as different.

4. *Weapons Systems.* Debates over defense costs and strategy have focused on the technology, costs, and capabilities of the most expensive element of Swedish defense materiel—aircraft. Given the lead time required for RDT&E, production, and delivery of new fighter aircraft, the decision as to which plane should follow the JA37 Viggen should have been taken in 1976 to ensure that the new aircraft would be in the air force inventory in the early 1990s. The Viggens are scheduled to be phased out about 1995. The new aircraft would remain in service until 2015. Debates on these future aircraft have been couched in memories of the past, especially the enormous cost overruns after the 1958 decision to produce the Viggen, an aircraft with a pricetag double the original estimates on which the parliamentary decision

was based. The Social Democrats who backed that decision have not forgotten this recent history.

5. *Survival of the Aircraft Industry.* The three principal firms in military aircraft production are Saab-Scania (airframes and systems integration), Volvo Flygmotor (design adaptation, reproductions, and engines), and L.M. Ericsson (target search and acquisition and display systems). Although industrially diversified, all three companies depend in part upon government defense contracts. The size and nature of the contracts make a great deal of difference to these firms. A decision to continue with a modified Viggen would have impacted adversely on their R&D programs. A decision for a limited number of a new aircraft involving new technology would have had an adverse impact on production programs. Either decision was related to the willingness and international political capability of the government to sell Swedish military aircraft abroad. Some quarters argued that an alternative to these bleak industry scenarios was a partial shift by the three aircraft industries into nonmilitary manufacturing. These debates began in the period prior to the introduction of the 1977–82 five-year defense program budget.

The B3LA was one of the two major aircraft under consideration in the debates surrounding the follow-on to the JA37 Viggen. In December 1978, after a bitter political struggle, the B3LA was found too costly. A similar, but less costly version, called SK38/A38 was proposed. The SK38 was a trainer version of the A38. The other major contender was the AJ37-A20, a modified Viggen. For reasons which will be developed throughout this chapter, these alternative aircraft became the center of disputes involving almost every aspect of the defense decision-making process until the issue was settled by a decision to produce the JAS39 multirole combat aircraft.

The Defense Community

A few basic considerations are central to understanding the institutions involved in decision making for Sweden's defense. The first is that despite a very large public administration sector the number of people involved in the decision-making process is small. Second, with the exception of the ministers, a very small number of others in a ministry, and members of the Parliamentary Defense Committee (some of whom change when a governing coalition changes), the vast majority of key people in defense decision making remain constant. Third, some of the civilians in key positions of the decision-making bureaucracy normally hold reserve military commissions, so that there is some commonality of background. Consequently, people in the defense policy decision-making process have known each other, many very well, over many years. This makes a difference in the way business is conducted.

The major institutions involved in decision making for total defense are portrayed in figure 5–1. At the highest level, the critical interaction is between

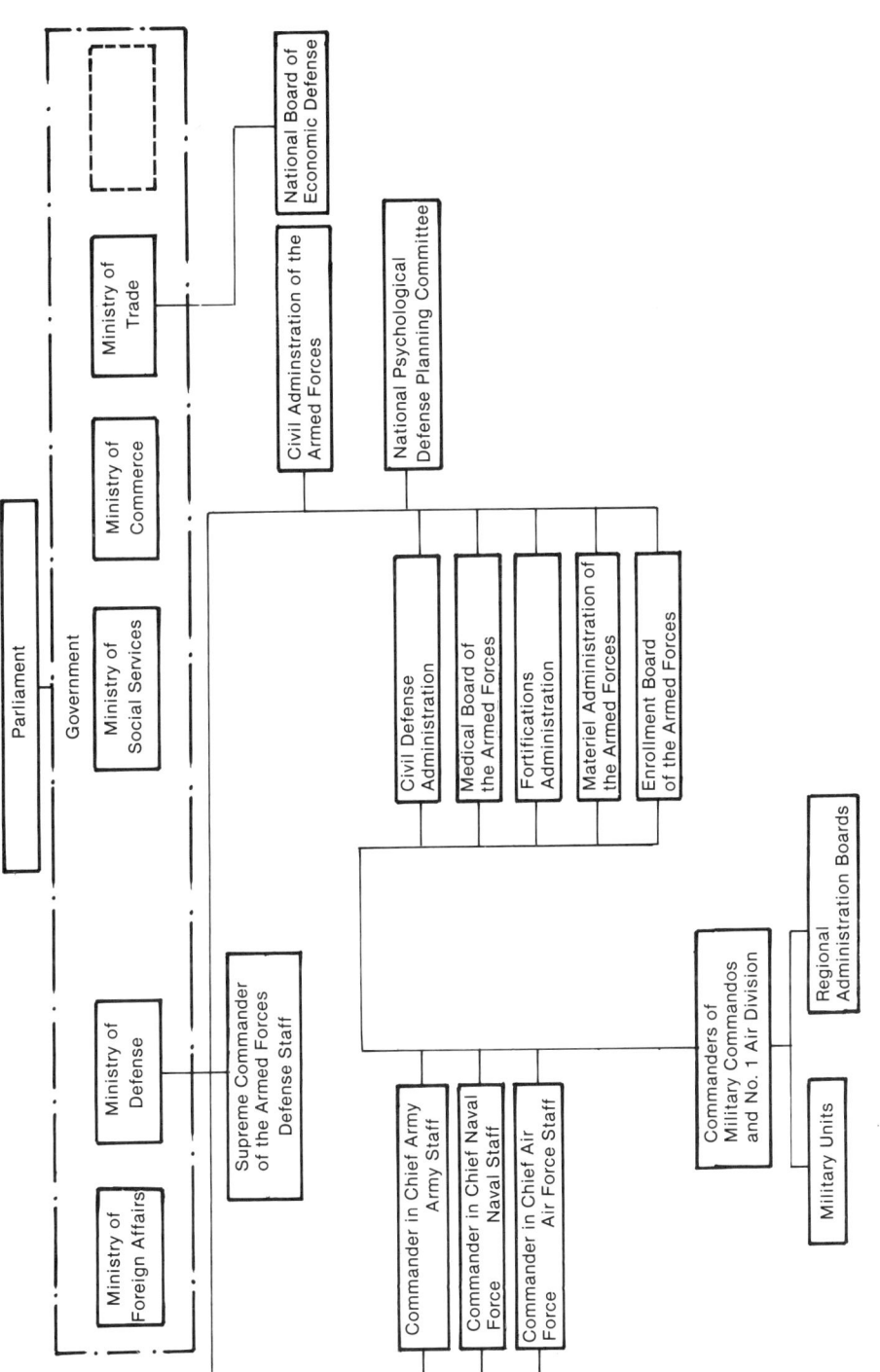

Figure 5-1. Swedish Organization for Total Defense

the government (governing coalition) and the Riksdag, because the latter must appropriate defense funds requested in the government's annual budget bill submitted by the minister of the budget each January. Each fourth year the parliament considers a five-year defense program budget. The Parliamentary Defense Committee is critical in forging the consensus and influencing the votes required for passage of a given defense bill.

The Parliamentary Defense Committee

In a unicameral Parliament of 349 voting members elected every three years on the basis of proportional representation, the Defense Committee is one of sixteen standing committees involved in studying legislative propositions. The committee has 16 members whose political affiliation is representative of the parliamentary distribution. Thus, reflective of the most recent 1982 national elections which allowed the Social Democrats to form a government, the Defense Committee includes eight Social Democrats, four Conservatives, two Center party members, and one member of the Liberal party.[20] Table 5–1 indicates the results of the 1982 elections and table 5–2 the October 1984 membership of the Defense Committee.

Committee membership does not change frequently. Since the mid-1950s, Defense Committee expertise on defense issues has grown.[21] However, given the miniscule staff available to the committee, a parliamentary premium on compromise, and the central role of the cabinet, the impact of the committee is not great. Given the fact that the Swedish voter votes for a party, not an individual, the committee does not have to play to the public in voting on defense matters. The selection of members is carried out by party caucus and members generally vote their party positions.[22] Selections for special parliamentary committees on defense matters are conducted in the same manner, and the voting behavior is predictable along party lines. The pressures for party conformity are great, as in most parliamentary systems, and unlike the U.S. system where party discipline over many issues is tenuous.

The constitutional mandate to the Defense Committee is to "prepare matters concerning military defense, civil defense, psychological defense, economic defense, noncombatant service, and financial benefits to conscripts." When parliament is in session, the committee carries out its duties in meetings twice a week on Tuesdays and Thursdays. Like meetings of all other parliamentary committees, all Defense Committee meetings are in closed session. The members of the committee conduct periodic visits to military installations and are in frequent contact with military officers assigned to positions in Stockholm. Individual members and the committee as a whole maintain contact with defense industry. For example, in 1984 the committee was in close contact with the newly formed Saab Comitech, a company com-

Table 5-1
The Swedish Parliament as of October 1984: Based on Results of National Elections Held September 1982

Party	Votes	Seats	Change from 1979	Percent of Votes
Social Democratic Workers Party (SD)	2,533,250	166	+12	45.2
Conservative Party (M)	1,313,337	86	+13	23.4
Center Party (C)	859,618	56	−8	15.4
Liberal Party (FP)	327,770	21	−17	5.8
Left Party Communists (VPK)	308,899	20	0	5.5
Total	5,606,603	349		95.3

Note: The total number of seats for the nonsocialist parties is 163 (−12) against 186 (+12) for the socialist parties. There are 349 seats in the Riksdag (parliament). The remainder of the votes (263,729, or 4.7 percent) went to other parties. None of these parties met the 4 percent national requirement or the 12 percent constituency requirement for representation in the Riksdag. The voter turnout was 92 percent.

Table 5-2
Parliamentary Defense Committee as of October 1984

Party	Committee Members
Center Party	Gunnar Björk i Gävle Ulla Ekelund
Conservative Party	Per Petersson (Chair) Göthe Knutson Olle Aulin Anita Bråkenhielm
Liberal Party	Eric Hägelmark
Social Democratic Party	Olle Göransson (Vice Chair) Åke Gustavsson Evert Hedberg Holger Bergman Karl-Erik Svartberg Mats Olsson Inge Carlsson

Note: There are 15 alternate members of the Committee who sit in the absence of a member; Center Party 2, Conservative Party 4, Liberal Party 1, and Social Democratic Party 8.

prised of many of the smaller concerns of Saab-Scania. Saab Comitech was formed based on the necessity for various parts of the defense industry to become more involved in specialized weapons production due to the high costs of foreign imports.[23] Given such a connection, the American observer tends to think in terms of a "military-industrial complex" and the activities of business lobbyists. Although the former exists in the special sense to be discussed below, the latter do not exist in any formal sense comparable to registration of lobby groups in the United States.

There exists a special cooperation between the Defense Committee and the Foreign Relations Committee which deals with some similar matters, especially in the context of considering the five-year defense program.

The Cabinet

Although the fundamental laws of the land are legislated by the parliament, effective political power resides with the cabinet and the parties of the governing coalition it represents. Parliament designates the prime minister who appoints all other ministers. Most of the ministers normally are also members of the parliament who vacate their seats and give up their right to vote during their tenure in the cabinet. However, a substitute from the same party fills the vacated parliamentary seat. In the fall of 1984 there were twenty ministers (including five women) represented in the cabinet. Olof Palme, the leader of the Social Democrats, returned to assume the duties of the prime minister when his party formed a government after the 1982 general elections.

The Ministry of Defense

The minister of defense (see figure 5–2) is charged with coordination among ministries in matters affecting national defense. In the fall of 1984, the defense minister was Anders Thunborg, former chairman of the Government Committee on Defense Materiel and also former undersecretary of defense. Thunborg's undersecretary was Per Olof Borg, principal manager of the work performed in the ministry.[24]

Unlike its counterparts in most countries, the Swedish Defense Ministry is responsible for policy framework and guidance, and the various central authorities, agencies, and boards concerned with defense matters are responsible for execution.[25] Although shown in figure 5–2 as "directing" these other agencies and boards, the defense minister, like each of the other thirteen heads of ministry, does not have the authority to issue formal instructions in his own name. All directives, including those to the military staffs, are issued in the form of decisions taken by the government as a whole. However, in practice, many defense decisions are made by the minister himself.[26]

Government decisions on defense and other matters are routinely made at Thursday meetings presided over by the prime minister and held in the Cabinet Office in Stockholm's Government Building. These meetings normally last less than a half hour and are generally a formality for ratifying decisions already taken. For exceptional issues which the minister feels require prior discussion within the government, there is the rather unique Swedish forum of frequent lunches in the Chancery, that are normally attended by

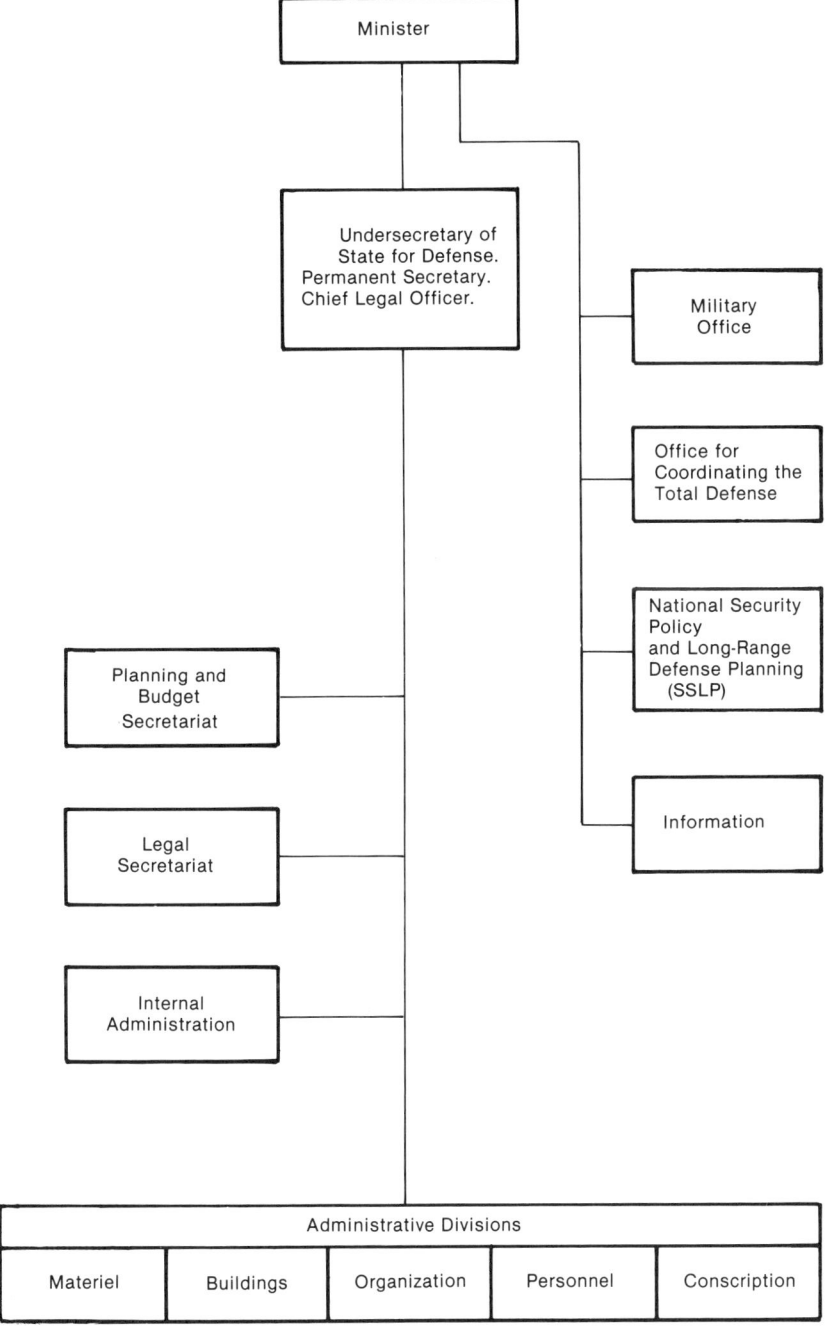

Figure 5-2. Swedish Ministry of Defense

members of the government. In this informal setting, the minister has the opportunity to test the waters on issue positions, iron out differences, coordinate approaches, and exchange information. Major questions are generally addressed at formal government meetings held several times a week for which agendas are distributed in advance. Agenda items are normally presented by a ministry civil servant who is a principal action officer for the item and who is best qualified to answer more specific questions. However, the civil servants do not remain for subsequent discussions among members of the government and there are no minutes for such meetings.[27]

Excluding armed forces personnel assigned to military units and personnel assigned to military district staffs, the number of people who work on defense matters might approximate 10,000 military and civil servants, depending on which organizations are counted under defense.[28] Civil servants enjoy almost complete tenure. They are appointed for life and can be removed before retirement only for cause and through legal process. The vast majority of defense employees are office and building staff assigned to the many agencies and boards shown in figure 5–1. As with all the ministries, only a very small number of individuals, about 150, are assigned to the office of the minister of defense, and only very few are involved in policy decision making (see figure 5–2). Some of the more important and influential of these are assigned to the Secretariat for National Security Policy and Long-Range Defense Planning (SSLP) created in 1972. This secretariat, totaling five people and headed by Nils Gyldén, is a prime mover in "perspective planning" (15–20 years into the future), although it is intimately involved also in defense system planning and program planning.[29] The secretariat's principal analytical approach is systems analysis. There has been a close connection between members of the SSLP and the National Defense Research Institute (FOA).[30]

The SSLP is organized into three ad hoc reference groups, International, Domestic, and Scenario Design, each with a director. The large number of studies conducted under the auspices of the SSLP clearly cannot be performed by their small staff. The procedure for performing the studies is analogous to the Interdepartmental Group system of the U.S. National Security Council staff. That is, members of different staffs, agencies, and boards are appointed to membership on study groups for the limited duration of a study project. Important in every step of defense planning is the Planning and Budget Secretariat (PBS). The few individuals in PBS are responsible for drafting the five-year defense plans and for coordinating the annual defense budget throughout all major organizations involved in the total defense.

Military Staffs

The armed forces of Sweden, like the agencies and boards, are not directly responsible to the minister of defense. Rather, in both peace and war they are under the overall command of the supreme commander (SCO) of the armed forces (currently General Lennart Ljung) who is directly responsible to the government. The commanders-in-chief of the three services are not in the operational chain of command. The command line goes directly from the SCO to seven military regional commanders and the Air Strike Group, then to the operational unit commanders.

The defense staff working directly for the SCO numbers approximately 512 people. The overall responsibility of the staff are those of the SCO:[31]

1. Operational war planning;
2. Readiness;
3. Those aspects of mobilization, training, tactics, organization, equipment, and personnel that relate to operations;
4. Coordination of long-term planning for development and direction of the armed forces;
5. Balance among the differing requirements of the armed forces;
6. Management of budgeting within the armed forces;
7. Execution of all operations in wartime.

The division of particular staff responsibilities is shown in figure 5–3. The service staffs number 225 army, 171 navy, and 230 air. Each has a chief of staff responsible to the service commander-in-chief for direction of peacetime administration, training, and organization of military units in the various services, as well as for force development and military research and development. Each of the service staffs has an augmentation of operations analysts from the National Defense Research Institute.[32]

National Defense Research Institute (FOA)

FOA (from the Swedish "Försvarets Forskningsanstalt") was established in 1958 to rationalize the fragmented operational research efforts of the three services which developed after World War II. With a staff of more than 1,350 (one-third with academic degrees), it is Sweden's largest research organization and it plays a major role in defense planning. FOA is organized into a planning and administration unit and five departments, as shown in figure 5–4.[33]

The Central Planning and Administration Unit has three bureaus which assist the Managing Board and director general and coordinate budgeting, research planning, personnel planning, and administration. It is important to note that this organization plays a major role in recruiting, training, and placing operations research specialists throughout the defense organization.

Department 1 performs studies and planning ranging from weapons systems to defense policy and is responsible for Operations Research, Systems Analysis (ORSA) organization and training across the defense organization.

140 • *Nordic Defense: Comparative Decision Making*

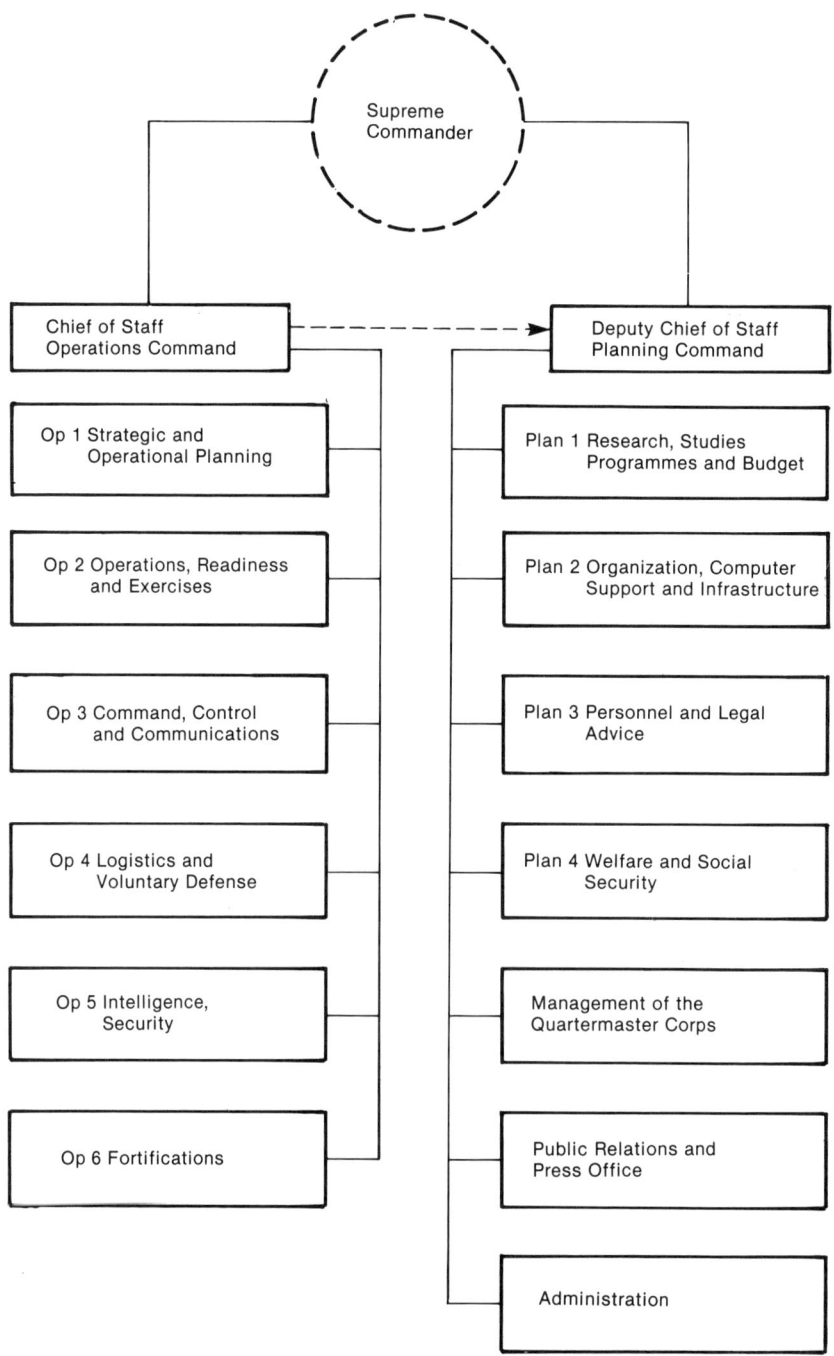

Figure 5-3. Swedish Defense Staff

Sweden • 141

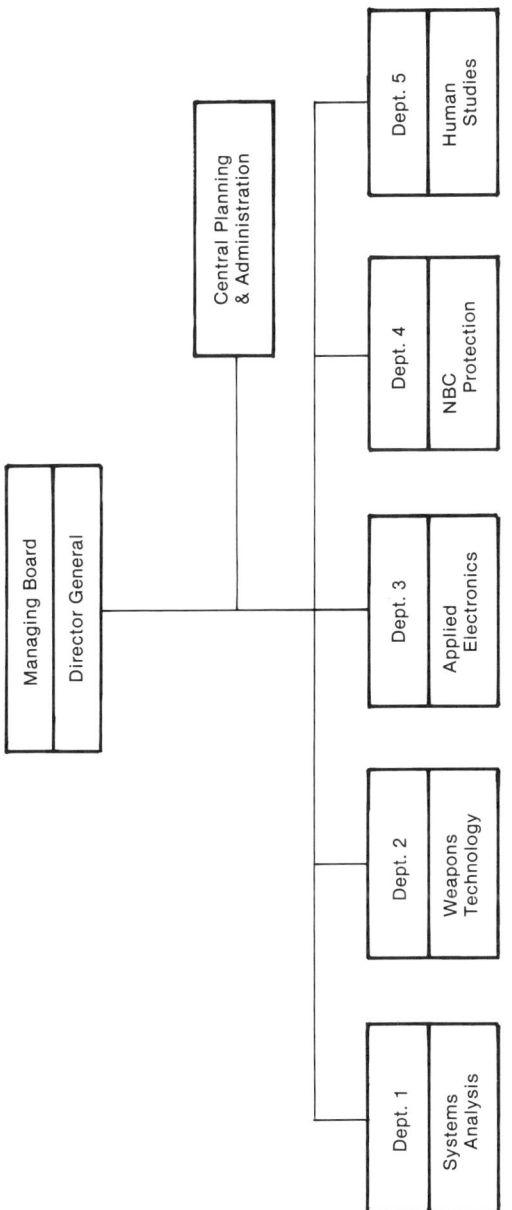

Figure 5-4. National Defense Research Institute

Department 2 deals in applied physics, chemistry, and mathematics centered on weapons and weapons systems research. Department 2 is also responsible for analysis and reporting on worldwide nuclear weapons technology and for operation of a seismological array station. Department 3 works on military and civilian applications of electromagnetic and acoustic waves in such fields as communication, guidance, and navigation. It also studies the electromagnetic and radiation effects of nuclear explosions and protective measures against them. Department 4 studies the effects of and protection against chemical and biological warfare agents and nuclear explosions. The scientific disciplines involved in these studies range from organic chemistry to applied physics. Department 5 applies the medical and behavioral sciences to the study of people in war and to the environment of total defense.

Like the heads of most agencies and boards, the director general of FOA is responsible directly to the government, but he reports to the minister of defense. The priorities for various research activities are assigned to FOA by the supreme commander and requests for allocations must pass through his defense staff. FOA has program responsibility for defense research in other agencies, meaning that this agency has a major role every four or five years in coordinating and developing a five-year program plan for defense research, as well as in preparing the budget for annual appropriations.[34] The OR people placed through the defense organization have close relationships with FOA. In fact, FOA appears to have a defense "omnipresence."

For fiscal year 1981/1982 the appropriated FOA budget was approximately $60 million.[35] Additionally, FOA received both public and private grants for specific research contracts. Unlike the defense research organizations of some other countries, FOA is concerned primarily with applied and some basic research, not with development of defense materials. The latter is the responsibility of the Defense Materiel Administration.

Defense Materiel Administration (FMV)

The Defense Materiel Administration is one of the largest defense organizations (a staff of over 3,380) and is the central authority for the procurement and maintenance of military equipment.[36] Project officers for major weapons systems work in this department and the liaison with civilian industry is close. Cost calculations and recommendations on budgeting for weapons systems from the director of FMV carry great weight in government decisions and paliamentary appropriations, although FMV requests to contract for weapons must go through the appropriate service commander-in-chief and the supreme commander.

A reorganization of FMV was initiated on July 1, 1982 and was completed about one year later. The new director, Carl-Olof Tenryd, became the first civilian to head the administration. One of the primary objectives of the restructuring process was to consolidate the procurement methods of the three services, the objective being improved cooperation with industry. In 1984, ninety percent of all contracts were given to domestic companies.[37]

The FMV director general has the potential for considerable power and influence. The position traditionally was occupied by an exceptional senior officer who has had a brilliant career. There is every indication that officers consider assignment in FMV to be career enhancing. In a military establishment where overseas operational action is largely confined to participation in UN peacekeeping activities, it appears that many of the brighter officers seek involvement in those organizations in Sweden that enjoy high priority and prestige. In the Swedish technocratic society FMV is such an organization and within FMV high priority is given to the position of project officer for a major weapons system.

Defense Commissions

The use of special commissions for program planning or to study current problems is a characteristic feature of the Swedish administrative system.[38] Although the number varies, there are generally in the neighborhood of three hundred commissions at work at a given time.[39]

Defense commissions are formed every four years to take a five-year look at defense programs. The 1978 Parliamentary Commission on Defense which developed the five-year plan for 1982–1987 was such a commission. The body was chaired by Mr. Gunnar Björk of the Center party and contained six Social Democrats, two Liberals and two Conservatives. The committee considered the objectives of Swedish security policies and submitted proposals to provide a background for program planning. In the final two phases the committee studied proposals for programs such as improved coordination between civil defense and local authorities and a price indexing system, and made decisions on overall planning for total defense during the five-year period.[40]

The second major type of commission to study problems is typified by "The B3LA Commission" which began its work in the spring of 1977 to consider the impact of a decision to adopt either a modified Viggen (A20) or a new aircraft (B3LA) to replace the Viggen 37. This committee was headed by Gunnar Nordbeck, the secretary of state for defense. Another example is the Air Industry Commission formed in 1978 to restudy the issue of the successor to Viggen 37. However, this fifteen-member commission, directed by retired Army General Sten Wahlin, studied the impact upon the entire aircraft industry of a decision *not* to produce either the A20 or B3LA—or both. This committee included members of government from the different parties, representatives from industry, representatives of the trade unions, and technical experts.

The reports of these commissions can carry great weight, and the course of commission deliberations are of much interest to all concerned in defense decision making.[41]

The Defense Industry

With a 1983 GDP of 695 billion Swedish kronor (in 1983, $1 = 7.69 Skr) Sweden spent 20.5 billion kronor ($2.59 billion) on defense. The percentage of GDP devoted to defense, approximately 3 percent, represents a significant decline from the 1960s when Sweden spent about 4.5 percent of GDP on defense.[42] A very high percentage, over 70 percent, of the defense budget is devoted to personnel costs. The reasons for this are several, including wage inflation and real-cost increases brought about through union pressures in a highly unionized, advanced industrial society.[43]

Unlike that of the other Scandinavian countries, Sweden's defense industry has long been relatively large and thriving. The four major corporations involved in defense R&D and production are Saab-Scandia in Linköping, Volvo Flygmotor in Trollhättan, L.M. Ericsson in Mölndal, and Bofors in Karlskoga. The first three companies are involved principally with military aircraft and Bofors deals with a wide variety of gun and missile systems. Each of these major corporations has a large number of subcontractors for weapons systems components.

Sweden's industrial productivity has been high indeed. By 1983 Sweden held third place in the world's GNP per capita, the main impetus for which has been increased output per capita.[44] There have been three principal trends in Swedish industry since the mid-1950s. First, there has been an increasing concentration of industrial production into larger firms through business mergers. Second, the traditional leading sectors of Swedish manufacturing based directly on iron and wood have gradually lost their importance and production emphasis has been shifted toward engineering and chemically processed goods that are based on high technology. Engineering has become the leading industrial sector, accounting for more than 37 percent of Swedish industrial sales. Five of Sweden's ten largest industrial firms are engineering enterprises. Third, Swedish manufacturing firms have expanded much more rapidly abroad than in Sweden, with engineering manufacturers leading the way.[45] The largest Swedish firms are multinational with hundreds of subsidiaries abroad and with much of their work force and sales in other nations.

Research and development expenditures involve approximately 2 percent of GNP. Roughly three-quarters is performed by industry, certain national authorities, and private and cooperative research institutes. The remaining quarter of all R&D work is undertaken within the higher education system. State grants for R&D in 1982 were about Skr 6.58 billion, 16 percent of which was given for defense and 40 percent for general scientific research.

A considerable amount of defense research is performed by corporations in the defense-related industries.[46]

Swedish industry is highly unionized at every level. The dominant organization for manual workers is LO (Swedish Confederation of Trade Unions) which has a membership of 2.16 million, about 90 percent of the organizable blue-collar workers. The principal organization for white-collar workers is the TCO (Central Organization of Swedish Employees) which has nineteen affiliated unions and a membership of about one million, or 70 percent of organizable white-collar workers. Today, two out of every five union members belong to the TCO. In an arrangement unusual in many countries, the dominant employer organization is SAF (Swedish Employers Federation) which has more than 40,000 member firms employing some 1,300,000 people.[47]

In 1984, the trade unions became increasingly restless over the policies of the Social Democratic party for which they have had a traditional affinity. In 1982 and 1983 the unions had even settled for modest pay raises at a time when many industrialists were making record profits. To mollify union leaders, the Palme government pushed through the controversial "wage-earner fund" plan. The plan was designed to increase taxes on company profits and place this money at the disposal of boards appointed by the government (with a majority of seats on each board filled by trade union members) to buy shares in Swedish firms. The arguments for and against the fund are many and complex, but almost no one was happy with it in early 1985—not the nonsocialist parties, nor industry, nor the unions. This occurred at a time when there were government attempts to cut public spending (to the dismay of the white-collar workers, most of whom work in the public sector); when the federal deficit was based increasingly on a large foreign debt; and when inflation remained high (1984 rate of approximately 9 percent). The unions became most frustrated. Thus, for the first time since 1950, Sweden's centralized system for pay bargaining broke down in 1984 and the unions chose to negotiate wages separately with private employers rather than through their union federations, where the LO, for example, would negotiate for all blue-collar workers with the SAF representing its member firms.

The unions figure largely in major business and government decisions on defense production. The leading defense manufacturers in Sweden do not formally lobby the government; this is not necessary for two major reasons. First, given Sweden's policy of nonalignment in peacetime, the traditional view has been that buying weapons systems in Sweden assists in keeping the nation independent of other advanced industrialized nations which are members of alliances. Second, given the movement toward concentrating industry through business mergers, there has been little room or need for competition in contract bidding. Rather, the relationship with government appears to be a matter of technology salesmanship among the relevant service staffs, the defense staff, the National Defense Research Institute, the Defense Materiel Administration, and contract negotiations principally with the latter.

Traditionally, lobbying in the cabinet and parliament has been unnecessary. Describing the situation of the late 1950s one observer noted, "by the time the politicians are brought into the process they usually have little option left but to justify the production order."[48] And one high official in government stated in an interview that "even if they had to lobby, they wouldn't be very good at it."[49] However, given downward pressures on the defense budget, the increasing political importance of decisions on major weapons systems, and a consequent necessity for earlier cabinet-level scrutiny of proposed defense expenditures, it is possible that business lobbying will increase. None of this is to imply that the defense industry and various government officials do not lobby with foreign industrial producers of weapons systems components over licensing arrangements; both do and in concert.

The News Media

Although there are no available data to support their assertions, many in the Swedish defense organization and in the defense industry are somewhat paranoid about the news media. Some assert that the media are "controlled" largely by the socialists and that it is very difficult for defense decision makers to get evenhanded treatment on policies and programs for total defense. Others deny that this is true, pointing out that the papers with the largest circulations are owned by the nonsocialist parties.

It is true that the media have traditionally tended to give short shrift to Swedish defense matters. To the extent that the media focus on foreign policy, they prefer to inform the public on detente, international arms control efforts, international peacekeeping, and international development assistance. Similarly, understanding that outspoken support for defense spending is unpopular or genuinely convinced that conditions for peace are not necessarily founded on strength or perhaps guilty of wishful thinking, many politicians have tended to focus on international peace. As Ingemar Dörfer expressed it in the late 1970s ". . . most likely Swedes tend to believe what their government has been telling them; that detente is here to stay."[50]

Television in Sweden is unique by U.S. standards. As in other European nations, there are rarely any daytime programs and only two channels. Production is controlled by an independent board (Board of Governors for the Swedish Broadcasting Company) which is subsidized 60 percent by the government. Programs appear to be selected or designed much more for their cultural value than for public leisure or public information. The board appears to believe that the Swedish public is not (or should not be) interested in defense policy. However, they do run programs on the horrors of nuclear war and on such matters as arms control and disarmament. Some Swedish defense officials have tried, unsuccessfully, to persuade the board that defense and defense information are important.

In general, Swedish newspapers are reticent to print articles on defense and, with the exception of *Svenska Dagbladet* which is conservative and comparatively prodefense, others, for example *Dagens Nyheter* (independent) and *Aftonbladet* (socialist) are generally skeptical or antidefense. The communist paper *Ny Dag* is clearly antidefense. Like the television board, the press argues that the Swedish public is not interested in defense.

An illustrative example of the general media position is the case of the press reporter, Maj Wechselmann, who gained notoriety several years ago for having "blown the cover" on the military-industrial complex involved in the high cost overruns (almost double original estimates) of developing and producing the Viggen 37 aircraft. An ardent opponent of defense spending in general, and especially in the case of the B3LA/A20 controversies, she was awarded the Peace Prize for 1978 from the Swedish Peace and Arbitration Society, a pacifist organization.[51]

Public Opinion and Civil-Military Relations

In light of the foregoing, it is not surprising that the ministers of defense have been outspoken concerning the lack of defense information received by the Swedish public. In 1978 Eric Kronmark criticized the inadequacy of defense information in the school system—to which the director general of the Swedish Board of Education replied to the effect that defense gets its prescribed share in the curriculum, but the pupils find the subject uninteresting.

Surveys indicate that the defense minister was and remains correct, even though there has been in recent years a concrete effort to better educate the public on defense matters, especially in schools and in conscript training. Recent trends in decentralization in the school system largely leave it to teacher discretion whether and how defense matters are taught.[52]

A basic problem is teaching teachers about defense policy. There are many organizations which long have tried, for example, the Central Organization for People and Defense which, funded about 90 percent by the government, organizes voluntary regional and local conferences on national security affairs. Very few teachers ever attend. Moreover, the Ministry of Education cooperates with attempts by the Ministry of Defense and the armed forces to educate about defense policy by permitting civilian or military experts a spot in the teachers' in-service training programs for which every community is authorized five days (never five consecutive days) during the school year. However, little really can be done in the short time provided. The 1980 Swedish Standing Committee on Defense proposal to include defense in the basic curriculum of the teachers' schools may be the best answer. Some feel that it is an essential responsibility of the Ministry of Education to emphasize support for defense as a duty of the nation's citizens.[53]

An exception is the limited amount of time devoted to training (or "education") on Swedish defense. The armed forces will get whatever benefit derives from distribution to 17-year-olds of a pamphlet on the Swedish total defense published by the Total Defense Information Committee (TAUN). The pamphlet cover, plain brown with block-type yellow printing and without illustration, is not exactly eye-catching. However, a young person who took the one minute required to read the front cover might find the brief statement and set of questions sufficiently interesting to turn the page:

> The earth is hardly a peaceful place to live. In our time, more than before, the superpowers are continuously on guard toward each other. Conflict and small wars occur constantly in countries of the world around us.
>
> The consequences of all this we have felt in our own time.
>
> But is there a risk of Sweden being attacked or becoming involved in war or being pressured? In that case must we defend ourselves? And what would such a defense look like? Is a military defense alone enough? What is the situation today?[54]
>
> We have few natural resources of importance that they would attack us to acquire. War is expensive. It would cost them much and yield little in return. But in geographic terms, we are in a bad place between NATO and the Warsaw Pact. The Warsaw Pact needs to come out to the sea in the north and through the Baltic. And NATO wants to stop this. Plus, both of them want to move their air forces forward toward each other. They are going to get as close to our country as possible. Besides, there is oil under the North Sea. And if they both start drilling for it, that also could be a factor leading to conflict. And Sweden lies in the danger zone.[55]

How does the Swedish public feel about defense? In the aftermath of the submarine hunt at Karlskrona in February/March 1984, the Psychological Defense Planning Committee (BN) interviewed 516 adults, asking among other things, "Do you feel that you received adequate information about the submarine hunt in Karlskrona?" This question was partly motivated by the fact that information was sometimes suppressed in the interest of national security. The results were:

	Adequate or *Nearly Adequate*	*Not Entirely Adequate* or *Insufficient*	*Don't Know*
1984	66%	29%	5%

This survey was taken against the background of repeated submarine violations. During the past thirty years, the index which indicates the willingness to engage in armed resistance has fluctuated between 70 to 80 percent. The changes which have occurred are due primarily to increased international tension or to swings in the domestic political debate. The following table shows that in March/April of 1984 the "will to resist" was in the middle of this range, 74.5 percent.[56] The recent increase in the Swedish will to resist can be partly attributed to the fact that the Swedish people believe that traditional armed forces provide the best means to deter aggression:

What type of defense do you think most deters a potential aggressor?[57]

	Military	*Guerrilla*	*Civil Resistance*	*Don't Know*
1983	60%	18%	9%	12%

Over the period 1968–1983, the percentage of Swedes who believe that Sweden can defend itself if war comes has increased from 21 to 27 percent. Over nearly the same period, confidence in civil, economic, and psychological defense has fallen while skepticism has risen:

How well do you expect the civilian elements of our defense to perform during a war?[58]

	Very Well or *Adequately*	*Badly* or *Very Poorly*	*Don't Know*
1969	67%	20%	13%
1973	51	28	21
1983	58	30	12

The percentage of Swedes who believe that Sweden must have a defense is high.

Given the way things are in the world today, do you think we should or should not have a defense?[59]

	Absolutely or *Should*	*Probably Shouldn't* or *Absolutely No*	*Don't Know*
1980	87%	10%	3%
1981	90	7.5	2.5
1983	93	4.5	2.5

Although these surveys do not distinguish between the utility of defense in the event of a conventional or nuclear war, confidence in defense has remained high even as concern over the degree of tension in the world has grown:

How much are you concerned over the political tension in the world? [60]

	Very Much	Not Much	Don't Know
1976	56%	39%	4%
1980	69.5	27.5	3
1983	70	27	2

It is worth noting that Sweden has one of the highest "will to resist" levels in the world.

If war comes, would you be willing to fight for your country? [61]

	Yes
Norway	82%
Sweden	78
USA	71
UK	62
Denmark	59
France	42
Japan	22

Yet at the same time Swedes say that they do not have information adequate to make decisions as to what they should do when war comes.

Do you think people in this country get enough or too little information about what each person should think about and do in the event of a war? [62]

	Enough or Nearly Enough	Largely or Totally Inadequate	Don't Know
1979	22%	73%	6%
1980	22	74	4
1983	21	77	2

There is a growing belief in Sweden that the armed forces are inadequate and should be augmented:

In today's world, is the strength of our total defense too small, or about right?[63]

	Too Small	About Right	Too Large	Don't Know
1963	12%	57%	8%	23%
1973	13	66	14	7
1978	22	52	9	18
1983	41	45.5	5.5	9

Do you think federal expenditures for defense should be raised, reduced, or left unchanged?[64]

	Raised	Kept Unchanged	Reduced	Don't Know
1957	9%	45%	26%	20%
1969	16	58	16	11
1979	20	51	19	9
1983	31	52	11	6

Likewise there is a growing interest in questions and issues concerning Swedish security:

How great is your interest in questions about Sweden's security, ability to deter war, and ability to resist threats and intimidation?[65]

	Very or Sort of Great	Very or Sort of Small	Don't Know
1979	48%	48%	4%
1980	46	49	4
1981	61	38	2

Finally, Swedes are not convinced that Sweden will be attacked or that World War III will break out before the year 2000.

Do you think Sweden will be attacked by a foreign power before the year 2000?[66]

	Very or Sort of Likely	Very or Sort of Unlikely	Don't Know
1979	14%	68%	18%
1981	27	62	11
1983	20	69	11

Do you think World War III will take place before the year 2000?[67]

	Very or Sort of Likely	*Very* or Sort of Unlikely	Don't Know
1979	21%	63%	16%
1981	33	57	9
1983	24	66	9

Absolute majorities believe in conscription, that disarmament is desirable only if it is multilateral, that Sweden will not be attacked with nuclear weapons, and that the easiest way to get information about what to do when war comes is to use the phone book or rely on local authorities.

This information shows that the Swedish public, though not generally well-informed about security matters, is beginning to become more appreciative of the military component of their total defense. Even in a period of growing inflation and increasing national debt the Swedish people believe that defense spending should be increased. There is a general tendency to doubt the threat of world war, but an increasing awareness of new forms of threat against Swedish security. There is no doubt that the public is increasingly interested in the role that force plays in Swedish diplomacy.

Finally, there is firm public support for current levels of defense spending, and a positive increase among those who think defense spending should be increased. This increase has occurred at the expense of the undecided cohort. It appears that if a clear case can be made concerning the nature of the threat and the utility of military force in meeting it, then the potential for public support for greater defense spending exists.

Decision-Making Constraints

As in any constitutional democracy, defense decision makers in Sweden bear the burden of systemic political constraints from which authoritarian regimes are relatively free. Also, their alternative choices in defense policy are shaped or conditioned by the geopolitical "facts" (as perceived) of strategy; by technological developments and trends only partially under their control; and by the increasing realities of resource scarcity.

Political Constraints

Governments in parliamentary systems usually wish to avoid taking stands on crucial political issues unless they are relatively confident they can win. The reason is obvious; in these systems, unlike the U.S. system, a vote on a major issue can result in the "no-confidence" vote which spells the demise of a governing coalition.

The Swedish government was faced with just such a crucial issue in October 1978—the necessity to make a fundamental decision on the expansion of nuclear energy. Prime Minister Fälldin's Center party repudiated a compromise he had struck with his coalition partners (who had pushed for expansion of nuclear energy) to delay putting two additional nuclear power plants on line until the nation's energy agency pronounced that safe means of waste disposal had been found. The Center party sought additional concessions which the prime minister could not get and Fälldin resigned.[68]

Another example was clear in the summer/fall 1979. A fundamental decision on the next generation of fighter aircraft to replace the Viggen should have been made in 1976 in line with the rationality of the R&D process. But there were political constraints involved. The decision had major implications for the future of Swedish defense, the defense industry, and the size of future defense budgets. No party wished to take responsibility before the 1979 elections. One political means of postponing decisions is the familiar tactic of having commissions undertake studies of the issue. A companion tactic might be to fund R&D alternative aircraft systems incrementally so that opponents would be confronted with sunk costs so great that a decision not to adopt a new Swedish-manufactured fighter aircraft would be clearly irrational on economic grounds. All Swedish political parties opted for one tactic or the other—or both—from 1976 to 1979, and they could rely on interservice rivalry to support both tactics.

Another alternative for future Swedish aircraft production and a means of reducing unit costs would be foreign sales. Two political constraints are operative in this respect. First, even if the defense establishment advocated this alternative, it would be constrained by the Foreign Ministry's intent to keep arms sales abroad below one percent of total Swedish production. (In 1983, 0.7 percent of Swedish exports were in arms and ammunitions.)[69] Second, such a position could run afoul of the foreign policy of neutrality—even if it could survive the onslaught of Swedish public opinion.[70] Defense Minister Anders Thunborg has stressed the intricate nature of negotiating arms exports, especially with developing countries. The problem lies in drawing the distinction between offensive and defensive weapons and determining whether a country is too closely tied to a major power bloc for legitimate trade considerations.[71]

Strategic Constraints

Sweden's policy of neutrality presupposes a "tous azimuts" (all directions) strategy under which total defense preparations should provide the capability to meet an attack from any quarter. A glance at a map underscores Sweden's strategic position between the superpowers and their allies. In the 1940s and 1950s Swedish forces were responsible for defense against attacks from both the Baltic and through Finland. These missions were redefined in 1963 to provide for either one or the other, not both simultaneously. In any case, three considerations would erode the "tous azimuts" strategy. First, Swedish defense planners have long considered the military threat to be from the Soviet Union and their sympathies clearly lie with the West.[72]

An illustrative example was the 1962 defense report of the supreme commander which was based on a Baltic attack from the east and showed the Soviet Union as the aggressor (of course, the Soviet ambassador protested strongly to the Swedish minister of foreign affairs). As we shall see, there has been every reason for Swedish defense planners to retain that view although they have gone to great pains in public pronouncements to either deny or obscure it. Second, it is impossible that Swedish planners have missed the qualitative buildup of Soviet forces on the Kola peninsula, with estimates of Soviet forces numbering as many as 70,000 men (seven divisions) with over 1,300 tanks. The disposition of Swedish units north of the Sundsvall-Trondheim line and recent prepositioning of U.S. military equipment in Norway are indicators that Sweden and NATO are taking this into account.[73] One might note here that the highly versatile JAS39 Gripen which will be the follow-on to the JA37 Viggen might be more suitable for the special defense considerations of northern Sweden. Whether or not the Gripen will appear more or less threatening to the southern flank of a Soviet land attack in northern Norway remains unclear.

Although operating with extreme uncertainties, Swedish defense planners traditionally have assigned the country a low strategic value, but this has been in a period prior to the realities of the gradual Soviet buildup on the Kola Peninsula. The principal strategic significance of a nation depends upon its location and its resources. In terms of location, it is the strategic significance of Norway that makes the major difference. There are two major schools of thought here. One school concludes that north Norwegian airfields are absolutely essential for extending the range of Soviet aircraft into the North Atlantic and that Norwegian (and Danish and Swedish) strategic utility resides in their positions behind the lines of Soviet strategy. The second school concludes that the deployment of new technology (mainly naval) on the Kola peninsula points to the nonutility of occupying territory.[74] To determine which school is correct, one must come to grips with five major considerations. First, it is possible that the Soviets would not want to commit major naval forces to large amphibious landings, preferring to hold them in reserve initially.

Second, the Soviets might consider that:

> The rapid transit of ground troups to the north could be facilitated by the use of Finnish territory and rail links, "doubling up" on Soviet capacity. Swedish

airspace could be utilized simply by over-flying for high priority missions or some form of "preemptive occupation" on the pretext of NATO's making use of Swedish facilities—a number of scenarios suggest themselves, all with the background that the Soviet Union could not leave Sweden out of its military calculations.[75]

Third, the Swedish transportation system might offer the Soviets the means of rapidly placing conventional forces in strategically important locations simultaneously in Norway and Denmark. Swedish air bases and airports might be viewed as having additional values.[76]

Fourth, a Soviet thrust through the Baltic into the Atlantic would necessarily mean elimination of Norway's coastal defenses and neutralization of Swedish coastal defenses.

Fifth, if Soviet military operations against Norway were completed successfully, it is difficult to imagine the Soviets ignoring Sweden, a "neutral" capitalist country with a mobilized, fairly sophisticated armed force of 850,000, intact in their newly acquired "front yard." The ideological and political costs of doing so might be viewed by Soviet leaders as simply too high.[78]

Despite, or perhaps because of, these strategic considerations, Swedish defense planners have few alternatives. They cannot formally align themselves against the Warsaw Pact, which must be perceived as the principal military threat, for at least two reasons. First, there is a clear public consensus in Sweden for a policy of neutrality; this is part of the Swedish psyche. Second, such alignment would almost guarantee the Soviet attack in time of war between the superpowers which Sweden seeks to avoid. However, even though they do not plan on direct NATO support, defense planners probably must consider the extent to which NATO force commitments to the northern flank reduce at the margin Soviet capabilities against Sweden. It should be noted that some have denied explicitly that the United States would come to Sweden's aid in the event of Soviet attack.[79]

Technological Constraints

Technological constraints are one of the major considerations for Swedish defense decision makers. As Ingemar Dörfer has pointed out so well, Swedish defense policy has little to do with science and a great deal to do with technology.[80] Sweden suboptimizes in the technology of weapons acquisition, relying on a balance of technological change between the superpowers. In practice this means that, as long as the East does not outstrip the West in weapons technology, Sweden can rely on Western technology to sustain Swedish defense requirements. This frees the Swedish government from the first two steps of a full-blown R&D program for weapons acquisition, steps Sweden cannot afford. The four R&D steps are:[81]

1. The formation and empirical verification of theories about parameters of the physical world.
2. The creation and testing of radically new physical concepts, components, devices, and techniques.
3. The identification, modification, and combination of feasible or existing concepts, components, and devices to provide a distinctly new application practical in terms of performance, reliability, and costs.
4. Relatively minor modifications of existing components, devices, and systems to improve performance, increase reliability, reduce cost, and simplify applications.

This means that Swedish weapons programs are for the most part "state of the art," thus eliminating many R&D uncertainties. However, it creates major external uncertainties and constraints. Sweden must purchase major weapons systems or their technology from either the Soviets or the advanced industrialized states of the West—principally from the NATO allies. Declining to purchase weapons systems on the principle of nonalignment in peace for neutrality in war, Sweden has purchased Western technology in the form of contract licenses for components of major weapons systems, because of its high quality and for several other reasons.

As the case of the Viggen JA37 coproduction agreement with the United States showed in the late 1950s and early 1960s (prior to Sweden's disenchantment with the U.S. war in Vietnam), the Social Democrats could find ways to rely heavily on U.S. technology without compromising Swedish neutrality. As the case of the JAS39 Gripen showed in 1983–84, the Social Democrats could rely on U.S. technology again, but to a lesser extent, diversifying more to European NATO sources.[82] In this case, seeking more European subcontracts was caused more by the strength of the U.S. dollar than by any aspect of preserving neutrality. When the basic JAS coproduction contract was signed with the United States, the Skr exchange rate was 4.5 to the dollar. By early 1985, the Skr was 9 to the dollar and many contracts for JAS parts were going to the United Kingdom and France for this obvious reason.

Another major defense problem of suboptimization involves Swedish coproduction and foreign sales. Again, the Viggen case is instructive. In 1977 and 1978 India seriously considered purchasing the Viggen. However, the U.S. license contract for the Viggen's Pratt and Whitney JT8D-22 (modified as the Volvo Flygmotor RM88) specified no sale to third parties without U.S. approval. In August 1978, U.S. Secretary of State Vance informed Minister of Commerce Burenstam-Linder that the United States opposed the sale.[83] This was clearly an important technological constraint which Swedish defense decision makers would have to suffer on aircraft systems as long as they suboptimized by purchasing the systems based on contracts with the West.

Largely because of such considerations, parliament chose in 1982 to approve the R&D and acquisition process for the JAS39 as proposed by the JAS Industries Group (Saab, Volvo Flygmotor, Ericsson, and FFV), calling for a production scheme that required foreign parts to be purchased in completed form without arrangements based on licensing and manufacture.[84]

The possible alternatives to coproduction are not happy ones: (1) optimizing by following steps 1 and 2 in the aircraft system acquisition process, which Sweden cannot afford; (2) purchasing the tactical aircraft in toto from the West, which would conceivably weaken nonalignment and would probably adversely affect the R&D component of Sweden's leading industrial sector—engineering; (3) contract or purchase from the Soviet Union, which would be politically untenable and disastrous for long term spare parts, and which probably would exacerbate Swedish arms sales problems, or (4) do without fighter aircraft, which would make Swedish deterrence of the marginal attack much less credible (a former Swedish Army commander-in-chief disagreed with this)[85] and probably lead to the demise of the aircraft industry and consequent loss of thousands of jobs for civilian technicians.[86]

Clearly, Swedish defense planners are not confronted with these technological constraints on most weapons systems, only on the ones most important to Swedish defense as presently conceptualized.

Resource Constraints

Aside from such human resource constraints implied by the potential loss of trained R&D personnel in the aircraft industry, there are other major resource constraints. The most obvious constraints on funding for military defense are real or politically perceived opportunity costs for domestic programs at a time when Swedish economic stability is unclear.

The Swedish economic performance for fiscal year 1983 painted an uncertain picture: the nation's balance of payment situation, although marginally better, was still a source of great concern; inflation was unacceptably high; and unemployment had risen for the fourth year in succession. Nevertheless, other aspects of the economy were showing reasonable success: GNP was up 2.5 percent to its highest level since 1979 and the balance of trade showed an incredible Skr 10 billion surplus. The significance of these figures is easier to understand when considering the recent effects of budget ceilings on defense spending. As inflation lingers around 8 or 9 percent the budget will be shrinking considerably in constant currency. The adverse effects loom even larger when one considers the 30–35 percent of development for the JAS39 that is contracted to foreign firms where rates are dependent on the dollar exchange. It is estimated that the Gripen will cost $6.7 billion more to produce between 1984 and the year 2000.[87]

The net result has been to force defense decision makers to make drastic reductions in military equipment and numbers of military units, to cut back in both conscript and refresher training, and to consider the possibility of early withdrawal of the J35 Draken before its estimated withdrawal date of 1995. The picture can be made to appear even worse if one contrasts recent forecasts of the future with the situation of the mid-1950s:

> The mobilizable frontline forces will decline into between half and one third of the force structure in the mid-1950s, one generation earlier. The air force will go from a 17 wing air force in 1955 (compared to a 26 wing U.S. tactical Air Force now) to a 7 wing essentially Viggen air force in 1988. The air defense fighter force, the strongest in Western Europe in 1955 with 33 squadrons, will eventually have 8 Viggen squadrons.[88]

Of course, one can argue that the more sophisticated weapons systems of the present and projected future have far greater capability than earlier generations and, thus, one needs far fewer. But this is a current and unresolved argument among military force development planners everywhere.

Military defense, albeit the largest part of total defense, comprising a wartime organization of approximately 210,000 people, is not the only area affected by resource constraints. In addition to military costs, other aspects of total defense, mainly economic and civil defense, are affected by resource constraints. Table 5–3 shows the appropriated amounts for total defense in fiscal year 1984 and the proposed amounts for fiscal year 1985.

Table 5–3
Summary of Appropriations
(million Swedish kronor)[89]

	1983/84 (appropriated)	1984/85 (proposed)	Change
The Defense Ministry	46.0	43.3	−2.7
Military defense:			
Army units	6,862.2	7,105.0[a]	+242.8[a]
Navy units	2,850.7	2,905.0[a]	+54.3[a]
Air Force units	5,950.5	6,475.0[a]	+524.5[a]
Operative command	738.4	815.0[a]	+76.6[a]
Joint agencies, etc.	4,091.7	3,435.7	−656.0
Total military defense	20,493.5	20,735.7[a]	+242.2[a]
Civil defense	854.5	1,083.0	+228.5
Economic defense	525.6	386.1	−139.5
Other total defense	97.3	136.8	+39.5
Rescue services	39.7	33.3	−6.4
Miscellaneous	23.9	150.8	+126.9
Total appropriations	22,080.5	22,569.0	+488.5

[a] preliminary figure

The most important figure in table 5–3 is the total change in defense spending, 488.5 million kronor (about $54 million), which is a 2.2 percent increase. When this figure is compared to the annual inflation rate of between 8 and 9 percent, it is clear that resource constraints do have an impact on the Swedish defense budget.

Civil defense is based on training for both men and women between ages 16 and 65. The size of the wartime organization was reduced in the Defense Resolution of 1982 from 200,000 to 150,000 people.

The civil defense mission is to protect the population against the effects of conventional warfare with a secondary mission of providing protection against ABC weapons within reasonable cost limits. Throughout the more highly populated areas, there is an impressive array of rock and concrete shelters. Under the direction of the Civil Defense Administration, primary responsibility resides with local authorities with all financing eventually to be provided by the national budget.[90] Resources for civil defense are constrained not only by opportunity costs, but also by public mood. For example, perceptions of detente and nuclear mutual assured destruction between the superpowers make it difficult for decision makers to convince the public and parliament that protection against ABC weapons requires much funding.

Economic defense planning, directed by the National Board of Economic Defense, is centered on Sweden's ability to independently withstand blockade and wartime situations involving essential resources such as energy supplies, raw materials, food, fertilizer, and clothing. It also entails quick conversion from peacetime to wartime industrial production. Caught in the typical economy-ecology dilemma of energy crisis which has been an issue that toppled two successive governments, the major emphasis in economic defense is on stockpiling crude oil.[91]

As with all industrialized nations, international trade and the international division of labor effect Sweden's prosperity in peacetime and economic security in war. Yet, as Prime Minister Olof Palme put it in his speech to the Congress of Foreign Policy and National Security in September, 1984:

> The cardinal rule of the policy of neutrality is that it must never be conducted in a way which can raise expectations on the one side, or apprehensions for divergences from the chosen course of action, on the other.[92]

Peacetime resource constraints are thus linked to the political constraints of a foreign policy of neutrality in war.

The miscellaneous costs of total defense include psychological defense, equipment for emergency hospitals in wartime, and the development of certain communcations capabilities. Swedish planners are properly concerned about the capabilities of an aggressor to penetrate their communications systems with all that implies for emergency command and control and psychological defense.

Resource constraints are real in Swedish peacetime defense planning. It is clear that Sweden is more or less constrained in defense capability based upon various crisis scenarios envisioning short or long wars.

Channels of Decision Making

The current long-range planning system for Swedish defense is based on a study begun in 1965 when the Ministry of Defense was reorganized. The system was applied on an experimental basis in 1968 and accepted in principle by Parliament in 1970. In 1972 the Swedish Planning, Programming, and Budgeting System was implemented fully (see figure 5-5). The system contains four major elements:[93]

1. Studies of international developments and construction of cases of agression in the form of "crisis scenarios."
2. Prospective plans dealing with a time perspective of fifteen to twenty years.
3. System plans for major weapons systems.
4. Five-year program plans, rolled every year.

Part of the Ministry of Defense responsibility for coordinating all defense matters in peacetime is to decide which types of threats to plan for. Should Sweden plan for deterrence and at what levels? For reducing the consequences of war and in what respects? For contributions to stability in the Nordic region and how? For territorial denial? To serve this function, *crisis scenarios* are developed on the basis of possible international developments which are of particular relevance for Swedish defense policy. Studies focus on international, regional, and national politico-military, technological, economic, and social developments which may lead to cases of aggression or crisis which affect Swedish interests. Study results are formally written as documents called "cases of aggression" or "crisis scenarios". This is primarily the work of the SSLP which manages these studies designed to suggest basic guidelines for planning.

Perspective plans are the basic frameworks for alternative defense structures which consider different budgetary constraints projecting fifteen to twenty years into the future. This work is done principally by the defense staff under the direction of the supreme commander. The plans consider alternative compositions of the armed forces derived from given goals (cases of aggression or crisis scenarios) including prescribed internal restrictions describing: (1) basic operational principles, (2) objectives of main allocation programs, and (3) characteristics of essential systems.[94] The studies of defense structures provide background for R&D policies, a basis for parlia-

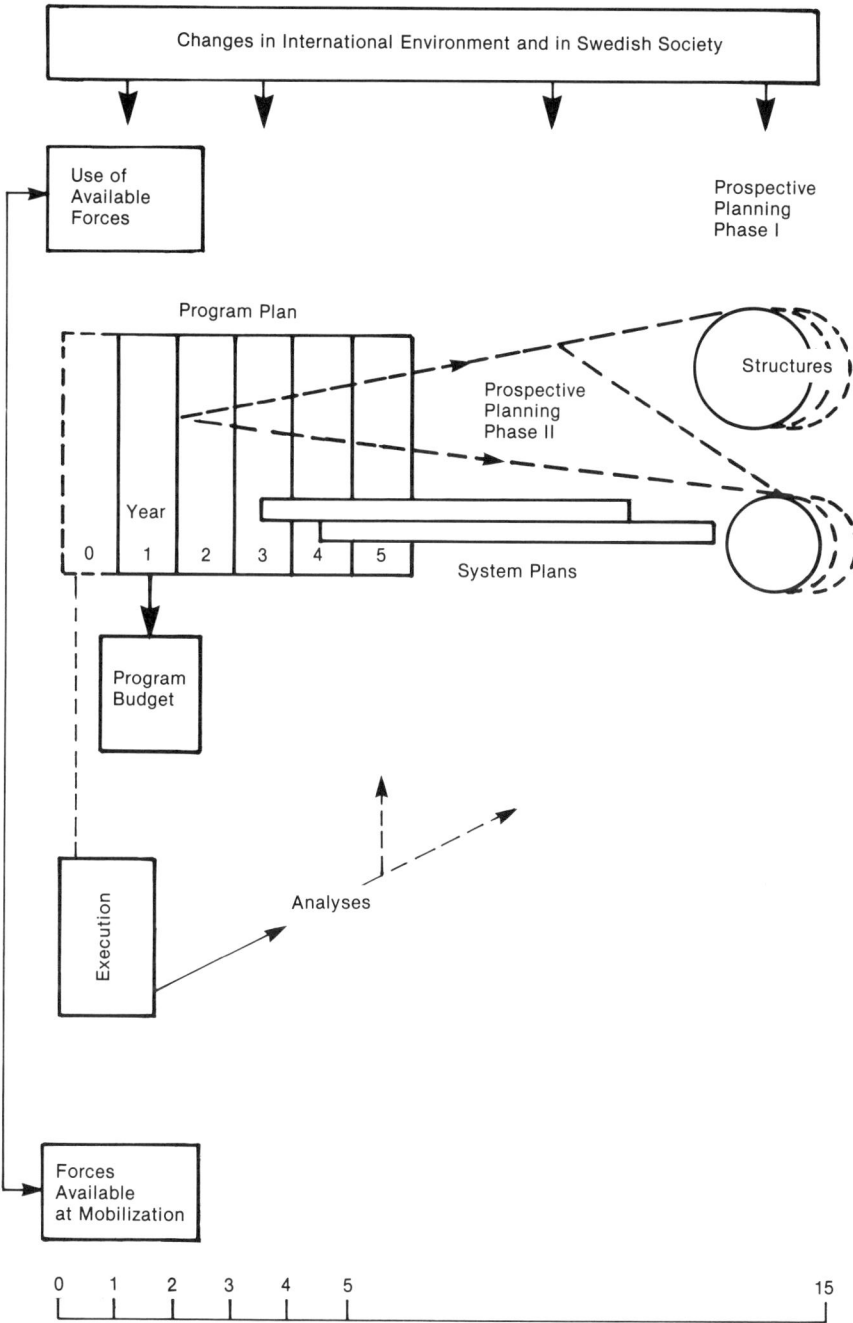

Figure 5-5. Main Links in the Swedish Planning, Programming, and Budgeting System

mentary decisions concerning defense five-year program plans, a long-term planning framework used by other branches of total defense, and background for military staff exercises and maneuvers. They serve also as mechanisms for coordinating the long-term planning activities of the many boards and agencies involved in total defense.[95] The perspective plan describes the most important relationships among system plans.

System Planning provides the link between perspective plans and program plans (see figure 5–6). The perspective plan outlines the ways in which future alternatives can be realized. A system plan is a detailed plan for the development of *one* such alternative system which can be as large as the armed forces as a whole, or main allocation programs, or as small as a specific weapon system (with subprograms, program elements, or equivalents) such as "Air Defense Units." Testing the feasibility of system plans against program plans provides the feedback loop for revision of the perspective plan which is provided to the ministry of defense and subsequently to parliament as a basis for program plan decisions.[96]

Five-year *program plans* are developed every fourth year to examine alternative means of developing different categories of defense capital over the planning period in order to satisfy specific operational goals. Included are considerations of commitments for the future based on ordered but not supplied materiel and assumed priority programs such as conscript training.[97] When defense capital equals demand, a program plan is feasible and rationally could be adopted. Whether or not a particular program budget will be adopted is, of course, a political decision.

Annual defense budgeting is based on the Swedish fiscal year which runs from July 1 to June 30 (see figure 5–7). The work of the ministry of defense for this budget begins during the winter of the preceding calendar year, based on directives from the ministry of the budget. All defense agencies must have their budget requests to MOD no later than August 31. These requests are formally registered in the ministry and, given the right to public information under the Freedom of the Press Act, often receive broad coverage. From August 31 to December 15 the defense budget is prepared and negotiated with the budget ministry.

The government's Budget Bill (about four thousand pages), including an economic policy statement, the draft budget, and a survey of the national economy, is submitted to parliament by January 10. The formal trace of the budget through parliament is shown in figure 5–8.

The channels of the Swedish defense decision-making process are rational and are followed formally. Whether or not the process works as intended is another matter. For example, it would be important to know what the correlation is between program budgets and actual defense expenditures from year one through year five. Unless the correlation is relatively high, given the opportunity costs of the resources devoted to program planning (and thus

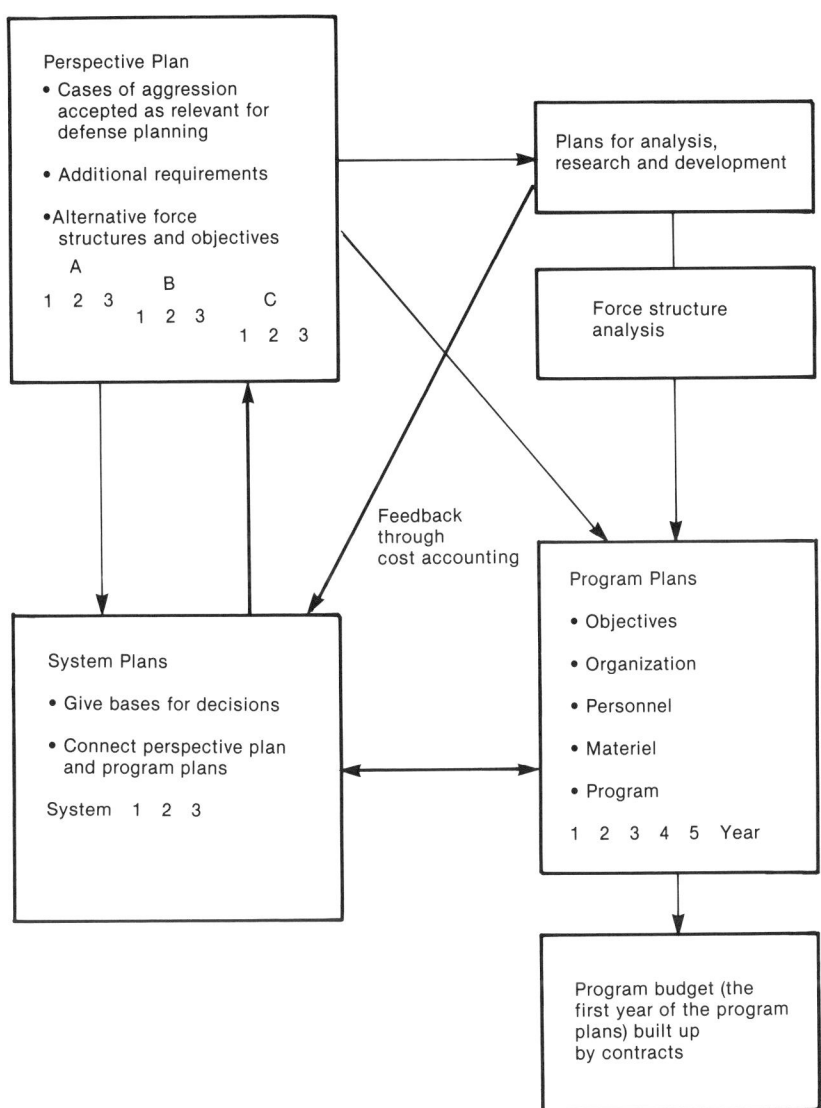

Figure 5-6. The Connection Between Plans

164 • *Nordic Defense: Comparative Decision Making*

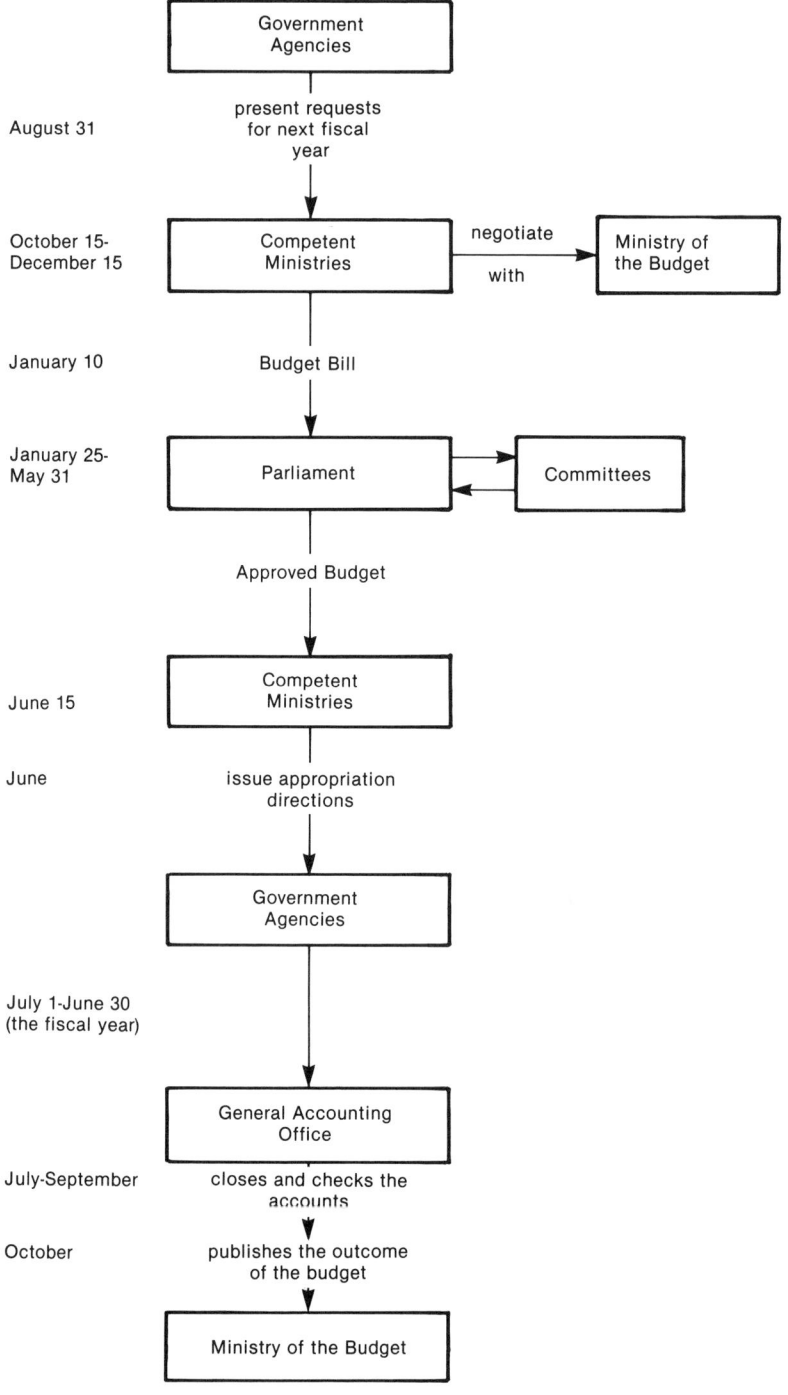

Figure 5-7. The Swedish Budget Procedure

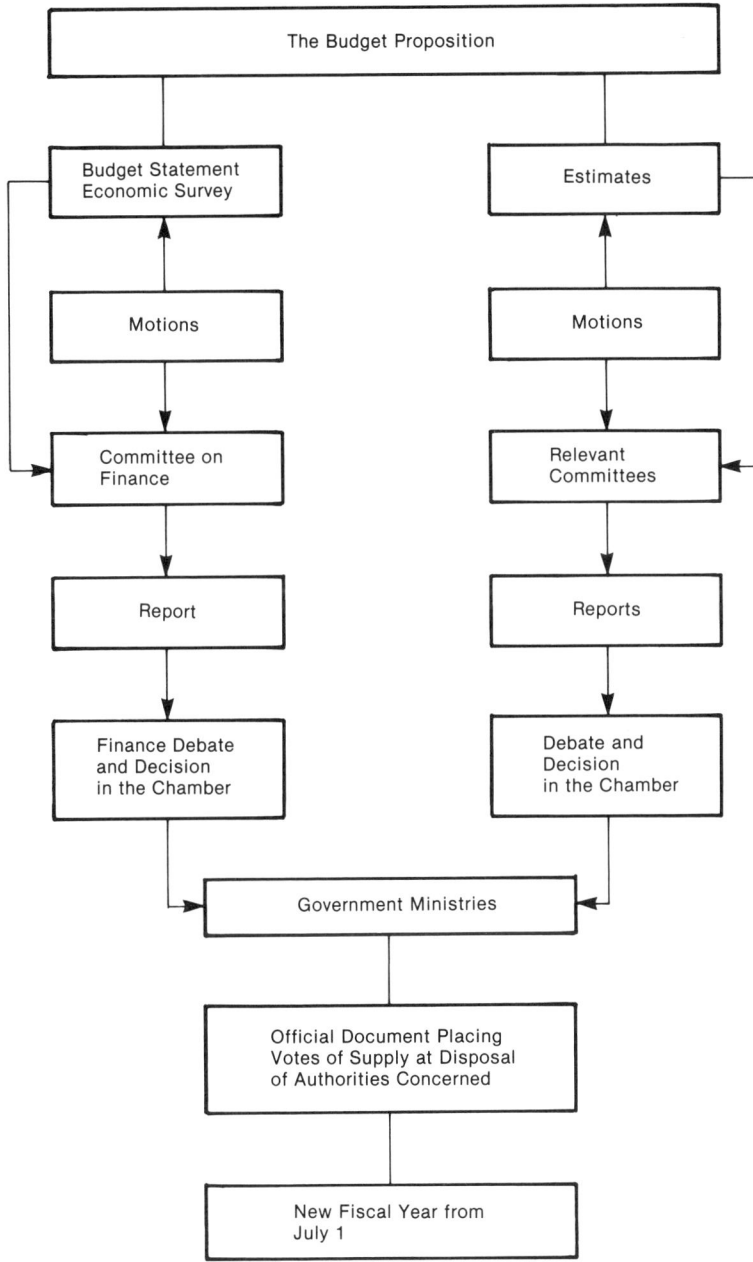

Figure 5–8. Swedish Parliamentary Budget Procedure

through the feedback loop through systems planning to perspective planning), alternative planning procedures may be in order. A thorough time-series analysis would be required for such analysis of the efficacy of the system.

Putting the Pieces Together: The Fighter Aircraft Controversy

The complexities surrounding a major decision on the future of Swedish defense are best illustrated by the debate over the follow-on aircraft to the JA37 Viggen. In the following section the issues involved in the debate are examined. Particular emphasis is placed on the bureaucratic and political constraints that inhibit a systematic approach. These constraints have served to build the aircraft decision into a landmark debate affecting not only defense planning, but the future of Sweden's policy of total defense. Sweden's future depends on its ability to integrate economic policy and social commitments into a cohesive long-term plan. The following case study demonstrates how the Swedes do this.

The Necessity for Choice

RDT&E and production require long lead times even in the Swedish system which suboptimizes in the weapons acquisition process. By 1992 the present Viggen system will be replaced by the JAS39. By then the Viggen 37 system will have become obsolete—structurally worn out and well behind the fighter aircraft technological power curve. The decision to begin the R&D process in order to have the follow-on aircraft in the inventory should have been recommended in 1974 or 1975 and made in 1976 or 1977. In February 1979, a decision was finally made by the Ullsten Government. In essence, the decision was to cease work on new aircraft alternatives and to develop the existing pursuit version of the Viggen to give it attack capability, to form another aircraft committee to study trainer aircraft alternatives and to examine the future possibilities for collaboration with other countries in developing fighter aircraft. The operative constraints preventing a decision were several.

There were the resource constraints described earlier based upon current and foreseeable conditions of the Swedish economy. There were important cost-benefit comparisons of the leading alternative systems, the A20 on the one hand and the B3LA or A38 on the other. However, available evidence suggests that, although the A20 may have been a less expensive alternative in the short run, the B3LA or A38 would have been less expensive over the long term.

The Aircraft Cost Comparison Concept

The B3LA/A38 included new technology involving the air frame, engine, instrumentation, and armament over the first five years. R&D would have cost an estimated $8.3 to $11.0 million more each year than the alternative.[99] The A20 involved significant modification of current Viggen technology. Included in these calculations was a major consideration of the state of aircraft research and development and alternatives to it at the time decisions would have to be made on the follow-on to either the A20 or the B3LA. Projecting alternative costs over the next five years is clearly more concrete (and, perhaps, more persuasive to the layman) than projecting for the long term. Most politicians taking stands on resource questions in the late 1970s involving RDT&E and production into the 1990s clearly would not be in the political arena in the long-term.

In 1973, with the deep involvement of the defense staff, air staff, FMV, and FOA, the system plan for air attack systems laid out alternatives which were narrowed into a "Systems Plan Number Two." In preparation for the 1977 five-year defense decision which would involve enormous commitments of Swedish resources, and in light of the controversy current at the time over the large cost overruns involved in the Viggen system, the Social Democrats created the Thunborg Commission in 1974 to examine the total defense picture. Given the timing for decisions on future aircraft production, that commission should have recommended, but did not, the follow-on to Viggen.[100] The Viggen controversy was still too hot politically.

Another commission was formed specifically to examine the aircraft issue. In the fall of 1976 the choice was between the A20 at relatively the same cost as the previous two years or the B3LA at added cost; however, politics intervened in the form of the September 1976 national elections. The Social Democrats were ousted and the B3LA issue went into limbo. Parliament decided not to fund the program for 1977-78 and to wait and see. In the spring of 1977, yet another group, the "B3LA Commission" or "Nordbeck Commission," was formed to look deeper into the issue of aircraft alternatives. This commission, headed by Undersecretary of State for Defense Gunnar Nordbeck, included representatives from the ministries of defense and budget, from the armed services, and from the defense industry. This group was to examine the alternatives and consequences of funding and to recommend an aircraft to be funded in the 1978-79 budget. Again, in the context of a Swedish economy in decline, parliament postponed decision.[101]

Yet another commission, referred to earlier, was formed in 1978 to restudy the issue, examining this time the consequences for the Swedish Air Force and the aircraft industry of a decision *not* to fund a Swedish-manufactured follow-on to the Viggen. This group, the "Air Industry Commission," submitted its report to the Ministry of Defense in October, 1978.[102]

Theoretically, this study of the B3LA would be available in mid-October 1978, to be used in finalizing the defense request for the budget bill to be submitted to parliament in January 1979; but this was not to be. The fundamental conclusions of the Air Industry Commission report were that the costs of alternative systems over the long-run were not significantly different and that, although the major aircraft corporations could absorb some of the impact of not producing a new fighter aircraft in Sweden, there would be significant adverse consequences for the Swedish aircraft industry.

A month before the Air Industry Commission Report was released, one of Prime Minister Fälldin's last moves prior to stepping down was to instruct Defense Minister Kronmark to find a less expensive alternative to the B3LA. Kronmark directed FMV to study such an alternative. Thus, even before the Air Industry Commission report had been submitted, the search for a new aircraft with essentially the same capabilities as the B3LA at a lower cost had begun; the new aircraft was the SK38/A38.[103]

The Politics of Choice

The second "wait and see" decision by parliament was a bit more than that. On April 25, 1978 the parliament approved a $7.1 million appropriation for the B3LA project,[104] or at least for pursuing R&D on alternative aircraft. However on May 30, 1978 the socialist, antidefense Stockholm daily *Aftonbladet* printed the story, "B3LA: Secret Contract Between Government and Saab." Allegedly, Minister of Defense Kronmark had, without consulting the Parliamentary Defense Committee, come to a secret understanding with Saab-Scania's chairman, Marcus Wallenberg, for contracts to be placed for a total of 119 pursuit Viggens (JA37) between 1978 and 1980. The price of those Viggens allegedly hinged on whether Saab were contracted to build the B3LA; if not, the Viggen price would be $10.7 million higher.

The reaction was immediate. The Social Democrats picked up on the story: "We have been deceived. The government should put its cards on the table concerning Wallenberg's and the defense minister's secret contract" demanded Social Democrat Maj-Britt Theorin in parliament.[105] On June 2, the prime minister confirmed in parliamentary hearings that such an agreement had been signed.[106] The minister of defense replied angrily that the leaked information was a security violation and that the offender should be punished.[107] Beneath the surface of this now-critical popular issue lay longer-term interests developed by competing factions.

The Social Democrats. The Social Democratic minorities in the various committees formed to consider the B3LA had consistently opposed the project and the increased defense budget expenditures involved. Their party leader, former prime minister Olof Palme, was especially irritated by the fact that the SDs had not been selected to participate on the Nordbeck B3LA Commission, despite the argument used by Prime Minister Fälldin that this group had not been politically composed.[108] The Social Democrats took the position that if the Fälldin government decided to go with the B3LA, the SDs would cancel the project if they returned to power in the fall 1979 elections. They knew that they were not without important support because the supreme commander, Stig Synnergren (an SD) had protested in writing against the nature of the government's negotiations with Saab-Scania linking Viggen 37 prices to future B3LA contracts.[109] The *Aftonbladet* expressed surprise on May 30, 1978 that the B3LA affair seemed to have a rapid momentum of its own and that flexibility for decision appeared to be diminishing rapidly.

The Armed Services: Conflict Over Roles and Missions. There are fundamental, now almost traditional, differences between the ways in which the Swedish armed forces view defense requirements. More than 85 percent of all Swedish commissioned officers of all services have supported the Conservative party and only 3.9 percent support the Social Democratic party.[110] However, army officers appear to be more inclined toward the philosophy of the Social Democrats, which is more traditional and more egalitarian. In fact, SD officers appear to be more typically Swedish. Navy and especially air force officers appear to be much more oriented toward the West and its technology, thus less traditional in outlook. The army is much more concerned with inner-directed territorial defense of Sweden. The air force and the navy focus on perimeter defense of Sweden well beyond its shores. These general predispositions have had significant influence on the stands the various services take on the alternatives to the follow-on to Viggen 37.

The army territorial defense advocates argued that:

> Total defense must take the form of a defense with staying power. . . . Capacity for stubborn and enduring defense is more important than great initial strength. . . .
>
> Military defense . . . should in the future continue to be built up so that in all essential respects it will be balanced and will make defense in depth possible with a concentration of forces on frontiers and coasts. . . .
>
> Priorities should be allocated . . . in accordance with the principle that it is better to obtain a larger number of technically less advanced weapons systems than a few technically advanced ones.[111]

Territorial defense, thus defined, does not require long-range, technologically sophisticated aircraft capable of striking an attacker at sea well beyond the Swedish coastline. Rather, weapons systems should be reoriented toward close support of ground units. The army, and especially the army commander-in-chief, General Nils Sköld, was aware that ever-higher costs of aircraft technology at a time of declining defense budgets and increasing manpower costs probably would result in diminished funding for army programs.

In 1978 interservice rivalry was intense.[112] The army fought to preserve the conscription system and reservist refresher training; to acquire funding for attack helicopters and surface-to-surface conventional missiles to attack tanks, armored personnel carriers, and troop concentrations; to modernize ground force weapons; and to arm aircraft then in the inventory (Saab 105 aircraft) for the close air support role.

This emphasis placed the army at odds with the air force and navy, both of whom argued for the importance of a strategy based on attacking ". . . the enemy's invasion units during the most vulnerable phase: the sea crossing."[113] The argument was for a "high-low" mix of attack aircraft in which the A20 stood for the high (expensive, technologically sophisticated, high altitude, supersonic) and B3LA or A38 for the low (relatively inexpensive, low altitude, subsonic).[114] Both air force and navy, but especially the former, were concerned that postponement of the aircraft decision would lead in the 1990s to an obsolete Viggen 37 and SK60 (modified Saab 105) air force with consequent high maintenance costs and flying hazards.[115] The air force and the navy found sympathy with those more technologically oriented in the Defense Materiel Administration and Defense Research Institute. A major problem for all the services was that budget appeared to be driving strategy. Strategy cannot be developed in the abstract but must consider current and projected force structures. Strategy without the weapons systems to carry it out is irrelevant at best.

The Defense Industry. The defense industrialists are Swedes interested in Swedish security; they are also businessmen interested in making a profit and preserving the future health and vitality of their corporations. Saab-Scania was representative in pushing for a quick decision on Swedish production of the new fighter or the A20. Saab's management argued that the costs could be kept reasonable because the B3LA or A38 would involve lighter materials and reduced size and complexity of electronic equipment. The industry arguments relied on the defense staff formula of "Effect plus survival equals efficiency in war" and cited added benefits of the new fighter for all the services, including its use as a support weapon for the army.[116] The position used as the bottom line in pressing for a favorable decision on the new aircraft was that "If the . . . project does not go through, the aircraft industry in Sweden will collapse and as many as 12,000 people could lose their jobs."[117] Despite the degree of validity of the Saab-Scania argument, the ardent defense critics countered that:

> The management at Saab has always known how to conduct extortion against the State. The most effective threat for ensuring continued orders has been to propose the closing down of the largest metal industry in Linköping.

The Saab directors themselves have also gone to the ministries, though as long as there was a Social Democratic government it was just as effective to work on the unions and utilize their access to government offices. Then the directors would also refer arrogantly to the workers' initiative.[118]

The Trade Unions. The potential impact of aircraft decisions upon the aircraft industry certainly is not lost on the major trade unions. The future of defense production for Saab-Scania, Volvo Flygmotor and L.M. Ericsson involves large numbers of employees. It makes a difference to the two major unions representing white-collar workers in R&D jobs (TCO and SACO) and the major union representing blue-collar workers concentrated in production jobs (LO) what kind of decisions are made. Unions rely on their parties to represent their views in the government. If the A20 were adopted alone, then much less R&D employment would be required. If the decision were made to purchase new aircraft abroad, both R&D and production jobs would be lost. In the event of the latter, some suggested retraining for employment in industries producing civilian manufactures. But this was not a viable solution for the unions which preferred the status quo and asked for examples of growing industry in the civilian sector which could train and absorb, for example, the 5000 people employed by Saab in Linköping. The unions had representatives on the Air Industry Commission, one each from LO, TCO and SACO. The representative from LO was a Social Democrat, the TCO representative (from Saab) was a Conservative, and the SACO representative leaned toward the Social Democrats. Any decision by the government must come to grips with union pressures through their political parties. In 1978 and 1979, the unions made these concerns very clear and their representatives argued predictably. In September 1978 the TCO representative Ben Ottoson (union chairman at Saab-Scania and a Moderate) insisted that adoption of the A20 would be disastrous for white-collar employment at Saab-Scania and Volvo Flygmotor, arguing that employment analysis by the defense ministry was one-sided.[119] At least from the unions' perspective, the best decision would have been the "high-low mix" the air force and navy advocated—the best of all worlds for both white- and blue-collar workers. In fact, over the not-too-long run, more technicians could be hired because the average age of the labor force was relatively old, over fifty in the case of Saab's technicians.[120]

Public Opinion. The general lack of knowledge concerning defense matters on the part of the Swedish public could only be made worse by what they may have read or seen on television about the B3LA/A38 controversy. Newspaper articles from 1976 through mid-1979 were confusing at best in portraying the issues involved. The costs involved were variously estimated; the B3LA was reported as a "go" and a "no-go"; *the* final decision was reported repeatedly as just over the horizon and the impacts of alternative decisions were reported in contracdictory ways. It is safe to say that there was no public consensus in Sweden for or against a B3LA/A38 or A20 or a program including both. One might hypothesize that this was an acceptable state of affairs for the government, permitting relative freedom of choice, and certainly better than a public consensus against a program the government might prefer.

The Government. Either the government spokespeople were inconsistent in their statements on the new aircraft or they were variously misinterpreted in press reports. Prime Minister Fälldin was reported as both for and against the program.[121] Minister of Defense Kronmark lent support to various alternative proposals, from Swedish manufacture of the B3LA to collaborative programs with Italy or Switzerland.[122]

Prior to the fall of Prime Minister Fälldin's Center party coalition on October 5, 1978, Kronmark was quite specific in stating the following about the aircraft decision:[123]

1. No one in the government had opposed the B3LA.
2. The only real skeptics were a number of younger Center party men and (even fewer) Liberal party people.
3. The program (presumably a high-low mix of A20 and B3LA) was costing 400 million Swedish kronor ($9.7 million) of which industry would pay 100 million kronor ($2.4 million) for fiscal year 1978.
4. The decision could not be postponed for another year for reasons of expense and long-term national security.
5. The problem of finding jobs for a couple of thousand displaced qualified technicians would be manageable.

Despite the vocal opposition of the Social Democrats and Prime Minister Fälldin's insistence that the aircraft decision would have to be founded upon broad political unity, Kronmark took the position in the summer of 1978 that the government had "confidence in the Defense Materiel Administration and aircraft industry people"[124] and that Prime Minister Fälldin would decide in favor of the B3LA without the cooperation of the Social Democrats if the basis for the project were sound.

However, the new minority government of Liberal party leader Ola Ullsten, with the weakest parliamentary support since 1936, did not have such confidence. Caught between strong SD advocacy of the A20 and Moderate party advocacy of the B3LA, by November 1978 the new defense minister, Lars de Geer, and his undersecretary, Gunnar Petri, saw the SK38/A38 alternative as a possibly attractive compromise. De Geer announced in the parliament on November 20, 1978 that the B3LA was no longer being considered.[125] By mid-December Prime Minister Ullsten had established two new aircraft committees. One was a parliamentary committee, with a Social Democrat as chairman, to study the employment situation and production alternatives in the Linköping region. The other was a committee under Supreme Commander Lennart Ljung to compare the operational and cost aspects of the A38 and A20 projects.[126] Appointment of the latter committee caused serious political conflict both within and outside the ministry of defense.

In late November, the director of the ministry's Materiel Section, Ingemar Engman, a known supporter of the Social Democrats' proposals for a guerrilla-type defense organization (and hence less spending on sophisticated and expensive weapons systems), went outside his line of authority to write and publish a letter to the supreme commander in which he indicted both the A38 alternative and the means by which the proposal for it was made. He cited the impropriety of FMV in forwarding the proposal directly to the government, rather than the supreme commander; he pointed to alleged inadequacies in the FMV analysis of the A38; he asserted that the A38 was a B3LA in disguise; he claimed that, because the A38 engine would be manufactured in the United States, the Volvo Flygmotor plant at Arboga would be closed down, and he joined in the Social Democrats' argument that a plane-for-plane comparison clearly favored the A20 over the B3LA or A38.[127] An FMV spokesman, Air Force Lieutenant Colonel Sven Hökborg, who was also the project officer for the B3LA and A38, quickly denied that either engine alternative (British or U.S. GE404) would be built abroad.[128]

The unions were quick to make their views known. As an indication of the issue's devisiveness, one element of the unions broke ranks with its own party. Ingvar Fahlsten, union chairman at the Saab Aircraft Division (largely a Social Democratic trade union) insisted that an A20 decision would be disastrous for white-collar employment in development work at Saab.[129] On the other hand, Olof Palme reiterated the Social Democrats' unanimous and irrevocable rejection of the B3LA and all its variants.[130]

By late December 1978, the supreme commander was committed to providing a February 1979 comparison of the A38 and A20 alternatives. Early on, he went on record stating that his report would take the form of a perspective plan to the year 2000; that negotiations with industry would be of decisive importance to his study; and that neither the A20 nor the A38 would be built in previously planned numbers within the present budget.[131]

Although there was mounting pressure from all quarters in early 1979 for an immediate decision on the next generation of fighter aircraft, and although the A38 option appeared to be a happy compromise, there appeared to be also increasingly sound reasons why the Ullsten government might find it politically prudent to stall the decision even further.

Given the weak parliamentary support of the Liberal party coalition, a major decision either way—to adopt the A38 alternative or to reject all alternatives—could have constituted in early 1979 a major election issue. This, in combination with other issues, would guarantee a Social Democratic victory in the fall 1979 elections.

How could a major decision be avoided? In theory at least, if a decision maker knows that the best case (a consensus in favor of a preferred policy position) is not possible, and if the decision maker wishes to avoid the worst case (a consensus against the preferred policy), there is a short-term option. That option is to fragment public opinion so that there is no consensus either way. How could this be accomplished in the case of the fighter aircraft controversy? Clearly, outright denial of a follow-on to Viggen would have had high political costs with FMV, FOA, the defense industry, some of the unions, the air force, and the navy. On the other hand, adoption of a high-low aircraft mix would have carried high political costs with opposition parties, the army, and with Sweden's pacifist groups. But there was a middle way which at least had the appearance of being a compromise. On February 24, 1979, *Svenska Dagbladet* reported the government's proposals:[132]

1. Discontinue the development work on the SK38/A38, formerly known as the B3LA.
2. Develop further the pursuit version of the Viggen and give it attack capacity.
3. Purchase a light armed trainer, simpler and cheaper than the A38.
4. Appoint the supreme commander to study these alternatives (aircraft committee number 12).
5. Increase work in the space industry field.
6. Set up an industrial fund of 300 million kronor to facilitate a changeover to civilian production.
7. Start work on heavy missiles.
8. Examine the scope for collaboration with other countries in the future.

By the time of these proposals, the defense community itself was fragmenting rapidly over the fighter aircraft issue. The head of the FMV, General Ove Ljung, criticized the supreme commander, General Lennart Ljung, for his economic analysis which permitted the government to equivocate on the fighter decision. The air force commander-in-chief, General Dick Stenberg, was also critical of the supreme commander's position.[133] Olof Palme abruptly summoned a press conference and indicated that the trainer aircraft alternative might be acceptable to the Social Democrats.[134] In the wake of the government's decisions, the chairman of the four trade unions at Saab-Scania and Volvo Flygmotor demanded employment guarantees for all employees in the aircraft industry.[135] Former supreme commander Stig Synnergren was reported to support a variant of the trainer alternative.[136] Former foreign minister Karin Söder was reported in March 1979 to have summed up the developing situation aptly:

Karin Söder considers that since there is no longer any proper agreement on the aircraft question, the Defense Committee should be able to study the question of what attack aircraft Sweden should have in the future.[137]

Given the conspicuous fragmentation of public opinion, interservice rivalry, and the divided views within and among the defense community and defense industry, it was difficult to envision the fighter aircraft question as a major issue in the fall 1979 elections. It was equally hard to believe that the fighter aircraft controversy had lost momentum. The government's decision to develop the J37 pursuit version of the Viggen with an attack capability was complicated in the spring of 1979 by U.S. policies on arms exports. Specifically, the United States prohibited the sale to Sweden of the AIM-9L Sidewinder advanced infrared missile which was to have been the major step in giving the J37 an attack capability.[138]

The Final Alternative: The JAS

In the federal election of 1979, the Social Democrats regained much of the ground lost in 1976. However, the nonsocialist parties were still able to build a majority coalition with 175 seats, but only by a one-seat margin.

The aircraft debate was still far from being resolved and various alternatives to the A38 emerged in the latter part of the year. For lack of a better domestic alternative, the nonsocialists were primarily in favor of purchasing the F-16 from the United States, while the socialists favored more research into a defense focusing on land-based air defense missiles coupled with extended production of a modified Viggen.

Nevertheless, the concept of a combined trainer/light-attack aircraft was not abandoned. The air force was determined to make its case for a plane that could fly low and operate independent of large permanent bases. In January, 1980 the air force commander-in-chief, Dick Stenberg, proposed that the government consider a new plane, the SK2, which was calculated to be 25 percent cheaper than the A38/SK38 and estimated to have fewer drawbacks than other alternatives. The air force pointed out that the other proposals calling for a modified Viggen and a missile-oriented defense would require extended use of the old J35 Draken. Furthermore, they argued that missiles could not be fully effective unless they could also be fired from aircraft.[139] In the short run the SK2 appeared to be a legitimate alternative but its future effectiveness was uncertain.

While the armed forces debated the relative feasibility of the SK2, Saab-Scania revealed a plan to develop a plane that would be based on the combined capabilities of the Viggen, the Draken, and the F-16. Saab's management realized the importance of concentrating resources on a system containing modern technology and requiring lower costs. This new system would involve a manufacturing plan that would take advantage of foreign cooperation and the use of ready-made components. The new plane would weigh only 50–60 percent of the Viggen and would cost about 40 percent less, an absolute necessity given the decreasing defense budget.[140]

Support for Saab's all-purpose aircraft, the JAS (Swedish acronym for fighter, bomber, and reconnaisance), gained momentum rapidly as Supreme Commander Lennart Ljung rejected the SK2, claiming that it would have shortcomings in the probable defense environment of the 1990s. Ljung instead supported proposals for the all-purpose JAS plane; the advantage being that the new system could use information from R&D on the earlier light attack aircraft proposals and, at the same time, stay abreast of new developments in the aeronautics field. According to development personnel at Saab, the JAS would be an excellent base for modifications made over a long period of time.[141] Another factor that supported the case for the JAS was Sweden's perception of the air threat that was beginning to include consideration of cruise missiles in the north.

Carl Bildt, a member of parliament and former undersecretary of state for planning and coordination, maintained that the air force needed an aircraft capable of intercepting low-flying systems, including cruise missiles. He argued that a missile defense system would be highly inadequate due to high costs and lack of mobility.[142] Gunnar Jerves pointed out in a January 1980 article in *Svenska Dagbladet* that Sweden's geostrategic position becomes more vulnerable in an environment dominated by cruise missiles. According to Jerves, NATO has a number of incentives to use cruise missiles to strike targets located in the Soviet Union. Many of these targets are best reached by trajectories crossing Swedish airspace. A combination of valuable targets and comparatively weak Soviet radar render the north a lucrative azimuth of attack. In addition to the NATO problem, it is likely that the Soviets would respond by moving radar stations into forward positions. In time of war this would mean using Finland or even Sweden for this purpose.[143]

Political and Economic Constraints. Given the numerous logistical benefits of the JAS, it appeared to be the perfect system to satisfy the multiple needs of the air force. Nevertheless, much would have to be settled before a decision on the aircraft could be reached in the parliament. The Social Democrats agreed to Supreme Commander Lennart Ljung's proposal on the JAS, emphasizing that much research work was needed so that the Defense Committee could make a recommendation by February 1981.[144] The government agreed to grant Skr 200 million to Saab so that they could evaluate the feasibility of purchasing parts abroad. At this juncture, it appeared that SD support for the JAS would be crucial given the slim majority held by the nonsocialists. Furthermore, because of extensive union support of the SDs in the aircraft industries, the problem of compensation for diminishing R&D work would have to be resolved. Saab estimated that as much as half of its R&D staff would have to be cut if the JAS were adopted.[145]

Typical of the uncertain and fragile nature of decisions relating to weapons systems costing large amounts of money, the government was forced to accept an Skr 500 million setback when a member of its nonsocialist coalition, Moderate Per Unckel, failed to appear for a crucial vote on funding for JAS research.[146] (He was taking his daughter to a day-care center and forgot that the vote was to be taken.) This incident emphasized the importance of acquiring a consensus concerning the acquisition of the JAS. The likelihood of the 1982 defense resolution being adopted without bipartisan support was extremely small.

Three possible procurement methods were studied in detail: first, a licensing arrangement whereby an aircraft could be produced in Sweden; second, an arrangement whereby an aircraft could be produced in Sweden using a large amount of foreign components; and third, an agreement to purchase the F16 from the United States. Of the three, the most desirable method was to build the aircraft in Sweden relying on a large percentage of foreign components. This was considered to be the most flexible approach for the government as it allowed greater leeway in scheduling and production. The other two alternatives relied on commitments to foreign contractors either in the form of a purchase agreement or a licensing arrangement to assemble the aircraft in Sweden.[147]

Regardless of the recommendations from the working group, the aircraft decision inevitably would become intertwined with the 1982 Defense Resolution. Hence, it was extremely important that the Fälldin government adopt a spending alternative that would provide enough funding for the initial stages of JAS development.[148] The estimated Skr 19 billion available for the aircraft until the year 2000 would be divided in the following manner:[149]

1980–85:	1.6 billion
1985–90:	4.7 billion
1990–95:	6.7 billion
1995–2000	6.2 billion

The two alternatives offered to the Fälldin government for the 1982–87 Defense Resolution called for Skr 65 billion and 71.5 billion ($1 = 7.6 Skr in 1982), the former being the proposal of the Social Democrats, the latter being that of the nonsocialists. In June, 1980 Lennart Ljung argued that both proposals were inadequate. Instead, he advocated an Skr 3 billion defense increase for a total budget of 74.5 billion. He claimed that only under this spending plan could the conscript system be saved without sacrificing the initial development phase of the JAS. Nevertheless, he still estimated that three regiments would have to be eliminated by 1982.[150]

In order to facilitate widescale agreement on the particulars behind production, the JAS industrial group was formed in 1980 and charged with the responsibility of putting together a firm offer for the aircraft's contract.[151] The Swedish newspaper *Dagens Nyheter* claimed that if the plane could not be manufactured in Sweden there was a possibility that as many as 6,000 jobs within the JAS industrial group could be lost.

The JAS Debate. In the fall of 1981 the next big obstacle to the adoption of the JAS system emerged. Army Commander-in-Chief Nils Sköld, who previously had endorsed the production of the JAS, began to express skepticism concerning the ability to modify the JAS given higher future performance standards. Meanwhile, Defense Committee Chairman Gunnar Björk called for "sound political unanimity" for the backing of the project. If Sköld continued to show reluctance to support the JAS, then the Defense Committee would not be able to recommend the project. In this case the Social Democrats would be certain to reject it in a parliamentary vote.[152]

The result of the debate was that the supreme commander backed production of the JAS with reservations, emphasizing that it was important for the Defense Committee to reach a consensus by December 1, 1981. The supreme commander's reservations centered on the uncertain projection that the plane would cost Skr 25 billion to produce by the year 2000. In addition, he showed much skepticism about the plane's effectiveness over the long run.[153] General Sköld had emphasized the drawbacks of the GE404 engine which left little room for modifications and would probably call for design changes as early as 1990.[154] Nevertheless, Ljung stipulated that despite the divergent viewpoints of the army commander-in-chief, a decision on the JAS had to be reached. The essentials of the report he submitted to the defense minister, Torsten Gustafson, on October 15, 1981 were:

1. A decision should be reached in 1982;
2. Deliveries of the JAS should replace the Viggen beginning in 1992;
3. The cost for acquiring 240–350 aircraft should not exceed Skr 25 billion.[155]

By early 1982, the survival of the JAS appeared to be in great jeopardy. In keeping with their intention to include the JAS decision in the 1982–87 Defense Resolution, the nonsocialists pressed the Social Democrats for a decision. Since a political consensus was imperative given the long-term significance of the aircraft decision, the Fälldin government was reluctant to forward the resolution to the Riksdag without a prior commitment from the SDs. The difficulty lay in convincing the Social Democrats that jobs could be created in the civilian sector by defense industries despite the large amounts of capital set aside for the JAS.[156] On February 8, Olof Palme met with Thorbjörn Fälldin to acquire reassurance on the employment issue. He was particularly concerned whether the JAS could be provided for within the Social Democrat's financial framework. He called for an additional Skr 400 million to improve allowances for conscripted men. Fälldin reassured Palme on the financial question surrounding the JAS and guaranteed that the five industries involved in plane production would present civilian projects creating many new jobs. In accordance with this directive, Saab and Volvo moved parts of their truck and automobile production to Norrbotten creating five hundred new jobs.[157]

Fälldin's proposals proved to be enough to satisfy Palme and the Social Democrats that the JAS project would be a positive addition to Sweden's defense capability. Hence, the Riksdag voted overwhelmingly in June 1982 to adopt the JAS program, and on June 30 a contract for development and production of the first batch of JAS39 aircraft was signed with the industry group.[158] After twelve years of debate over a successor to the JA37 Viggen, the Swedish government finally had decided on a new system.[159]

Conclusion

Sweden continues to struggle to preserve its neutrality while simultaneously seeking to avoid increased vulnerability to changing world conditions. The solution lies in resolving the apparent dilemma between maintaining Sweden's traditional defense posture, anchored to a strong military deterrent, and a growing desire to keep military spending at a constant level, roughly 22.5 billion kronor for FY 1984/85 or 7 percent of the national budget.[160] In March 1984 the Government and three opposition parties (Moderate, Center, and Liberal) agreed on a three-year increase in the defense budget amounting to approximately Skr 600 million per year. By December 1984 that consensus appeared to be fragmenting as the government sought to curtail defense spending in the 1985/86 budget bill, based on excessively modest previous forecasts of inflation and the dollar exchange rate. Specifically, the government sought to curtail materiel procurement authorizations deemed vital by the supreme commander.[161] Increased costs might require the government to reduce the number of JAS aircraft it had originally planned to acquire (140) or else withdraw the Draken squadron as early as 1987. As Sven-Olof Hökborg, JAS project leader of FMV explained: "When aims and means no longer balance out, the politicians must be prepared to provide more money or else revise the aims. Otherwise there will be no stability in long-term projects like JAS."[162]

Hökborg's statement accurately describes the prevailing question in Swedish defense decision making: with less money available will Sweden be able to develop a legitimate military strategy or will it be forced to alter strategy to compensate for rising costs?

Given the politics of compromise in Sweden's parliamentary system, the government must guard itself against inaction on, or dilution of, major defense programs resulting from a lack of consensus on strategy. Given the evidence, few could doubt that there is a strong Swedish consensus on total defense in the abstract. However, largely missing from the public debates on the follow-on to Viggen over the past ten years has been the critical question of defense strategy. The role of strategy is to transform the total capabilities of a state into instruments of policy. In its simplest form, strategy must tell defense planners what kinds of capabilities they must create and convince the parliament and public alike what levels of defense spending are required. The absence of a clear statement of Swedish defense strategy goes far to explain the tortuous path to the long-overdue decision on the follow-on aircraft to the Viggen 37.

The decision to proceed with the follow-on aircraft to the Viggen was a necessary step in preserving the deterrent capability of the Swedish defense system. However, the issues and events surrounding the decision must be viewed in the context of Sweden's decreasing ability to pursue a foreign policy of neutrality based on a clear strategy supported by a strong total defense without larger defense spending outlays. There is much at stake:

1. The future of an independent Swedish aircraft industry, "the very source of pride of the technostructure," as Ingemar Dörfer has stated.
2. The future direction of Swedish nonalignment, to the extent that strategy is affected by the sources of acquisition for major weapons systems.
3. The viability of Sweden's military manpower system required to support total defense.
4. The future of the Nordic balance.

Notes

1. Ingemar Dörfer, *System 37 Viggen: Arms, Technology and the Domestication of Glory* (Oslo: Scandinavian University Books, 1973), 13–14.
2. "Swedish Industry," *Fact Sheets on Sweden* (Stockholm: The Swedish Institute, 1983), 3.

3. "Sweden, Time for a Cull," *The Economist,* October 6, 1984, 17.

4. Nils Andrén, *The Future of the Nordic Balance* (Stockholm: Ministry of Defense, Secretariat for National Security Policy and Long-Range Defense Planning (hereafter SSLP), 1977), 85. For further background, see Johan Jørgen Holst, *Five Roads to Nordic Security* (Oslo: University Press, 1973), 208–12.

5. Olof Palme, Speech on foreign policy and national security, to the Swedish Social Democratic party, September 17, 1984.

6. See ÖB *1984–1989* (Stockholm: Ministry of Defense), 24–26, 36–39.

7. Olof Palme, "Security and Stability in the Nordic Area," a speech to the Paasikivi Society (Helsinki: June 1983), 8.

8. *The Future of the Nordic Balance,* 94.

9. Ingemar Dörfer, "The Nordic Balance in Perspective: Sweden," a paper prepared for the seminar on International Security Problems in the Nordic Area, Georgetown Center for Strategic and International Studies, June 15–16, 1978, 7–23.

10. "Swedish Defense System," *Fact Sheets on Sweden* (Stockholm: The Swedish Institute, 1983), 1. Shows full-time salaried officers plus conscripts in one year.

11. "The Swedish Army," produced by the Information Department of the Army Staff and the Defense Forces' Center for Educational Aids (Stockholm: 1983), 7.

12. *The Military Balance 1984–1985* (London: International Institute for Strategic Studies, 1984), 54.

13. Ibid., 54.

14. Ibid., 54.

15. "Sweden, Time for a Cull," 4.

16. William J. Taylor, Jr., "Issues in Military Unionization," in *Blue Collar Soldiers?* Alan Ned Sabronsky, ed. (Philadelphia: Foreign Policy Research Institute, 1977), 24; and William J. Taylor, Jr., "Military Unions for the U.S.: The Irrelevance of the European Experience," in *Naval War College Review* (Winter, 1978), 85–86.

17. An objective assessment needs to be made, however. It appears that assessments of Swedish capabilities by military planners in some NATO nations are both impressionistic and overly optimistic.

18. See John Erickson, "The Northern Theater: Soviet Capabilities and Concepts," *Strategies Review,* vol. IV, No. 3 (Summer 1976), 70–72; *Aviation Week and Space Technology,* May 15, 1978, 16; and Nils Ørvik, "Scandinavian Military Doctrines," in *Comparative Defense Policy,* Frank B. Horton III, Anthony C. Rogerson, and Eduard L. Warner III, eds. (Baltimore: Johns Hopkins University Press, 1974), 265–67.

19. See "New Economy Demands on Defense," *Svenska Dagbladet,* December 12, 1984. Also see *The Swedish Economy: Facts and Figures 1984* (Stockholm: Swedish Institute, May 1984).

20. Figures obtained from Swedish air attaché to the United States, General Hans Neij, in a conversation on Swedish defense.

21. *System 37 Viggen,* 30.

22. Ibid., 28–30.

23. David A. Brown, "Budget Cuts Could Affect Sweden's JAS," *Aviation Week and Space Technology* (December 12, 1983), 74.

24. "Close Up Sweden," *Military Technology,* Vol. VII, 1983, 5.
25. Based on an interview in the Swedish Ministry of Defense, June 28, 1978. Also see Pierre Vinde and Gunnar Petri, *Swedish Government Administration* (Stockholm: The Swedish Institute, 1978), 36.
26. Ibid., 13–14. Also from interviews with representatives from the Swedish Parliamentary Defense Committee and Committee on Foreign Affairs, July 5, 1978.
27. Ibid., 32–33.
28. *The Swedish Total Defense* (Stockholm: The Total Defense Information Committee, undated), 14.
29. Interview with air attache, Gen. Hans Neij, 1984.
30. Sven Hellman, "Use of International-Security Studies," in *Trends in Planning,* C.G. Jennergren, Stephen Schwartz, and Olov Alvfeldt, eds. (Stockholm: Swedish National Defense Research Institute, 1977), 95–96, and *System 37 Viggen,* 95–96.
31. Notes from interview with Swedish Defense Planning Staff member, June 16, 1978.
32. See "Operations and Systems Analysis: A Special Issue in English on a Series of Surveys," published by the Research Institute of National Defense (FOA) (Stockholm: National Defense Research Institute, 1969), 9–10; and "FOA in a Nutshell" (Stockholm: National Defense Research Institute, 1978), 1–2.
33. *Research in Sweden* (Stockholm: Ministry of Education and Cultural Affairs, 1982), 14.
34. Carl Gustav Jennergren, "The Planning Division of FOA, Its Development and Role," in *Trends in Planning,* Jennergren, Schwarz, and Alvfeldt, eds. 19–23.
35. Försvarets Forskningsanstalt, (National Defense Research Institute), Central Planning and Administration, (Stockholm). Figures for FY 1984–1985 were provided in response to a letter requesting budget information.
36. "Close up Sweden," 29.
37. Ibid., 22–28.
38. The terms "committees" and "commissions" are used interchangeably in Sweden. Where this paper refers to Defense Committee, the reference is the Standing Parliamentary Defense Committee.
39. *Swedish Government Administration,* 24–25.
40. *Sweden's Total Defense 1982–1987* (Stockholm: Ministry of Defene, 1981), 1–2. A summary of the final report by the 1978 Parliamentary Committee on Defense, November 1981.
41. Based on interview with Swedish Ministry of Defense, June 16 and July 3, 1978, and with Ministry of Economic Affairs, June 26, 1978.
42. *The Military Balance,* 1984–1985, 54.
43. "Close up Sweden," 3, and *Swedish Industry,* 2.
44. *Economic Surveys, 1983–1984* (Washington, D.C.: Organization for Economic Cooperation and Development, February 1984).
45. *Swedish Industry,* 1.
46. *Research in Sweden,* 8–9.
47. "Labor Relations in Sweden," *Fact Sheets on Sweden* (Stockholm: Swedish Institute, 1984), 2.

48. *System 37 Viggen,* 21.
49. Interview in the Swedish Ministry of Foreign Affairs, June 27, 1978.
50. "The Nordic Balance in Perspective: Sweden," 19.
51. *Swedish Digest,* No. 31, August 15, 1978, 2.
52. *Encouraging Debate About Defense Policy* (Stockholm: Ministry of Defense Report No. 1980), a translation by Brigadier General Nils-Fredric Haegerstrom, 7–10.
53. Interview with Sven Hendrickson, Ministry of Education, Stockholm, Sweden, June 13, 1980.
54. *The Earth is Hardly a Peaceful Place* (Stockholm: Total Defense Information Committee, 1980), 3.
55. Ibid.
56. "Beredskapsnämnden för Psykologiskt Försvar" (National Psychological Defense Planning Committee), hereafter "BN", August 28, 1984.
57. BN, *Opinion 83,* 30.
58. Ibid., 32.
59. Ibid., 35.
60. Ibid., 23.
61. Ibid., 45, citing results published in the Norwegian journal *Førsvarets Forum,* No. 22, October 31, 1983, 13.
62. Ibid., 60.
63. Ibid., 48.
64. Ibid., 49.
65. Ibid., 57.
66. Ibid., 53.
67. Ibid., 55.
68. *The Washington Post,* October 6, 1978, A22.
69. "Sweden's Foreign Trade," *Fact Sheets on Sweden* (Stockholm: The Swedish Institute, 1983), 3.
70. From interview in Ministry of Foreign Affairs, June 27, 1978; also see extract from Swedish Government Proposition 1971: 146, establishing the 1971 Principles on Arms Transfers. For a discussion of the implications for Swedish neutrality, see Björn Hagelin, "The Margins of Security: Politics and Economics in Sweden," *Policy Sciences* (Amsterdam: Elsevier Publishing Company, 1978) Vol. 9, 217–19.
71. "Close Up Sweden," 2–5. Interview with Defense Minister Anders Thunborg.
72. Katarina Brodin, *Surprise Attack Problems and Issues* (Stockholm: SSLP, 1973), 15–16; North Atlantic Assembly, "Defense of the Northern Flank," November 1972, 39, and Thorbjörn Fälldin, *Swedish Security Policy* (Stockholm: Ministry of Foreign Affairs, Press and Information Department, 1978), 2.
73. Tomas Ries, *The Nordic Dilemma in the 80s: Maintaining Regional Stability Under New Strategic Conditions,* PSIS Occasional Papers, November 1 (Geneva: Graduate Institute of International Studies, 1982), Appendix H.
74. Arthur E. Dewey, "The Nordic Balance," *Strategic Review,* Vol. IV, No. 4 (Fall 1976), 7–8.
75. John Erikson, "The Northern Theater," *Strategic Review,* Vol. IV, No. 3 (Summer 1976), 8. See also 76, 79 on the place of Sweden in probable Soviet calculation.

76. Nils Andrén, *The Security and Defense of Sweden* (Stockholm: National Defense Research Institute, 1976), 79, and Ørvik, "Scandinavian Military Doctrines," 265–66.
77. Erickson, "The Northern Theater," 70.
78. Ørvik, "Scandinavian Military Doctrines," 266.
79. For example, see the denial at a meeting of the Swedish Institute of Foreign Affairs reported in *Svenska Dagbladet,* May 4, 1977.
80. Dörfer, *System 37 Viggen,* 17–18.
81. Merton J. Peck and Frederick M. Scherer, *The Weapons Acquisition Process: An Economic Analysis* (Boston: Harvard Graduate School of Business Administration, 1962), 24, quoted in Dörfer, *System 37 Viggen,* 17–18.
82. See interview with Carl-Olof Ternryd, general director of FMV, in *Military Technology,* 27.
83. *Swedish Digest,* No. 30, August 8, 1978, 1.
84. "The Dollar Exchange Rate and JAS Armament," *Svenska Dagbladet,* December 7, 1983.
85. From interview in Defense Materiel Administration, June 22, 1978. Some air force officers are almost paranoid about the politics they suspect the army commander-in-chief might be playing to block the B3LA or A20 in order to get support and funding for attack helicopters.
86. The Air Industry Committee should yield some sound estimates of the impact on civilian technicians.
87. *The Swedish Economy, Facts and Figures 1984* (Stockholm: The Swedish Institute, 1984), 10, 19, 22, 31.
88. Dörfer, "The Nordic Balance in Perspective: Sweden," 6.
89. *The Swedish Budget 1984–85* (Stockholm: A summary published by the Ministry of Finance, 1984), 76. This table shows the summary of appropriations for defense as it appears in the publication.
90. *Facts About Civil Defense* (Falköping: Information Department of Civil Defense Administration, 1984), 14–15.
91. *The Swedish Budget,* 75.
92. Unofficial translation of a speech by Prime Minister Olof Palme to the Congress of Foreign Policy and National Security, September 17, 1984.
93. Brita Schwarz, "Programme Budgeting and/or Long Range Planning," in Jennergren, Schwarz, and Alvfeldt, eds., *Trends in Planning,* 41.
94. *The Defense Planning System: Planning and Planning Documents* (Stockholm: SSLP, 1970), 13–14. For a précis of the perspective plans developed in 1969, see *Svenska Dagbladet,* May 7, 1979.
95. Hellman, "On the Use and Usefulness of International Security Studies," 101–03, and Schwarz, "Programme Budgeting and/or Long-Range Planning," 46.
96. *The Defense Planning System: Planning and Planning Documents,* 17–19.
97. Ibid., 19. Some suggest that the assumptions of the present conscript system should be reexamined. See Dörfer, "The Nordic Balance in Perspective: Sweden," 16–18.
98. Figure from *The Swedish Parliament* (Stockholm: The Administrative Office of the Riksdag, 1978), 11.
99. For different estimates, see *Aftonbladet,* May 30, 1978 (the high figure) and *Dagens Nyheter,* June 1, 1978 (low figure).

100. From interview in the Swedish Defense Materiel Administration, June 22, 1978.
101. From interview in the Swedish Ministry of Economic Affairs, June 26, 1978.
102. *Dagens Nyheter,* July 2, 1978. Retired Army General Sten Wahlin, former director of the Defense Materiel Administration, was chairman of this committee. The committee was to report, not recommend.
103. See Nordbeck's statement in *Svenska Dagbladet,* November 16, 1978; also the statement of the FMV project officer (Sven Hökborg) for the B3LA and A38 in *Svenska Dagbladet,* November 7, 1978; and the statement of air force commander-in-chief Dick Stenberg, in *Dagens Nyheter,* December 5, 1978. All make the point that both the SK38/A38 and B3LA are based on the fundamental principles for light attack aircraft operational requirements approved by the supreme commander in the 1977 systems plans.
104. *Aftonbladet,* May 2, 1978.
105. *Aftonbladet,* June 3, 1978.
106. Ibid.
107. *Dagens Nyheter,* May 3, 1978.
108. See Olof Palme's statement in *Svenska Dagbladet,* October 19, 1977.
109. *Aftonbladet,* May 30 and June 3, 1978.
110. Annika Brickman, "Military Trade Unionism in Sweden," *Armed Forces and Society,* Vol. 2, No. 4 (Summer 1976), 537.
111. Quoted in Adam Roberts, *Nations in Arms: The Theory and Practice of Territorial Defense* (London: Praeger Publishers, 1976), 95.
112. *Defense and Foreign Affairs Digest,* Vol. VI, No. 10, October 1978, 47.
113. General Hans Neij, chief of the air force staff, quoted in *Svenska Dagbladet,* February 17, 1977.
114. Ibid.
115. Ibid.
116. Tore Gullstrand, head of Saab-Scania's Aeronautical Division, quoted in *Svenska Dagbladet,* April 24, 1977.
117. Ibid.
118. Maj Wechselman quoted in *Dagens Nyheter,* May 3, 1978.
119. See *Svenska Dagbladet,* September 19, 1978.
120. *Expressen,* September 9, 1977.
121. *Dagens Nyheter,* July 2, 1978.
122. Ibid.
123. Summarized from *Dagens Nyheter,* July 2, 1978.
124. Ibid.
125. *Svenska Dagbladet,* November 21, 1978.
126. Ibid., December 21 and 23, 1978.
127. *Dagens Nyheter,* November 28, 1978 and *Svenska Dagbladet,* November 29, 1978.
128. Ibid.
129. *Svenska Dagbladet,* December 18, 1978.
130. *Dagens Nyheter,* December 2, 1978.
131. *Svenska Dagbladet,* December 23, 1978.
132. Ibid., February 24, 1979.

133. Ibid., February 14 and 21, and May 8, 1979.
134. Ibid.
135. Ibid., March 20, 1979.
136. *Dagens Nyheter,* April 3, 1979.
137. *Svenska Dagbladet,* March 9, 1979.
138. Ibid., April 2, 1979.
139. *Dagens Nyheter,* January 10, 1980.
140. *Svenska Dagbladet,* January 13, 1980.
141. Ibid., January 27, 1980.
142. Ibid., January 31, 1980.
143. Ibid., January 20, 1980.
144. Ibid., February 6, 1980.
145. *Dagens Nyheter,* February 8, 1980.
146. *Svenska Dagbladet,* May 22, 1980.
147. Ibid., June 26, 1980.
148. *Dagens Nyheter,* February 6, 1980.
149. Ibid., February 2, 1980.
150. *Svenska Dagbladet,* June 11, 1980.
151. *The New Swedish JAS 39 Multi-Role Combat Aircraft,* pamphlet from the JAS Industry Group, Saab-Scania Aerospace Division, undated.
152. *Svenska Dagbladet,* October 12, 1981.
153. *Dagens Nyheter,* October 14, 1981.
154. Ibid., October 20, 1981.
155. *Svenska Dagbladet,* October 15, 1981.
156. Ibid., January 30, 1982.
157. Ibid., February 8, 1982.
158. JAS Industry Report on JAS 39, see note 153.
159. *Svenska Dagbladet,* February 8, 1982.
160. Ibid., December 7, 1984.
161. Ibid., December 7, 1983.
162. Ibid., December 7, 1983.

6
Comparative

Paul M. Cole

Recent events confirm that the security environment in the Nordic countries is undergoing fundamental changes that require the United States to reevaluate its policies toward what used to be known as Europe's "quiet corner." But as security planners, business leaders, politicians, and other analysts begin the process of reevaluation, they will discover that very few studies—American or European—address the critical issue of how Denmark, Iceland, Finland, Norway, and Sweden make defense and security decisions.

There are many indications that the United States, the Soviet Union, and their respective allies all have reasons to be concerned about developments in the Nordic nations. A list of current political-military issues that are cause for concern includes the following:

1. The growing Soviet military presence at Murmansk and on the Kola Peninsula;
2. Actual and potential North Sea oil resources;
3. The strategic and resource issues associated with the Spitsbergen Archipelago;
4. Soviet submarine activity, including special forces training (Spetznaz), in and around the Nordic countries;
5. The impact of emerging technology on the defense structure, particularly on the future of air defense, in the Nordic countries;
6. Technology transfers where Nordic nations are used as transit points in the West-to-East flow of high-tech goods; and
7. The sea boundaries between the Soviet Union and Nordic countries in the Barents and Baltic Seas.

This partial list indicates that the security system in the north is changing rapidly. Recommendations for U.S. policy changes that can accommodate these developments must be based on correct impressions of Nordic defense decision making, or they will probably fail. Policy changes must reflect also an understanding of how the Nordic nations perceive and react to the shifts that are occurring in the existing security system. Each Nordic nation is adjusting in its own way to the changes in the regional and global security environment. This chapter shows how these changes are similar and dissimilar, both in form and substance.

The Setting

What is the setting for defense decision making in the Nordic countries? What are the characteristics of the region and how are decisions and policy made?

By U.S. standards the Nordic nations are not considered large. The following table illustrates how each country fits into an American frame of reference:

Country	Population (1983)	U.S. Geographic Equivalent
Iceland	236,000	Kentucky
Finland	4,800,000	South Dakota and Nebraska combined
Denmark	5,100,000	Vermont and New Hampshire combined
Norway	4,100,000	New Mexico
Sweden	8,300,000	Nebraska and Kansas combined

Yet when combined with one another, the total population (22.5 million) of the Nordic nations is about equal to that of California. The combined geographic area of the Nordic states is 92,000 square miles *smaller* than the state of Alaska alone. Thus the first similarity shared by the Nordic countries is that compared to the United States each is small indeed.

Beyond geographic comparisons one finds many similarities among the Nordic states. Except for Finland, these nations are basically homogeneous with respect to the state church (Lutheran denomination) and the common Germanic (but not German) heritage including a wide range of cultural and linguistic traits whose history is intertwined. Finland shares strong cultural historical and linguistic ties with the Baltic Soviet republic of Estonia. Throughout most of their history, the current five Nordic states were only two, Denmark-Iceland-Norway and Sweden-Finland respectively. In the past, these two conglomerate nations spent most of their time fighting for supremacy in the region. In recent time, the competition has been of a more peaceful nature. Their cultural and ethnic homogeneity has to some degree, of course, been influenced by recent immigration from many other European countries. For example, almost 10 percent of Sweden's population is now foreign-born. But, as half of these are Finns and other Scandinavians, the basic characteristics of the Scandinavian setting remain relatively unchanged.

Moreover, the setting also includes a more undefined, but extant nevertheless, strand of skepticism about the intricacies of world politics and about the merits of defense expenditure. As citizens of small countries that have experienced the whims of history in the past, many people living in the Nordic states now feel that they have something to contribute toward the construction of a new, more stable international system. Outsiders to the region often find these aspirations perplexing or even irritating. However, such aspirations should be understood in the context of nations that, in sociological terms, have in many ways evolved from war societies to postwar societies. This contention means simply that these nations have achieved a degree of "security community" among themselves. Such a community entails inclination to settle differences by means other than war. But it does not mean that the Nordic countries have in any way given up the notion of national security as a military concept. They will defend themselves if attacked, but they also measure their national security in economic and social terms.

Most Nordic citizens feel that their countries can, whether as members of NATO such as Denmark, Iceland, and Norway, or as neutrals such as Finland and Sweden, express their opinions quite freely, without necessarily being suspected of advancing only their own narrow national interests. Since these states are in relatively fortunate positions economically and in many other respects, it might even be natural for them to voice concerns of a more general nature, for example, expressing certain moral or idealistic tenets of international politics. Rather than giving in to the temptation to castigate the Nordic nations for meddling in international issues that some consider to be none of their business, it is useful to consider the policies that motivate the foreign policies of these nations.

At the same time, the Nordic nations can be very hard-nosed when it comes to their own security. Although the idealist tradition in foreign policy has had its impact on Nordic defense discussions, the realist tradition always coexists with the idealist. The mixture of idealist and realist elements in the foreign and defense policies of the five nations may vary with time according to domestic political situations and levels of tension in the relations between the major powers.

No doubt there is a connection between these philosophical tendencies and the fact that parties on the moderate left have dominated the Nordic scene since the end of World War I. Although they have not been in power for the entire period, the Social Democrats and various parties of more radical liberal persuasions have been clearly dominant. These parties have in general tended to be more idealistic than the more conservative groups. Since the advent of universal franchise, conservatives have not been as successful in obtaining governmental power in these countries as in many other European nations. Whether Social Democrats and Liberals have become politically ascendant as a result of widely held beliefs in the foreign policy or national security areas is clearly debatable. But, through their policies they may have reinforced existing public sentiment in those fields. The public believes by and large that there is a very close connection between domestic and foreign policy. One tends to influence the other. In Europe, therefore, a moderate leftist is likely to hold world views which might be labelled "dovish" by U.S. standards.

However, despite the many characteristics shared by the Nordic countries, there are obvious differences. Denmark has always had a dual foreign policy orientation: toward the Nordic states, a region in which Denmark was often the dominant power; and toward the continental European states with which Denmark, in the past, formed various alliances. Norway has had a dual orientation toward the Nordic states on the one hand and toward the sea or, more specifically, toward Great Britain and other dominant sea powers on the other hand. Iceland is distantly located and its national interests have always been defined by its dominant industry, fisheries. Finland has had a dual orientation as well. Although the Finns share the same fundamental values and traditions of Scandinavia in general, Finland suffered greatly when it was Sweden's borderland with Russia from the early thirteenth century and subsequently under Russian rule from 1809 until independence in 1917. Sweden's convenient geographic location partly accounts for its monistic foreign policy since the time of Napoleon, although Sweden was active on the continent prior to the early nineteenth century. This was, no doubt, partly a consequence of Sweden's wish to break out of a confined Scandinavian setting. Today, Swedish participation in the international arena avoids militarily entangling alliances, focusing instead inter alia on trade, United Nations activities, and political engagements in foreign policy issues outside Europe.

What is important, however, is that the Nordic region has always been a separate and distinct part of Europe. The results of various referenda and debates concerning the relations of the Nordic nations to the Common Market demonstrate a degree of aloofness from continental Europe. Any person from this region is a Dane, Norwegian, Icelander, Finn, or Swede first, a Nordic citizen second, and a European third. This tends to be borne out in the different national security solutions for which the nations in the area have opted. It may suffice at this juncture to recall that Denmark, Iceland, and Norway are members of NATO, whereas Finland and Sweden pursue distinct policies of neutrality. These five countries share the common view that their individual policies are in the interest of each Nordic nation, and that these policies are also in the interest of the superpowers and their allies.

Structures

The preceding chapters indicate that the decision-making structures (or defense communities) of the Nordic nations are alike in many ways. The cabinet exercises political authority in accordance with the parliamentary system as long as it enjoys the support or tacit acceptance of a majority of the parliament. In the cabinet, a very small number of ministers are involved in defense decision making. In addition to the minister of defense, the prime minister, foreign minister, and minister of finance have major roles in defense policy. An important role is played by the small defense bureaucracy in each country and by the supreme commander (or commander-in-chief) of the armed forces.

The powers of the supreme commander have in recent times been enlarged at the expense of the heads of services in both Denmark and Sweden, and he is consequently a key figure in the defense decision-making structure. The military bureaucracy that serves the supreme commander is also a very important element in the defense community. In Sweden, as elsewhere, a major role is played by the research and development segment of the defense bureaucracy which, for obvious reasons, maintains close contacts with the armaments industries in the country. Among defense critics, many claim that Sweden's relatively strong defense is a function of a factual fusion between the research and development bureaucracy and its military supporters on the one hand and the arms industry on the other.

Compared to the congressional committees of the United States, the standing parliamentary committees on defense play a more limited role in the Nordic nations. This follows logically from the parliamentary system in which the cabinet, as noted above, remains in power only so long as it retains the sympathy or tolerance of the majority of the house. Therefore, individual members are not expected to inject too much expertise into the process. If they did, it would tend to develop the system in the direction of a division of power, a basic constitutional principle of the United States. If the standing committees of the parliament had large staffs, this could lead to scrutiny not only of the principles, but also the minute details of a particular bill. This could not only challenge the positions taken by the cabinet on policy, but would jeopardize fundamental provisions as well. Such challenges on an annual basis would also undercut the long-term planning system that is particularly useful in defense, given the enormous expenditures involved over long periods of time.

What the members of parliament (MPs) are supposed to do is to exercise their good political judgment in the discussion of defense bills. There is a delicate balance here, since the MPs clearly must have some staff to acquire the information and perspectives which underpin sound judgment. But the basic principles of parliamentarism must not be infringed upon while the powers of the individual MP and his right and duty to screen the government's proposals for expenditures are retained.

Clearly, the political systems in the Western world should be viewed as a continuum, not as opposing poles on a scale. The difference between the North American and the European democratic systems is one of degree, not of kind. However, the degree of difference is important when it comes to analyzing the roles and functions of parliamentary systems and, in particular, their standing committees. In the U.S. system, a division of power clearly necessitates large committee staffs that enable Congress to act as an independent branch of government. Parliamentary theory implies that the parliamentary majority has, conditionally to be sure, delegated to the cabinet some of the people's authority in the formulation and implementation of policy.

The decision-making structure also encompasses something that is very typical of the Nordic nations: instruments for political compromise located outside the formal structure. In Denmark, the factual framework for defense decisions are the so-called *forliger* (literally, "compromises") that are formed every four years or so. This kind of group, the *forlig,* consists of representatives from all the major parties as well as those from the Danish ad hoc defense commissions that are appointed every four or five years. Its purpose is to agree on defense programs for the ensuing five-year period and to defuse the political status of defense discussions.

Interestingly enough, however, Norway has had only two such commissions during the postwar era and, in Sweden, the real political power has tended to slip away from the ad hoc commission. Despite their composition of parliamentary members, the commissions are no longer the preeminent instruments of compromise they once were. During the height of the Cold War there was a definite interest on the part of the non-Communist parties to arrange a political compromise so that the country could demonstrate a united front to the outside world and avoid spilling political blood over major issues. When it was believed that détente had come to stay, the sense of threat to Swedish interests changed. The threat perception altered from a singular military threat to Sweden's security in a Cold War context to a much more diffuse and complex perception of threat to Sweden's economic well-being and prestige. As a consequence of this development, the Social Democrats began to disassociate themselves somewhat from the consensus on Swedish defense policy. They were the first to recognize new international trends and concluded that the changing nature of the threat merited a somewhat different defense policy. The impact of these differing perceptions among political parties was felt at the cabinet level and among its parliamentary support.

This does not mean that the traditions of compromise have all disappeared; far from it. But the defense issue has become more political in the nations concerned, especially in Sweden, and this has had its effects upon structures. The more technical elements in the structure have seen their influence reduced in recent years as the politicization of defense debate has become more evident.

What roles do the trade-union movement and the press play? Are they part of the structure and, if so, what importance should be attached to them? The LO (the Confederation of Swedish Trade Unions), for example, is a very powerful institution. Union membership, very high in all Nordic countries, is in Sweden as high as 90 percent for blue-collar workers. Moreover, the unions and their central organizations are a most important source of electoral campaign financing for the Social Democratic parties. One would expect, therefore, that they would be an important part of the defense decision-making structure in these states. But that is not really the case, even in Sweden, where the armaments industry employs a fair number of people and arms exports amount to some 1.175 million kronor (0.6 percent of GNP in 1983) per year.

Defense has been left to the party branch of the labor movement in the Nordic states. Traditionally, the trade-union movement concentrated its efforts more on immediate domestic interests than on foreign policy and defense. It is true that it has in recent years ventured out into foreign policy, particularly in solidarity actions for oppressed fellow workers in other countries, and also on such questions which have generally attracted the attention of important segments of public opinion, such as Vietnam, Central America, or Southern Africa. However, it is possible that as the arms industry is squeezed by a somewhat diminished volume of orders from local armed forces and by restrictions on arms exports that are not very likely to be lifted, Swedish and Norwegian unions will show a more substantial interest in defense policy. One reaction by some unions with members in the arms industry has been to press their companies to try to make themselves less dependent on arms sales. These companies should, it is often suggested, try to differentiate production and turn to more civilian output. One additional reason for union reluctance to engage in defense issues may well also be the "skeptical" streak that is mentioned above. This particular tradition may contribute to the feeling that defense, as a symbol of the old hierarchic political system, is a matter one does not busy oneself with too much.

Public opinion and the mass media are participants in the defense decision-making structures in varied ways. Until very recently there has been very little debate on defense and national security issues in Denmark and Sweden. In both countries there has been a general reluctance to engage in defense debates. In Denmark, the country's relative smallness may contribute to a feeling among some people that there is not much Denmark can do militarily to reinforce its own security. This is reflected in the positions taken by the *Radikale Venstre* (Radical Liberal party) or the famous statement by the leader of *Framstegspartiet* (Progressive party) that the only money Denmark needs to spend on defense is for a telephone answering machine that would play a recording of "We give up" in Russian. Although this is far from a dominant feeling in Denmark, it has been traditionally of some importance.

In Sweden, support for national defense has until recently been relatively uncontroversial, but as noted in the Swedish chapter, aside from the very pro-defense *Moderata Samlingspartiet* (Conservative party), most parties generally have seen defense as something of a necessary evil. Such a climate has not fostered debate, especially since the policy of neutrality has been interpreted by some people as an inhibition to public discussions of sensitive defense issues. However, spurred by the number of submarine incidents, this has changed somewhat. As of late people who engage in defense debates have found it easier to have their articles accepted by the newspapers, and journalists seem to find it more professionally rewarding to write about defense issues.

This change can be traced to two different and unconnected developments. First, like most other industrialized nations, Sweden has experienced a tightening grip on the public purse. It has become more difficult recently to allocate the same proportion of the GNP to defense because the international economic situation has been unstable and tight. This has resulted in a debate on the proper allocation of resources. The question being asked is, do the threats to Swedish security justify the rather comprehensive defense expenditures that Sweden has been committed to for so long? The second development is related to the increasing strategic interest in northern Europe that has occurred in recent years. Both these developments have meant that public opinion will play a larger role in Swedish and Danish defense decision-making structures from now on.

In Norway, public involvement in defense debate has been a fact for quite some time. This can be traced to a number of individuals and institutions, for example, *Norsk Utenrikspolitisk Institutt* (NUPI) and the Peace Research Institute of Oslo (PRIO). Both have stimulated the mass media and informed the public community toward debate on defense issues for at least the past ten years. The activities and research reports of both these institutes have had considerable influence also on the national security and defense debates in all the Nordic countries, where similar institutions have either come later or been engaged in different forms of activity.

In Finland, the populace favors a credible defense to protect their national interests and the existing pluralistic political structure. This support for a reasonable national defense is apparent in public opinion polls. Defense and political authorities who have vested interests in defense seek to enhance this popular support by educating the public on security issues. Recent Soviet attempts to exert pressure on the Finnish security policy process have met with resistance and resulted in a shift to the right in Finnish public opinion polls on defense and security issues.

In Iceland, public interest in defense issues is low. This disinterest is partly explained by Iceland's long history of pacifism. For example, in 1949 Iceland declared its policy to neither raise an army nor maintain any native military forces of any kind. This cultural and historical bias against defense is underscored by the linguistic barrier to informed discussion of defense issues. The Icelandic language lacks the basic military terminology needed in the discussion of defense concepts. Compounding the problem is the politicization of defense issues and security policy. This politicization is evident in Iceland's six major newspapers, all of which have ties to one of the major political parties. The result of these political affiliations is that defense issues are editorialized along party lines—news coverage of defense issues amounts to political propaganda rather than objective analysis. In sum, however, the average citizen of Iceland is unconcerned and uninformed about defense issues.

Defense Issues

Even if the settings and the structures which underpin defense decisions are alike in most vital respects in these five countries, the issues are somewhat different. However, the specific issues do tend to hinge on two major variables: the allocation of resources to defense in the face of mounting demands from other parts of the public sector; and on threat perceptions.

First the matter of resource allocation. International economic developments in the 1970s and early 1980s have had different impacts on the Nordic states. Inflation, at one point reaching nearly 15 percent, was more or less alarming in Denmark and Sweden. Very significantly, this meant higher unemployment in societies that traditionally have had a high stake in maintaining full, or very close to full employment. Inflation also meant a progressively tighter squeeze on the public purse, particularly to support faltering key industries. This led to larger budget deficits. The net result was a demand to save funds by cutting sectors other than those immediately affecting direct economic interests. Since public support for development assistance to the less developed countries (LDC), also a result of the idealist tradition in Nordic foreign policy thinking, remained strong despite financial pressures, it was only natural that some political interest would call for measures to lower the defense burdens of the LDCs. Most Swedes consider development assistance as a mechanism with which to redistribute global wealth and as an element of national security policy. This view, hitherto somewhat alien to U.S. thinking, assumes that it is in the interest of the entire industrialized world to try to minimize the risks of future North-South conflicts and thus reduce the threat to the supply of raw materials.

In Sweden there traditionally has been general public support for defense expenditures. Most people of the older generation (politicians tend to be of that age group) remember that Sweden was spared during World War II. It is not known to what extent this resulted from the fact that Sweden, after some initial problems, had built up a rather impressive military apparatus that provided a shield from outside pressures. But in recent years it has not been easy for politicians to withstand the pressure to reduce defense expenditures in order to satisfy demands in other areas. Even the improvement of the Swedish economy since 1978 has not reduced public pressure to cut defense expenditures, though the trend has been somewhat reversed as a result of the growing awareness of the persistent submarine threat. The problem has been even more evident in Denmark, but Norway's case is different. Norway emerged relatively unscathed from the mini-recession of 1973/1974, and its recent status as an oil-exporting nation has given it increasing economic leverage. Thus there has been little pressure to diminish the Norwegian defense burden. However, Norway was forced to increase government spending and to introduce tough wage and price controls to stop inflation.

In Finland the public supports defense spending and favors a credible national defense. The populace is willing and able to fight in the event of an attack on Finnish territory. To ensure the integrity of Finnish defense capabilities within the limits set in Helsinki, defense spending during the postwar period has consistently ranged between 1.3 and 2.0 percent of the GNP. While the present level of defense spending is acceptable and desirable to the Finnish people, the rapid expansion of the economy during the postwar period and the subsequent increase in the standard of living have produced greater demands on the limited national resources. This constraint limits the amount of resources the Finnish people are willing and able to commit to defense.

Iceland lacks a national military complex. Although Iceland is a member of NATO and permits the stationing of U.S. troops at Keflavík, the only funds allocated for defense go to the coastguard. Iceland maintains a coastguard consisting of 160 men and five gunboats which serves a constabulary function by policing Iceland's fishing zones. The current politics of defense policy and the present public disinterest in matters pertaining to defense seem to ensure that the present situation in Iceland will not soon be amenable to change.

It should also be borne in mind that Sweden has voluntarily undertaken a heavier defense burden than its two NATO neighbors, who for many years have been able to profit from their NATO membership and U.S. financial support. Of course, alliance membership should, in theory, allow member nations to coordinate defense programs and maintain a somewhat less expensive defense than a neutral state that has chosen a policy of armed neutrality.

The allocation problem has been a real issue in Denmark and Sweden, while recent Norwegian defense discussions have had no strong traces of economic constriction. Whatever the likely direction of the Norwegian economy, the country has experienced a marked change in threat perception and is thus not likely to undergo public pressures for reduced defense spending. A major reason for this is that Norway bears the brunt of a number of important changes in the Nordic geopolitical subsystem that have taken place in the last ten years or so. Those changes are not related to each other but are nevertheless interdependent. There are four basic changes in threat perceptions, each of which is mentioned in the preceding chapters. The first is the growing importance of the Kola Peninsula base system and the consequent Soviet interest in safeguarding that area from foreign surveillance and intervention. A second change concerns existing or potential oil deposits in Norwegian territorial waters west and north of mainland Norway. Third is the relationship with the Soviets concerning the administration and exercise of sovereignty in the islands of Spitsbergen (or Svalbard as they are called in Scandinavia). And fourth is the new focus on the division of the waters and continental shelves of the Barents Sea in the vicinity of the Kola Peninsula. Together, these changes have surfaced an impressive array of issues that have caused diplomatic conflicts between Norway and the Soviet Union. Norwegians have developed an increased sense of exposure.

This is primarily a Norwegian problem, but it concerns the entire region and, no doubt, will be perceived as such as time goes by. At present, the situation is not generally perceived as reflecting any Soviet strategic designs on the Nordic region. However, Norwegian defense policy has been modified in response to the situation, primarily through the strengthening of forces in northern Norway and, above all, the navy. The increasing activity in the Norwegian sea territory demands close surveillance by naval forces. Increased political activity by Finland, such as the Kekkonen plan for a Nordic nuclear-free zone, is also a part of the picture. There has not yet been any marked change in Swedish defense policy, but the signs are that some reevaluation is coming. Sweden does envisage a relative strengthening of the forces in the north as compared to other parts of the country, for instance.

As mentioned above, the character of the threat perception in Sweden has changed from a purely military threat in a Cold War context to include a number of diffuse and nonmilitary threats. The concurrent advent of the oil crisis and its demonstration of the vulnerability of the Western industrial system on the one hand, and the détente policy between the superpowers on the other, led many Swedes to conclude that military adventures will be less likely in the future. The submarine debate has challenged this perception. There is little credibility in scenarios based on direct superpower military confrontations in an age of strategic nuclear parity. There is greater credibility in the growing importance of nonmilitary conflicts over commodities such as oil. While Swedish threat perceptions by no means exclude the risks of military attacks, they tend to diminish the importance of such threats compared to, say, the 1950s.

Defense debates in the five Nordic states must be viewed against this general strategic background. But the major defense issues in recent years have not been strategic. Rather, they have focused on military hardware and especially the acquisition of aircraft. Denmark and Norway experienced lengthy public and private debates for several years concerning the aircraft they should buy to replace the aging F-104s that both nations had in their inventories. In Sweden, the defense debate centered on whether or not to build a new light ground-attack aircraft to replace the Viggen JA37 fighter-bombers in the 1990s.

It is not surprising that aircraft acquisition engenders such debate in each of the three countries. The sums involved are enormous and the commitments undertaken are very long term indeed, since the planes are supposed to be in the inventory for at least fifteen years. Aircraft are also symbols of technological sophistication and it is assumed that aircraft research, development, and production include beneficial spin-offs in other technical fields.

For Denmark and Norway, it was a choice between the French (Mirage F-1), the Swedish (Viggen 37) and two American (General Dynamics F-16 and Northrop F-17) systems. The selection in some ways symbolized the basic choices in foreign policy orientation of the two countries. Politically there was much to be said for the acquisition of a French or a continental European system. Denmark and Norway (the latter had just decided not to join the Common Market) could have demonstrated their "Europeanness" and actively contributed toward the further improvement and maintenance of an independent European aircraft industry. Denmark could have reinforced its membership in the EEC by choosing a French system. Norway could have similarly showed its basic Europeanness by doing the same thing, despite the fact that Norway chose by referendum not to become a member of the Community. In addition to the technical qualities of the Mirage F-1, this was the argument that the French were particularly stressing.

But the Mirage never had much of a chance in Denmark and Norway. Partly as a consequence of those countries' Scandinavian orientation, the choice was between the Swedish Viggen and the American F-16 or F-17. In turn, the choice of the U.S. aircraft was a result of internal studies and discussions in these countries as to which of the two planes would be better. What were the arguments for going Swedish? There seems to have been a stronger pull in Denmark for the Swedish model than there was in Norway. Purely economic considerations were important. These included which country could provide the more favorable compensation contract, and which would be more generous when it came to coproduction. The Danes and the Norwegians already knew the Swedes well in this respect and evidently it would have been easy to establish joint production arrangements and facilities. Given their traditional cooperation across national boundaries, the trade unions in Scandinavia were viewed as a potential factor in favor of the Swedish option.

Other considerations favored selection of U.S. aircraft. This would have demonstrated NATO solidarity and, in particular, the ties between the United States and Europe. For very clear reasons the two small NATO nations look to the United States to provide the mainstay of support for their security. And the manufacturers of the U.S. aircraft, General Dynamics and Northrop respectively, could provide Danish and Norwegian industries with useful injections of technological expertise. Of course, both countries could have profited from the infusion of Swedish technological know-how, but continued cooperation with leading U.S. firms in the field might have a greater spin-off effect than corresponding Swedish cooperation.

These general considerations most certainly played a major role in decision making. There is no evidence of any serious dissention among various agencies in the Norwegian defense apparatus or decision-making structure. In all probability, the military and civilian leaderships were united in their preference for the F-16 once it had become clear that the U.S. Air Force itself would chose the F-16 rather than the F-17. In Denmark, it was rumored that some of the unions were in favor of the Swedish alternative. But in the end, the general orientation of the national security policy in the two nations proved to be decisive. No doubt it was important that the acquisition of U.S. aircraft would also guarantee continued production of the plane in question for the foreseeable future. On the contrary, buying from a neutral state with a small aircraft industry mostly or wholly dependent upon purchases from the Swedish Air Force would seem a somewhat less attractive proposition, Nordic or Scandinavian affinities notwithstanding.

In Denmark aircraft acquisition was obviously the leading defense issue during the 1970s. However, a new issue has arisen. This centers on the increase in strength and numbers as well as the new exercise patters of the Soviet Baltic fleet. The nature of threat perceptions in Denmark have an impact upon resource allocations. The director of the Danish Home Guard (an independent service of the Danish Defense Forces) has suggested that Denmark will not be able to finance four independent services in the future. This would mean that Danish resources would have to be concentrated in some of the services, letting NATO, or realistically, the Federal Republic of Germany, assume responsibility for the rest. This raised a furor in Denmark and has been widely repudiated, but it may be to some extent symptomatic of the continuing allocation debate.

Norway has not had any defense debate more intense than the aircraft acquisition issue which was resolved by the decision to purchase the F-16. Since that debate, an even wider consensus on Norwegian defense appears to have developed. As mentioned above, the vital issues in Norway concern the problem of maintaining Norwegian sovereignty over Spitsbergen and the various territorial delineation problems with the Soviets.

As the preceding chapters suggest, the liveliest defense debate has been going on in Sweden. It concerns the future of the Swedish aircraft industry and reflects various strategic differences. The B3LA aircraft and a variant of it called the SK38/A38, which was under debate, did represent a departure from earlier, high-technology-oriented aircraft designs. The Viggen fighter-bomber now in use is an expression of high-technology orientation. It is a heavy, sophisticated plane (the U.S. A-7 and the French Mirage-1 may be the closest counterparts to the fighter-bomber versions) designed to attack targets at sea or along other invasion routes. Military, tactical, and strategic issues aside, there remains the view held by many that without a new aircraft (as opposed to a modification of Viggen), the present research and development capability of the Swedish aircraft industry will be jeopardized. In this view, although the production line would be kept busy building any of the four Viggen versions or, for that matter, any foreign plane that could be built under license, these alternatives would place insufficient demand on the research and development side. There would also be a high risk that this capacity, which if once lost is not easily regained, would evaporate altogether. However, it must be emphasized here that the Swedish aircraft industry is not necessarily a precondition for neutrality. The important thing is that Sweden must have fighter aircraft available during times of crisis, not how or where they are obtained. Other neutral nations such as Finland, Austria, and in particular, Switzerland have been able to retain an air force by either buying abroad off the shelf or by producing aircraft under license. Ironically, while the B3LA was designed to get away from the very expensive systems that generally are supposed to characterize the so-called peripheral or "shell" defense system, it became synonymous with some of the philosophical underpinnings of perimeter defense. Thus, proponents of territorial defense argued for rejection of the B3LA, whereas proponents of the peripheral defense system suggested just the opposite, despite the fact that B3LA or SK38/A38 would have served primarily to support ground forces once an enemy had entered Swedish territory.

The Swedish defense establishment is certainly a tight-knit community. It had developed many arguments for adopting the new aircraft. A major argument rested on the fact that the research and development capabilities of the Swedish aircraft industry (outside the great-power group, one of the very few independent ones) was at stake, involving enormous "sunk costs." But the Social Democratic party announced its opposition to the project, and support for a completely new aircraft among the four other parties (with the exception of the moderate Conservative party) was scant. At that time the chances were slim indeed for the Liberal minority cabinet to get a decision in favor of a new aircraft through the parliament. So, Sweden was faced with a proposal with major support in the establishment's military, technological, and business circles, but with lukewarm support from the politicians. The decision to reject B3LA/A38 was made in a much tighter economic situation than was the decision to proceed with the Viggen—a child of the more prosperous 1950s and 1960s.

It was a politically difficult decision. The choices were, fundamentally, either to acquiesce in downgrading the nation's aircraft research and development capability or to attempt to get public and parliamentary support for higher defense expenditures at a time when public opinion did not take into account a changing strategic environment. In the end, the Liberal government chose not to build the B3LA or SK38/A38.

An interesting implication of the government's decision was that the proponents of peripheral defense were given support which was perhaps unintended. The modified Viggen would have been better suited for defense at or beyond Sweden's borders. The B3LA or SK38/A38 were designed primarily as close air-support aircraft for army forces fighting on Swedish territory once an enemy had penetrated Swedish borders. By *not* funding the very expensive research and development required for a new aircraft in January 1979, the Liberal cabinet may have saved the proponents of peripheral defense from themselves. Indeed, it decided to study further a new version of the Viggen (A20), the construction of a new Swedish trainer aircraft, and to restudy future modes of aircraft acquisition. It may well be that the decision taken by the Ullsten Liberal cabinet was in conformity with important trends in the Swedish defense debate.

The 1978 ad hoc Defense Commission published a report containing eleven independent essays on Swedish defense problems. A significant thread in that collection of essays is that, regardless of political affiliation, there is increasing criticism of the territorial defense model. Fundamental to Sweden's policy of total defense is the concept that there must be a public consensus that defense is a burden to be shared by all Swedish citizens and that military conscription is a necessary condition. But the concept has its critics. The territorial defense model presupposes an expensive manpower training organization which has, in recent years, tended to divert funds away from investment in weapons systems. The territorial defense model also has drawbacks from a purely military point of view, according to its critics, because it envisions a large Swedish army fighting on Swedish soil against an enemy with increasingly sophisticated weapons. The argument is, of course, that it would make better sense to fight outside Sweden's borders against invading forces and with smaller but highly mobile and technical forces.

The decision not to build the B3LA tended to support those who argued in favor of peripheral defense for the foreseeable future. In the very long run, it is at least possible to argue the other way around; that is, by reducing Sweden's capacity to build its own airplanes, the cabinet opted in fact for the territorial model. The implications of either interpretation would depend upon estimates of the changing threat.

In 1980 Saab–Scania revealed the plan which, ostensibly, defused the doctrinal arguments on both sides, or viewed another way, accomodated the preferred doctrines of both. The plan took advantage of foreign cooperation and ready-made components (such as the British Martin–Baker ejection seat) in order to produce a new aircraft at a cost below that of a modified Viggen. The new aircraft would have an advanced engine, modern electronics, precision-guided weapons, and would have only half the weight of the Viggen. Thus the new all-purpose aircraft, JAS–39 "Gripen," was born. The JAS (the Swedish acronym for fighter, *Jakt;* bomber, *Attack;* and reconnaissance, *Spaning*) would serve both as an interceptor in support of peripheral defense at or beyond Sweden's borders, and as a ground support aircraft suited for territorial defense.

Unfortunately, by 1984 it was clear that the eight-year search for a cheap alternative to the Viggen would not produce substantial savings. The Swedish krona had lost a great deal of ground against foreign currencies during the interim. As a result, the total cost for the 140 new JAS aircraft, including support systems and ancillary equipment, has already exceeded projections out to the year 2000 by 2.8 billion kronor (approximately 400 million dollars). The U.S. dollar is to a large extent responsible for this miscalculation. Swedish plans anticipated a worst-case exchange rate in 1984 of 5.5 kronor to the dollar. The actual rate turned out to be between 8.5 and 9.0 kronor per dollar. The effect of fluctuations in the exchange rate can also be measured this way: a fluctuation of one krona means a difference of 1.5 billion kronor in the Gripen project.

Due to the squeeze on Air Force funds, the Parliament agreed to make a supplemental defense appropriation in 1984. Before the supplemental appropriation the number of fighter squadrons had dropped from 12 to 11. If the supplemental appropriation had not been approved, three Draken squadrons would have been eliminated to help pay for the JAS. Given dramatically rising costs of the JAS, a major question for the future is whether Sweden will be able to afford the weapons that the JAS is designed to carry. Depending on the strength of the krona, other cost reduction options include savings on spare part inventories, elimination of some equipment, or the elimination of the two-seat JAS version. The eight-year wait may be a case of the better becoming the enemy of the good.

More important, the JAS decision has not resolved the fundamental question of defense strategy. A multi-purpose aircraft is not the only ingredient of military capability that underpins strategy. Military doctrine, whether perimeter defense or territorial defense, should be designed to support strategy. A clear statement of Swedish defense strategy has not been forthcoming. And it is important to note that, simultaneous with larger expenditures for the JAS, ground forces have been reduced and training for the reserve forces, the vital foundation for a rapid defense mobilization capability, has been curtailed significantly.

Lessons from the Study of Nordic Defense Decision Making

A common assertion in the Swedish defense debate is that defense decisions often are made on the wrong pretexts. Whereas decisions should be made in the light of threat estimates, they are often influenced by supposedly irrelevant aspects such as the employment situation in a given region of the country, or the policy preferences of a skillful bureaucraty on a wide range of domestic considerations. But it is naive to assume that defense decisions in a modern state can be taken irrespective of such other national concerns. Defense policy is a branch of public policy and it cannot possibly be exempted from the strictures of political analysis and political decision making of a more general nature. In the Nordic context of strong Social Democratic parties (and in any real democracy) public support for defense expenditure would suffer if policy makers were to act on the pretext that defense decision making is something special, and that defense decisions should be taken without concern for domestic matters.

The foregoing analysis of the Nordic nations suggests many similarities, both in settings and structures. Similar issues are at hand, but those issues, depending on differing economic situations and threat perceptions, tend to be discussed in a slightly different fashion in the five countries. The security arrangements that each nation has selected constrain the range of choice in each nation. Neutrality in Sweden and Finland, and the membership of Iceland, Denmark, and Norway in NATO have a bearing upon choices; so do other constraints that have been discussed, such as the economies, the existence of a modern arms industry, and the idealist tradition in Nordic approaches to foreign policy.

Defense choices in the five countries are made in a way that is very different from the complex system prevalent in the United States where the decision-making apparatus is enormous and the number of participants almost infinite. But there is a growing similarity in that political parties in the Nordic states have become much more interested in defense in recent years. At least in Sweden and Denmark, heretofore small, exclusive, defense communities are becoming increasingly open to new voices and concerns. Increasingly, given international interdependence and economic constraints, and without détente, allocation arguments will continue to have an impact on the once-special province of defense. This is an important change compared to the environment of the 1960s and 1970s.

Index

A-17, 200
ABC weapons, protection against, 159
Academic experts: Denmark, 9–10; Finland, 51; Iceland, 71, 80; Norway, 102
Afghanistan, Soviet invasion of, 22–23
Aftonbladet (Sweden), 147, 168, 169
AIM-91 Sidewinder missile, 175
Aircraft acquisition: Denmark and Norway, 198–199; Sweden, 200–202
Allison, G., and P. Szanton, xii
Alpytublatit (Iceland), 78
Althing. *See* Iceland, parliament
Alusuisse (Swiss multinational), 69–70
American National Security (Jordan and Taylor), xi
Andren, Nils, 129 (quoted)
Arms sales (Sweden), 153, 156, 175, 193, 198, 199
Arnarson, Ingólfur, 63
Austria, xix, 128, 200

BALTAP (Baltic Approaches), 3, 19, 26, 29
Baltic Sea, xiv–xv, 2–3, 40, 131, 154, 187
Barents Sea, 92, 111–112, 187, 197
Belgium, 115, 117
Bilateral Defense Agreement Iceland–U.S., 1950), xvi–xvii, 66, 74, 75, 86
Björk, Gunnar, 143, 178
Bofors (Sweden), 144
Borg, Per Olof, 136
Bowman–Holst Study (U.S.–Norway, 1979–1980), 118, 119, 120

Brateli, Trygve, 117
Brezhnev, Leonid, 48
Brown, Harold, 12, 23
Bruland, Bjørn, 119
Brundtland, Arne, xiii
Brundtland, Gro Harlem, 111
Burenstam-Linder, Minister of Defense (Sweden), 156
Bye, Ronald, 97

Cabinets. *See* Executive Branches
Centurion tank (British), 130
Clemmesen, Michael H., 32 (quoted)
Cod Wars, 64, 87
Cold War/detente, 1, 65, 192, 197
COMBALTAP (Commander Baltic Approaches), 17, 19
Common Market. *See* European Economic Community
Communist parties: Denmark, 7–8, 12; Finland, 44, 50, 59; Iceland, 82, 83; Sweden, 147
Conscription: Denmark, 15, 27, 30; Finland, 55–56; Sweden, 130, 170, 178, 179, 201
Constitutions: Germany, 80; Iceland, 73, 80; Norway, 92, 98, 109
Cruise missiles, 42, 103–104, 112, 176
Czechoslovakia, 97

Dagblatit Vísir (Iceland), 78
Dagens Nyheter (Sweden), 147, 178
Damgaard, Knud, 27, 28, 29
Danish straits, 3
Defense budgets: Denmark, 14–30, 192; Finland, 44, 51–52, 196; Norway, 112–113, 196–197;

Defense budgets: *(continued)*
  Sweden, 131, 134, 144, 152, 157–159, 162, 170, 179–180, 194, 195–196, 201
Defense Policy Formulation (Roherty), xiii
"Defensive defense," 33
De Geer, Lars, 172
Delta class vessels, 112
Denmark: xiv–xv, 1–36, 129, 154, 155; air force and F-16s, 14, 24, 29, 30, 33, 115, 117, 198; Atlantic Association, 9; BALTAP/COMBALTAP, 3, 17, 19, 26, 29; Center Democratic party, 6, 28; Christian People's party, 6; Commission on Security and Disarmament Affairs, 6; "Committee of Eleven," 24, 27, 29; Communist party, 7–8, 12; conscription, 15, 27, 30; Conservative party, 5, 6, 13, 28, 33; Coordinating Committee for Security Questions, 5; "Defend Denmark," 9; Defense Command/Defense Department/Ministry of Defense, 4–5, 16–17, 20; defense "establishment" demise, 13; "defense settlements" (Defense Acts/defense budget), 14–30, 192; "Denmarkization," 23; and European Community/European Political Cooperation, 2, 198; foreign policy 2, 190; and Germany, 1, 3, 23, 26, 32, 199; Home Guard, 9, 17, 29, 199; and Iceland, 63–64, 70, 87, 188; interpellation debates, 8; Kalmar Union, 63; Left Socialist party, 7, 24; Liberal party, 5, 6, 13, 21, 28, 33; military unions, 9, 30; and NATO, xiv, 1, 2–4, 5, 6, 10–12, 14, 18, 19, 22–23, 26, 27, 29, 32, 33–34, 189, 190, 196, 198, 203; naval Standard Flex units, 24, 30, 33; news media, 10; oil crisis, 21; parliament (Folketing), 1, 6–9; peace movement, 3–4, 9, 12–13, 22; political parties, 6–9, 13, 14, 22, 24,, 28, 32–33; population and size, 188; pressure groups/lobbies, 9–10; Progressive party, 8, 24, 194; public opinion, 10, 12; Radical party, 7, 14, 16, 21, 22, 23, 24, 27, 31, 32, 193; resource allocation, 195, 196, 199; and Scandilux, 13; Seidenfaden Committee, 5; Social Democratic party, 1, 6, 7, 9, 10, 12, 13, 16, 21, 22, 23, 24, 27, 28–29, 30, 31, 32, 33; Socialist People's party, 7, 24; submarines, 27, 29, 30, 33; trade unions, 9, 23, 30, 199; and U.S., 2, 3, 4, 196, 198–199; and USSR, xiv–xv, 2–3, 12, 199
"Denmarkization," 23
Developmental assistance to LDCs, 195
Dörfer, Ingemar, 146, 155, 158, 180
Draken (J35) aircraft (Sweden), 130, 158, 175, 180, 202

Eastern Europe, 42
Economies: Finland, 43–44, 52; Iceland, 69–70, 85, 86–87; Sweden, 127, 131, 145, 156, 157, 194, 195, 202
Eduskunta. *See* Finland, parliament
Energy crisis: Denmark, 21; Sweden, 159, 197
Energy resources (Iceland), 69, 85
Engell, Hans, 27, 28, 29, 30, 33
Engman, Ingemar, 173
L.M. Ericsson (Sweden), 132, 144, 157, 171
Erikson, John, 154–155 (quoted)
Estonia, 40, 188
European Economic Community (EEC)(Common Market), 190; and Denmark, 2, 198; and Iceland, 87; and Norway, 103, 104, 110, 198
European Political Cooperation, 2
European Security Conference, 38
Evensen, Jens, 92
Executive branches (prime minister/cabinet), 191, 192; Denmark, 4–5; Finland, 46, 47–48, 51, 52; Iceland, 73; Norway, 92–97, 99, 105, 106; Sweden, 136, 172–175, 179–180

F-16 fighter (U.S.): Denmark, 14, 29, 30, 33, 198; Norway, 96, 114–117, 198–199; Sweden, 175, 177

F-17 (Northrup Cobra), 115, 117, 198
F-104 fighter, 115, 198
Fahlsten, Ingvar, 173
Fälldin, Prime Minister (Sweden), 153, 168, 169, 172, 177, 178, 179
Finland, xv-xvi, 37-62, 129, 131, 154, 200; academic experts, 51; armed forces, 37, 54-56; arms industry/arms procurement, 50-51, 52-53; Association of Finnish Metal Industries, 49; Communist party (SKP), 44, 50, 59; Confederation of Finnish Employers (STK), 49; Confederation of Finnish Trade Unions (SAK), 50; Confederation of Finnish Wood Processing Industries, 49; conscription, 55-56; Council of State (cabinet), 46, 47, 51; defense budget, 44, 51-52, 196; Defense Council, 46; economy, 43-44, 52; and Estonia, 40, 188; Federation of Finnish Industries, 49; Finland's Trade Union Organization (SAJ), 50; Finnish People's Democratic League (SKDL), 44; Foreign Affairs Committee, 51; foreign policy (neutrality), 38, 189, 190, 203; Foreign Policy Institute, 51; Frontier Guards, 46, 55; geographic/ climatic constraints, 43; interest group system, 49-50, 52; and Nordic nuclear-free zone plan, 197; and Norway, 39-40, 41, 42, 60, 91, 93, 110; officer training, 56-57; Paris Peace Treaty (1947), xv, 37-38, 43, 44; parliament (Eduskunta), 46-47, 48, 51; Parliament Defense Commission, 47; political parties, 44; population and size, 188; presidency, 46, 47-48, 51, 52; public opinion, 46, 54, 59, 194, 196; Social Democratic party, 50; Supply Committee, 47; and Sweden, 39-40, 52, 60, 188, 189, 190; trade unions, 50; Treaty of Friendship (1948), xv, 38; and USSR (*see also* Paris Peace Treaty *and* Treaty of Friendship *above*), xv-xvi, 39, 42, 46, 48-49, 51-52, 54, 59-60, 176, 190, 194; veto power, 48; War College, 56; war reparations, 43
"Finlandization," 43, 44-46, 59
Fishing industry/fishing rights: Iceland, 64, 69, 70, 85, 87, 190, 196; Norway, 91, 92, 112, 114
Folketing. *See* Denmark, parliament
Foreign policy, 190, 193
France, 12, 156; Mirage fighter, 115, 116, 117, 198, 200
Frydenlund, Knut, 119

GE404 aircraft engine (U.S.), 173, 178
General Dynamics, 198, 199. *See also* F-16 fighter
Geographical size comparisons, 188
Germanic culture and language, 188
Germany: and BALTAP, 3, 26; Basic Law (Constitution), 80; and Denmark, 1, 3, 23, 26, 32, 199; and Norway, 93, 105; peace movement, 3, 13; and Scandilux, 13; Social Democratic party (SPD), 13, 33
Glistrup, Mogens, 8
Great Britain: and Iceland, 64, 65, 70; and Norway, 113, 121, 190; and Sweden, 156, 173
Gröndal, Benedikt, 76, 82
Gulf of Finland, 40
Gustafson, Torsten, 178
Gyldén, Nils, 138

Helgason, Hörtur, 74, 82
Helicopters (Sweden), 170
Hökborg, Sven-Olof, 173, 180
Holst, Johan, 97, 102, 118

Iceland, xvi-xvii, 63-89; Bilateral Defense Agreement (1950), xvi-xvii, 66, 74, 75, 86; cabinet, 73; coast guard, 71, 196; Cod Wars, 64, 87; Commission on Security and International Affairs (CSIA), 76-78; Communist party, 82, 83; Constitution, 73, 80; culture/language, 68-69, 81, 195; Defense Committee, 75; Defense Council (with U.S.), 75-76; Defense Division, 74-75; and Denmark, 63-64, 70, 87, 188; economy, 69-70, 85, 86-87;

Iceland *(continued)*
energy resources, 69, 85; and European Community, 87; fishing industry, 64, 69, 70, 85, 87, 190, 196; geographic isolation/climate, 63, 64, 85; and Great Britain, 64, 65, 70; Icelandic Defense Force (IDF), xvii, 66, 74, 75, 78, 79, 86, 196; Independence party, 71, 78, 83; Kalmar Union, 63; Ministry for Foreign Affairs, 73–76, 81–82, 85, 86; and multinational corporations, 69–70; and NATO, xvi, xvii, 63, 64, 65, 66, 67, 70, 73, 74, 78, 82, 83, 84, 86, 87, 189, 190, 203; news media, 78–79; and Norway, 63, 70, 87; pacifism, 66, 70–71, 80–81, 195, 196; parliament (Althing), 63; People's Alliance, 71, 73, 75, 78, 83–84, 85–86; political parties, 71–73, 78, 82–84, 195; population and size, 188; Progressive party, 71, 78, 83; public opinion, 79–80, 195, 196; resource constraints, 65, 69, 85; Social Democratic Alliance, 84; Social Democratic party, 76, 78, 84; State Broadcasting Service/Broadcasting Council, 79; Union Act (1918), 64; and U.S. (*see also* Bilateral Defense Agreement *and* Icelandic Defense Force *above*), 65, 68–69, 70, 73, 75–76, 82, 83, 84, 87; and USSR, xvii, 63, 66–67, 70, 83, 86; Women's League, 84
Icelandic Defense Force (IDF), xvii, 66, 74, 75, 78, 79, 96
Immigration, 188–189
India, 156
Inflation, 195
Intermediate-range Nuclear Force (INF) talks (1979), 3–4, 6, 21, 27, 98
Italy, 172

Jaguar fighter, 115
Jan Mayen Island, 70, 87
JAS39 (Gripen)(Sweden), 132, 154, 156, 157, 166, 175–179, 202
Jerves, Gunnar, 176
Jóhannesson, Ólafur, 86
Jordan, A.A., and W.J. Taylor, Jr., xi

Jørgensen, Anker, 9, 22, 24, 28, 29, 30

Kalmar Union, 63
Karjalainen, Ahti, 49
Karlskrona, Sweden, 148
Kekkonen, Urho, 39, 42, 47, 48–49, 52, 197
Kemuri Oy (Finland), 51
Koivisto, Mauno, 38, 39, 47, 49
Kola Peninsula, USSR, 131, 154, 187, 197
Kronmark, Eric, 147, 168, 172
Krushchev, Nikita, 48

Latvia, 40
Law of the Sea, 92, 112, 121
Lebanon, 98
Leningrad, 40
Less developed countries (LDCs), assistance to, 195
Liberal party, 190; Denmark, 5, 6, 13, 21, 28, 33; Sweden, 134, 143, 172, 173, 200, 201
Lithuania, 40
Lobbies and interest groups: Denmark, 9–10; Finland, 49–50; Sweden, 136, 145–146
Ljung, Lennart, 139, 173, 174, 176, 178
Ljung, Ove, 174
LORAN C station (Norway), 105
Lupuan Patruunatehdas (Finland), 51
Lutheran church, 188
Luxembourg, 85

Military unions: Denmark, 9, 30; Norway, 102, 130; Sweden, 130
Mirage fighter (France), 115, 116, 117, 198, 200
Møller, Orla, 16
Monaco, 85
Morgunblatit (Iceland), 78
Multinational corporations, 69–70
Murmansk, USSR, vii, 40, 131, 187

NATO: BALTAP/COMBALTAP, 3, 17, 19, 26, 29; and Denmark, xiv, 1, 2–4, 5, 6, 10–12, 14, 18, 19, 22–23, 26, 27, 29, 30, 32, 33–34, 189, 190, 196, 199, 203; F-16 consortium, 114–117, 199; and

Iceland/Icelandic Defense Force, xvi, xvii, 63, 64, 65, 66, 67, 70, 73, 74, 75, 78, 79, 82, 83, 84, 86, 87, 188, 190, 203; and INF, 3–4, 6, 21, 27; Long-Term Defense Plan (LTDP, 1978), 4, 18, 19, 22; and Norway (including prepositioning of U.S. military equipment), xvii–xviii, 40, 41, 42, 60, 91, 92, 93, 98, 103, 104, 105, 108, 109, 110, 111, 113, 114–120, 121, 154, 188, 190, 196, 199, 203; Rapid Reinforcement Program, 3, 4, 23, 24; SACEUR, 24; and Sweden, 148, 154, 155, 156, 176; and Warsaw Pact, xv, 67, 148
Netherlands, 115, 117
Neutrality. See Finland, foreign policy; Sweden, foreign policy
News media, 193; Denmark, 10; Iceland, 78–79, 195; Norway, 103, 116, 119, 194; Sweden, 146–147, 171
Nokia group (Finland), 51
Nordbeck, Gunnar, 143, 167
Nordic Balance, xiii–xiv, xix–xx, 110, 128, 180
Nordic Cap, 40, 41
Nordic Council, xix, 39
Nordic defense pact (1948), 1, 114
Nordli, Odvar, 97, 117, 118, 119
North Atlantic, 63, 154
North Sea oil, 148, 187
Northrup, 198, 199. See also F-17
Norway, xvii–xviii, 91–125, 154, 155; academic groups, 102; air force (see F-16 decision below); armed forces/conscripts, 93, 98, 102, 109; "base and ban" policy, xviii, 118, 119; Bowman–Holst Study (1979–1980), 118, 119, 120; Bruland Committee, 119; chief of defense, 93; commanders, South Norway/North Norway, 93; coastal resources/continental shelf boundaries, 91, 92, 111–112, 114; Cooperation Committee, 101; Defense Advisory Group, 96–97; defense budget, 112–113, 196–197; Defense Commission (1946), 97; defense commissions, 192; Defense Committee, 99; Defense Review Commission (Nordli/Bye Commission), 97, 113, 117; Defense Staff, 93; Defense White Paper, 112; and EEC, 103, 104, 110, 198; Eidsvold Constitution (1814), 92, 98, 109; Exclusive Economic Zone, 91; executive branch (prime minister/cabinet), 92–97, 99, 105, 106; Expanded Foreign Affairs Committee, 99, 108; F-16 decision, 96, 114–117, 198–199; fishing industry, 91, 92, 112, 114; and Finland, 39–40, 41, 42, 60, 91, 93, 110; Foreign and Constitutional Affairs Committee, 99; foreign policy, 190; foreign troops ban, 93, 98, 104, 105, 109, 110; and Germany, 93, 105; Government Security Committee, 96, 106; and Great Britain, 113, 121, 190; Home Guard, 93; and Iceland, 63, 70, 87; Intelligence Steering Group, 96; Kalmar Union, 63; Kongsberg Weapons Factory, 96, 116; Labor (Social Democratic) party, 97, 100, 101, 104, 119, 120; and Law of the Sea, 92, 112, 121; LORAN C and OMEGA stations, 105; military unions, 102, 130; Ministry of Defense, 92, 93, 105, 115, 120; Ministry of Education, 103; Ministry of Finance, 92, 113; Ministry of Foreign Affairs, 92, 93; national intelligence organization, 93–96; national trade-union council (LO), 101, 108, 116; and NATO, xvii–xviii, 40, 41, 42, 60, 91, 92, 93, 98, 103, 104, 105, 108, 109, 110, 111, 113, 114–120, 121, 189, 190, 196, 199, 203; news media, 103, 116, 119, 194; Norwegian Defense Research Establishment (NDRE), 96, 115; Norwegian Foreign Policy Institute (NUPI), 103, 194; nuclear weapons ban, 104, 109, 129; oil, 91, 111–112, 121, 196, 197; parliament (Storting), 97–100, 105–106, 108, 109, 112, 113, 117, 120; Peace Research Institute of Oslo (PRIO), 103, 105, 194; political parties,

Norway *(continued)*
  100–101, 108; population and size, 188; prepositioning of U.S. military equipment in, 117–120, 154; public opinion, 103–104, 108, 194; and Scandinavian Defense Union (1948), 1, 114; senior civil servant committees, 96; Social Democratic party (*see also* Labor party *above*), 3; Svalbard (Spitzbergen), vii, 114, 121, 187, 197; and Sweden, 91, 104; trade unions, 101, 108, 116, 193; and U.S., xviii, 103–104, 111, 112, 113, 114–120, 121, 196, 198–199; and USSR, xviii, 40, 41–42, 60, 91, 92, 93, 104, 111–112, 114, 117, 118, 119–120, 131, 197, 199; and Warsaw Pact, 91; World War II, 110, 111, 114, 120–121
Norwegian Military Academy, 82
Norwegian Sea, 41, 112
Nu Tíminn (Iceland), 78
Nuclear energy (Sweden), 153
Nuclear-free zone, 3, 27, 129, 197
Nuclear freeze, 98. *See also* Peace movement
Ny Dag (Sweden), 147

Oil, offshore: North Sea, 148, 187; Norway, 91, 111–112, 121, 196
Oil crisis: Denmark, 21; Sweden, 159, 197
Olesen, Kjeld, 22, 24, 29
OMEGA station (Norway), 105
Ottoson, Ben, 171
Oy Sako-Tikka AB (Finland), 51
Oy Sisu-Auto AB (Finland), 51
Oy Tampella AB (Finland), 50–51

Paasikivi, J.K., 48
Pacifism (Iceland), 66, 70–71, 80–81, 195, 196
Palme, Olof, 128, 136, 145, 159, 168, 173, 174, 179
Paris Peace Treaty (USSR-Finland, 1947), xv, 37–38, 43, 44
Parliaments, 191–192; Denmark, 1, 6–9; Finland, 46–47, 48, 51; Iceland, 63; Norway, 97–100, 105–106, 108, 109, 112, 113, 117,

120; Sweden, 128, 134, 160, 167, 168, 179
Peace movement (Denmark), 3–4, 12–13, 22. *See also* Nuclear freeze
Pershing II, 10, 42
Petri, Gunnar, 172
Pjótviljinn (Iceland), 78
Poland, 42
Political compromise, 192
Political parties, 189–190, 203; Denmark, 6–9, 13, 14, 22, 24, 28, 32–33; Finland, 44; Iceland, 71–73, 78, 82–84, 195; Norway, 100–101, 108; Sweden, 134, 153, 192, 194, 200
Population statistics, national, 188
Poseidon missiles, 112
Pratt and Whitney JT8D-22, 156
Precision guided munitions (PGMs), 112
Public opinion, 190, 193–194, 203; Denmark, 10, 12; Finland, 46, 54, 59, 194, 196; Iceland, 79–80, 195, 196; Norway, 103–104, 108, 194; Sweden, 148–152, 171–172, 195–196, 201

Reagan administration, 3
Remaking Foreign Policy (Allison and Szanton), xii
Research and development (Sweden), 144–145, 155–157, 191, 200, 201
Resource allocation, 195–196, 199, 203
Riksdag. *See* Sweden, parliament
Rogers, Bernard, 46
Roherty, James, xiii

Saab/Saab-Scandia (Sweden), 116, 132, 135, 144, 157, 168, 169, 170–171, 173, 174; Comitech, 134–135; JAS, 175–179, 201–202
Scandilux, 13
Scandinavian Defense Union (1948), 1, 114
Schlüter, Poul, 28, 29, 30
Sea boundaries, 187; Norway, 92, 114; violations of Swedish territorial waters, 127, 128, 131, 148–149, 194, 196, 197
Shaastad, Anders, 102
Sköld, Nils, 169, 178

Social Democratic parties, 13, 33, 189, 190, 203; Denmark, 1, 6, 7, 9, 10, 12, 13, 16, 21, 22, 23, 24, 27, 28–29, 30, 31, 32, 33; Finland, 50; Germany, 13, 33; Iceland, 76, 78, 84; Norway (see also Norway, Labor party), 3; Sweden, 127, 132, 134, 136, 143, 145, 156, 167, 168–169, 171, 172, 173, 176, 192, 193, 200
Söder, Karin, 174–175
Søgaard, Poul, 18, 22, 23, 24, 29, 32,
Soviet Union: Afghanistan, invasion of, 22–23; in Baltic Sea, xiv–xv, 2–3, 40, 187, 199; in Barents Sea, 92, 111–112, 187, 197; and Denmark, xiv–xv, 2–3, 12, 199; and Eastern Europe, 42; and Finland (see also Paris Peace Treaty *and* Treaty of Friendship *below*), xv–xvi, 39, 42, 46, 48–49, 51–52, 54, 59–60, 176, 190, 194; and Iceland, xvii, 63, 66–67, 70, 83, 86; Kola Peninsula, 131, 154, 187, 197; Murmansk military complex, vii, 40, 131, 187; and Nordic countries, vii, 40–41, 197; and Norway, xviii, 40, 41–42, 60, 91, 92, 93, 104, 111–112, 114, 117, 118, 119–120, 131, 197, 199; Paris Peace Treaty (Finland, 1947), xv, 37–38, 43, 44; sea boundaries, 92, 114, 187; Spetznaz special forces/submarine activity, 131, 187; and Spitzbergen (Svalbard), vii, 114, 121, 187, 197, 199; and Sweden, 41, 131, 154–155, 176, 197; Treaty of Friendship (Finland, 1948), xv, 38; and U.S., 1, 42, 59, 65, 192, 197
Spitzbergen Archipelago (Svalbard), vii, 114, 121, 187, 197, 199
Stenberg, Dick, 174, 175
Storting. *See* Norway, parliament
Submarine-launched ballistic missiles (SLBMs), 112
Supreme commanders, 191; Sweden, 139
Surface-to-surface missiles (Sweden), 130, 170
Svalbard (Spitzbergen), vii, 114, 121, 187, 197, 199

Svenska Dagbladet (Sweden), 147, 174, 176
Svinhufvud, P.E., 48
Sweden, xix, 127–186, 192–193, 195–196; air force (see also fighter aircraft controversy *below*), 130, 139, 158, 169, 170, 171; aircraft industry, 132, 156–157, 170, 172, 174, 179, 180; Air Industry Commission, 143, 167–168, 171; armed forces (personnel/equipment), 129–130, 138–139, 169–170; arms sales, 153, 156, 175, 193, 198, 199; army, 130, 169–170; "B3LA (Nordbeck) Commission," 143, 167, 169; cabinet/prime minister, 136, 172–175, 179–180; Center party, 134, 143, 153, 172, 179; Central Organization for People and Defense, 147; Central Organization of Swedish Employees (TCO), 145, 171; Civil Defense Administration, 159; Communist party, 147; Confederation of Trade Unions (LO), 145, 171, 193; conscription, 130, 170, 178, 179, 201; Conservative party, 134, 143, 169, 171, 194, 200; defense and service staffs, 139; defense budget, 131, 134, 144, 152, 157–159, 162, 170, 179–180, 194, 195–196, 201; defense commissions, 143–144, 167–168, 192, 201; defense employees, 138; defense industries, 52, 144–146, 155–157, 170–171, 191, 193; Defense Materiel Administration (FMV), 142–143, 146, 168, 170, 172, 173, 174, 180; Defense Resolution (1982), 159, 177, 178, 179; development assistance to LDCs, 195; economy, 127, 131, 145, 156, 157, 194, 195, 202; education, 147–148; energy crisis, 159, 197; fighter aircraft controversy, 131–132, 143, 147, 153, 166–179, 198, 200–202; and Finland, 39–40, 52, 60, 188, 189, 190; Folk party, 179; foreign policy (neutrality/nonalignment), xix, 128, 180, 189, 190, 194, 203; Foreign Relations Committee, 136; and

Sweden *(continued)*
France, 156; Freedom of the Press Act, 162; and Great Britain, 156, 173; "high-low" aircraft mix, 170, 171, 172, 174; Home Guard, 130; immigration, 188–189; JAS Industries Group, 157; Liberal party, 134, 143, 172, 173, 200, 201; lobbies, 136, 145–146; military staffs, 138–139; military unions, 130; Ministry of Defense, 129, 136–138, 147, 153, 160, 162; Ministry of Foreign Affairs, 153; Ministry of Trade, 129; Moderate party, 171, 172, 177, 179; National Board of Economic Defense, 159; National Defense Research Institute (FOA), 138, 139–142, 146, 170; National Telecommunications Administration, 127; and NATO, 148, 155, 156; navy, 130, 169, 170, 171; newspapers, 147, 171; and Norway, 91, 104; nuclear energy policy, 153; parliament (Riksdag), 128, 134, 160, 167, 168, 179; Parliamentary Commission on Defense, 143; Parliamentary Defense Committee, 132, 134–136, 168, 175, 176, 178; Planning and Budget Secretariat, 138; political parties, 134, 153, 192, 194, 200; population and size, 188; Psychological Defense Planning Committee, 148; public opinion, 148–152, 171–172, 195–196, 201; public sector (employment/expenditures), 127–128, 145; research and development, 144–145, 155–157, 191, 200, 201; resource allocation, 195–196; SACO, 171; and Scandinavian Defense Union (1948), 1, 114; Secretariat for National Security Policy and Long-Range Defense Planning, 138; Social Democratic party, 127, 128, 132, 134, 136, 143, 145, 156, 167, 168–169, 171, 172, 173, 174, 175, 176, 178, 179, 192, 193, 200; Swedish Employers Federation (SAF), 145; Swedish Planning, Programming, and Budgeting System (SSLP), 160; Swedish Standing Committee on Defense, 147; supreme commander (SCO) of the armed forces, 139; television, 146–147; territorial vs. peripheral defense, 129, 131, 169, 200, 201, 202; territorial waters violations, 127, 128, 131, 148–149, 194, 196, 197; Thunborg Commission, 167; Total Defense Information Committee, 148; total defense policy, xix, 128, 129, 180, 201; "tous azimuts" strategy, xix, 153–154; trade unions, 145, 171, 173, 174; and U.N., 143, 190; and U.S., 156, 173, 175, 177; and USSR, 41, 131, 154–155, 176, 197; Viggen aircraft *(see also* fighter aircraft controversy *above)*, 115, 116, 130, 154, 156, 157, 158, 180, 199; "wage-earner funds," 128, 145; and Warsaw Pact, 155
Swedish Peace and Arbitration Society, 147
Switzerland, xix, 69–70, 128, 172, 200
Synnergren, Stig, 169, 174

Technology transfers, 187, 199
Tenryd, Carl-Olof, 142
Territorial waters, 187; Norway, 92, 114; violations of Swedish, 127, 128, 131, 148–149, 194, 196, 197
Theorin, Maj-Britt, 168
Thoroddsen, Gunnar, 73
Thunborg, Anders, 136, 153
Tornado fighter, 115
Torpedo boats (Sweden), 130
Trade unions: Denmark, 9, 23, 30, 199; Finland, 50; Norway, 101, 108, 116, 193; Sweden, 145, 171, 193
Treaty of Friendship, Co-operation and Mutual Assistance (TFCMA)(Finland–USSR, 1948), xv, 38
Trident missiles, 112
Trondheim/Trønelag, Norway, 119

Ullsten, Ola, 166, 172–173, 201
Unckel, Per, 177

United Nations, 2, 53, 98, 109, 143, 190
United States: Air Force, 199; Bilateral Defense Agreement (Iceland, 1950), xvi–xvii, 66, 74, 75, 86; Bowman–Holst Study (with Norway, 1979–1980), 118, 119, 120; cruise missiles, 42, 103–104, 112, 176; decision-making process, 98, 99, 102, 191, 192, 203; and Denmark, 2, 3, 4, 196, 198–199; F-16 fighter, 14, 29, 30, 33, 96, 114–117, 198–199; and Iceland (*see also* Bilateral Defense Agreement *above and* Icelandic Defense Force *below*), xvi–xvii, 65, 68–69, 70, 73, 74, 75–76, 82, 83, 84, 87; Icelandic Defense Force (IDF), xvii, 66, 74, 75, 78, 79, 86, 196; Marine Amphibious Brigade, 118, 119; National Security Council, 138; and Norway, xviii, 96, 103–104, 111, 112, 113, 114–120, 121, 154, 196, 198–199; Pershing II, 10, 42; Poseidon/Trident SLBMs, 112; precision guided munitions (PGMs), 112; and Sweden, 156, 173, 175, 177; and USSR, 1, 42, 45, 59, 192, 197

University of Reykjavík (Iceland), 71, 80

Valmet group (Finland), 50
Vance, Cyrus, 156
Viggen Aircraft (Sweden), 115, 116, 130, 131–132, 143, 147, 153, 154, 156, 157, 158, 166–179, 180, 198, 199, 200–202
Volvo Flygmotor (Sweden), 132, 144, 157, 171, 173, 174, 179; RM88, 156

Wahlin, Sten, 143
Wallenberg, Marcus, 168
Warsaw Pact, 59; and NATO, xv, 67, 148; and Norway, 91; and Sweden, 155
Wärtsilä group (Finland), 50
Wechselmann, Maj, 147, 170–171 (quoted)
WEU, 12
World War II: Denmark, 1; Finland, 37; Norway, 110, 111, 114, 120–121; Sweden, 196

Yankee Class SSBNs, 112

About the Contributors

John R. Fairlamb is a lieutenant colonel in the United States Army at the Office of the Supreme Allied Commander Europe (OSACEUR). He received his B.A. in political science at the Citadel, his M.A. and his Ph.D. in international relations at the University of South Carolina. His Ph.D. dissertation was titled "The Evolution of Icelandic Defense Decision Making." He has taught at the United States Military Academy at West Point (1979–82) and has served in a number of commanding positions in Germany and Vietnam as well as at Fort Campbell, Kentucky. He is the author of numerous articles on European defense, especially the Icelandic situation, in *Problems of Communism, Naval War College Review,* and *The Christian Science Monitor.* He also has been a panelist and colloquium speaker at several conferences on Western European defense issues.

Trond Gilberg is professor of political science and associate director of the Slavic and Soviet Language and Area Center at Penn State. He has been a visiting professor at the Christian-Albrechts-Universität in Kiel, West Germany; the University of Washington; the U.S. Military Academy at West Point; and the U.S. Army War College at Carlisle, Pennsylvania. His publications include two books, over two dozen book chapters, and numerous articles on communist studies, Soviet and East European politics, and the governments of northern Europe. A native of Norway, Dr. Gilberg has travelled extensively throughout Eastern and Western Europe and the Soviet Union. He has a thorough knowledge of a number of languages, including Russian, Romanian, and several western European languages.

Nikolaj Petersen is associate professor at the Institute of Political Science, University of Aarhus. He is also a member of the Danish Commission on Security and Disarmament Affairs, the board of the Danish Institute of International Studies, the Nordic Cooperation Committee for International Politics, and the International Institute for Strategic Studies. He is co-editor (with Christian Thune) of *Dansk Udenrigspolitisk Årbog* and (with Hans-Henrik

Holm) of *The European Missiles Crisis: Nuclear Weapons and Security Policy,* and author of numerous monographs and articles on comparative foreign policy, defense policy, and international security policy.

James R. Stark is a captain in the United States Navy and is currently a staff member at the National Security Council. He has also served in Washington on the navy staff in the areas of political-military affairs and systems analysis. His operational tours have included duty in cruisers, destroyers, and frigates and he has completed deployments to both the western Pacific and the Mediterranean Sea. Upon graduation from the U.S. Naval Academy at Annapolis, he was selected as a Fulbright Scholar and attended the University of Vienna, Austria, where he studied history and German. He received his M.A., M.A.L.D., and Ph.D. in political science at the Fletcher School of Law and Diplomacy, Tufts University, and wrote his dissertation on U.S.–Scandinavian security relations. He is fluent in German and Danish.

Christian Thune is associate professor at the Institute of Political Studies, University of Copenhagen. He is chairman of the board of the Danish Institute of International Studies, and a member of the Danish Commission on Security and Disarmament and the International Institute for Strategic Studies. He is co-editor (with Nikolaj Petersen) of *Dansk Udenrigspolitisk Årbog* and editor of *Konflikternes Verden 1984,* and is the author of publications on Danish foreign policy, European cooperation, and Third World countries in international political economy.

About the Editors

Paul M. Cole is currently a fellow in International Security Studies at the Center for Strategic and International Studies. He holds degrees from Gustavus Adolphus College (B.A.) and the Graduate School of Foreign Service, Georgetown University (M.S.F.S.). He is currently pursuing his Ph.D. degree in the School of Government, Georgetown University. He attended the Universities of Stockholm and Örebro, both in Sweden. He is fluent in Swedish, having taught and translated Swedish on a number of occasions. In 1979 he worked on the largest public opinion poll ever conducted in Sweden while at the Kennedy School of Government, Harvard University. He has travelled extensively in Europe, including the Nordic countries. His recent publications include the following: *Northern Europe: Political Military Issues for the 1990s,* (co-editor), (forthcoming 1985); "Nuclear Policy, Nuclear Protest," in *Conventional Deterrence,* (Lexington Books, 1984); "Europe," in *Strategic Requirements for the Army to the Year 2000,* (Lexington Books, 1984); "Vilseledande om USAs Utrikespolitik," in *Svenska Dagbladet,* (June 1984); and "The American Nuclear Weapons Freeze Movement and Its Contribution to the American Peace Movement," in *The Peace Movements,* (Rome: FIUC Research Center, 1984). He is a frequent contributor to the Swedish Broadcasting Corporation and is a consultant to London Weekend Television.

Dr. William J. Taylor, Jr. is executive director, chief operating officer, and director of Political-Military Studies, Georgetown University Center for Strategic and International Studies. He holds a Ph.D. from The American University, Washington, D.C. and has done postgraduate work at The American University of Beirut. Until retirement in 1981 as an army colonel, he served in Germany, Korea, and Vietnam, completing his final ten years of professional military service as a professor of Social Sciences, director of National Security Studies and director of Debate at West Point, and as a visiting professor at the U.S. National War College. He is a member of the Council on Foreign Relations and the International Institute for Strategic Studies. Author or co-author of over forty-five publications, he has published three books in

1984, *Strategic Responses to Conflict in the 1980s; Strategic Requirements for the Army to the Year 2000;* and *American National Security: Policy and Process* (2nd ed.). His 1983 publications include *The Future of Conflict in the 1980s; The Future of Conflict: U.S. Interests;* and *The Nuclear Freeze Debate: Arms Control Issues for the 1980s.* He is also author of the highly regarded "The Defense Policy of Sweden," in Murray and Vlotti (editors), *The Defense Policies of Nations,* (Baltimore: Johns Hopkins Press, 1982).